Little Ireland

*A family's journey from
Co. Sligo to Co. Durham*

by Philip Lees

Published by Philip Lees

First published 2004

© Philip Lees

All rights reserved

No reproduction permitted
without the prior permission of the publisher:

Published by Philip Lees

ISBN 0-9548273-0-9

Design & Typeset by Philip Lees
Printed by Hughes & Co, Kempsey, Worcestershire

Contents

Dedication		Page iii
Foreword		Page v
Acknowledgements		Page vi
List of Photographs, Maps and Illustrations		Page vii
List of Colour Plates		Page xi
Chapter 1	Tragedy for the young Gray Family	Page 1
Chapter 2	Connaught's History	Page 8
Chapter 3	Gaelic Roots	Page 26
Chapter 4	Early 19th Century Connaught	Page 36
Chapter 5	Hard Times	Page 50
Chapter 6	Early Days in England	Page 74
Chapter 7	Work in the Mines	Page 80
Chapter 8	The Development of *'Little Ireland'*	Page 90
Chapter 9	The Move to *'Little Ireland'*	Page 96
Chapter 10	A New Generation	Page 102
Chapter 11	The 20th Century Opens	Page 120
Chapter 12	The Great War	Page 138
Chapter 13	Frank's Story	Page 148
Chapter 14	Jubilation and Depression	Page 160
Chapter 15	John Mattimoe's Family	Page 178
Chapter 16	Stephen Mattimoe's Family	Page 192
Chapter 17	Peter Mattimoe - A Pillar of the Community	Page 198
Chapter 18	Tha Hannon Family	Page 204
Chapter 19	Life Continues	Page 218
Appendix A	Irish Records	Page 220
Appendix B	Census of Gordon Gill, Ramshaw	Page 226
Bibliography		Page 233
Index		Page 234

In memory of Julia Bell who sadly died during the writing of this book. I wish we had met sooner.

Foreword

It was with some trepidation in August 2002 that I rang Betty Lees. Betty had left her phone number at the nearby Bridge Inn in the hope of making contact with someone who knew the Mattimoe family. My concern was unnecessary. I was absolutely delighted to make contact with Betty and Bernard and their son Philip. Just a few weeks earlier I had been speaking to my cousin Maureen and we had reluctantly concluded that we would never know anything about our Grandmothers ancestors so it seemed unreal when I met with Betty, Bernard and Philip and we all swapped stories and compared our old family photographs, pooling our knowledge, putting names to previously anonymous faces.

Since then during the past two years I have been enthralled as we unravelled the story of the Mattimoes and pieced together their lives. What has emerged is the story of a close, warm Catholic family. Everyone who has been contacted who knew members of the family or are descended from them speak well of them, how generous hearted they were and how generous they were with their hospitality. The work during the past two years has put me in contact with many of the distantly related family and it is pleasing to see that this generous nature has been passed down undiminished to later generations.

My childhood memories of my Aunt Sally's house full to bursting with visitors, all of whom would be well fed on Aunt Sally's home cooking, echoed those of Philip's visits to his Aunt Nora's despite the distance of several generations from our common ancestor, and that these gatherings were by then taking place at different ends of the country.

It is a special feeling to be part of such a warm, caring family and to have had that reinforced by the contacts, some new and some just renewed, during these two years. The common regret of all who embark upon this research is that they wish they had started sooner and Philip and I are no exception to that rule. However we could so easily have missed this opportunity and our lives would have been the poorer so we are enjoying, and will continue to enjoy, our new friendships.

I hope all those that read this book can share at least part of the enjoyment we who have contributed to it had in its preparation and will perhaps be encouraged to embark upon a similar journey and reap its benefits.

Angela Seagrave October 2004

Acknowledgements

I am grateful to many people who contributed their stories, information and photographs to enable this book to be produced. I am particularly endebted to Angela Seagrave, without whose encouragement, personal memories and happy knack, tirelessly pursued, of locating those who could contribute further information, this book would not have been produced and the story of Thomas Mattimoe, his family and descendants would have remained untold. I thank my mother for her help, support and background to her family. My thanks to Mary Eales, Thomas Mattimoe, Jackie Moran, Irene Welsh, John Bell and Tom Seagrave for the stories of their families and life during the 20th century. I thank Kathleen Hannon for an entertaining morning when she related the story of her family, Bernard Hannon for his help and amusing telling of the story of the air raid on Ramshaw, and Tommy Woods for the story of the day my Grandfather died in a mining accident. I am grateful to Joan Hannon for the copy of the recording of Suzie Tate and others made in the 1970's which illustrates the value of such recordings for future generations. I thank Maureen Doyle, Brian Armstrong, Peter Ward and Michael Hannon for their stories and use of family photographs. I am grateful to Pa Mattimoe, Mai Hannon, Sylvester Hannon and Assumpta Giblin for their help in researching the background of the families in Ireland. I thank Vanessa Barnard for allowing me to remove family photographs from their lovely frames for copying. I thank my brother Stewart for the illustrations for the story of the air raid on Ramshaw and Richard McGhee of Taylors, Jewellers of Boyle for use of the illustration of the church on Trinity Island, Lough Key. I thank Kevin Richardson for access to his wealth of material on the history of the Gaunless Valley.

I acknowledge the Durham County Record Office and its staff for their help during my research and for permission to use extracts from the minutes of the Bishop Auckland Board of Health (UD/BA 1) and sections of the Ordnance Survey maps scale 1:2500 covering Ramshaw dated 1855, 1887, 1921 and 1939. I also acknowledge the permission of the Director of Education, Durham County Council for use of transcripts from the log book of Ramshaw School 1866-1937 (ref: E/SW105 and E/SW106).

I am particularly endebted to Newsquest (North East) Ltd for permission to include without charge copyright material from the newspapers which are part of their publishing heritage and about communities which remain at the heart of their daily and weekly newspapers.

I acknowledge and thank Beamish The North of England Open Air Museum, Woodhorn Colliery Museum and The Scottish Crannog Centre for kindly providing photographs for use in this book.

I thank the Roman Catholic Diocese of Elphin for permission to use the poems recorded in the Parish Register of Ardcarne and reproduced on pages 37 and 49. The poem on page 73 is published with permission of the Head of the Department of Irish Folklore, University College, Dublin as are the images attributed to that university which appear in this book..

I thank the Commissioner of Valuation of the Valuation Office, Dublin for permission to use the extracts from the Griffith's Valuation.

My research into the Mattimoe name has been greatly helped by the volunteers and facilities of the Family History Centre of the Church of the Latter Day Saints, Crawley. Similarly this book could not have been produced without the help of the staff and facilities of the Newspaper Library and Map Room of the British Library, The Family Records Centre, Islington, the Public Record Office, Kew, the photographic library of the Imperial War Museum and the National Library of Ireland.

List of Photographs, Maps and Illustrations

Chapter 1

1.	The Gray children outside the house in Coronation, Co. Durham.	Page 2.
2.	Molly Gray and Monica in the Rose Garden at Bushey, Hertfordshire.	Page 3.
3.	Molly Gray in the garden of Chiltern Avenue, Bushey.	Page 4.
4.	Author outside the Gray family home in Chiltern Avenue, Bushey.	Page 5.
5.	Willy Gray's grave , Bishop Auckland.	Page 6.

Chapter 2

6.	Megalithic passage tomb, Carrowmore, Co. Sligo.	Page 8.
7.	Crannog, The Scottish Crannog Centre, Loch Tay, Perthshire.	Page 8.
8.	Ballinafad Castle, Co. Sligo.	Page 10.
9.	Round Tower, Killala, Co. Sligo.	Page 11.
10.	Sweat House, Drumkeeran, Co. Sligo.	Page 11.
11.	Celtic cross, Drumcliffe, Co. Sligo.	Page 12.
12.	Ballindoon Friary, Co. Sligo.	Page 13.
13.	Gallowglass	Page 14.
14.	Boundaries of the ancient kingship of Moylurg.	Page 15.
15.	Boyle Abbey, Co. Roscommon.	Page 17.
16.	Trinity Island, Lough Key, Co. Sligo.	Page 19.
17.	Statue of Gaelic Warrior above Lough Key, Co. Sligo.	Page 21.
18.	Open air Mass at the Mass Rock at Milford, Co. Sligo.	Page 22.
19.	Map of Co. Sligo and Co. Roscommon, 1831.	Page 25.

Chapter 3

20.	The spread of the Mattimoes through Co. Sligo and Co. Roscommon.	Page 28.
21.	General Humbert's march through Co. Sligo.	Page 34.

Chapter 4

22.	Labourer's cottage, Gweedore, Co. Donegal.	Page 38.
23.	Tithe Applotment entry for Thomas Mattimoe at Aghacarra, Co. Sligo.	Page 40.
24.	Tithe Applotment map of Aghacarra, Co. Sligo.	Page 43.
25.	Rockingham House, Co. Sligo.	Page 44.
26.	Evicted family, Western Ireland.	Page 44.
27.	An Irish Farmer	Page 46.

Chapter 5

28.	'Lazy beds'.	Page 51.
29.	Market scene in Ireland.	Page 54.
30.	Irish farmer and his wife.	Page 55.
31.	Group of Irish barefoot women.	Page 57.
32.	Old Irish woman in traditional dress.	Page 60.
33.	Eviction at Kilrush with the cottage 'tumbled down'.	Page 63.
34.	Irish eviction scene with police and troopers.	Page 64.
35.	Strawboy dress.	Page 66.

36.	Uillean Piper.	Page 67.
37.	Slag heaps, Arigna, Co. Sligo.	Page 68.
38.	Cottage in Carrigeenroe, Co. Sligo.	Page 69.
39.	Sligo Harbour.	Page 71.
40.	Advert for steamer sailings from Sligo to Liverpool, Glasgow and Ballina.	Page 71.

Chapter 6

41.	Thomas Mattimoe and Anne Gaffney.	Page 76.
42.	Patrick Mattimoe.	Page 77.
43.	Bishop Auckland market place.	Page 78.

Chapter 7

44.	Sandhole drift.	Page 81.
45.	Pony putters, Railey Fell Colliery.	Page 83.
46.	Pony putter riding the limmer, Ashington Colliery.	Page 84.
47.	Putters, Railey Fell Colliery.	Page 85.
48.	Hewer, Ashington Colliery.	Page 86.
49.	Miners, Houghton-le-Spring Colliery.	Page 87.
50.	Coal sorting belt.	Page 88.

Chapter 8

51.	Tithe map of Gordon Gill and Ramshaw, 1842.	Page 91.
52.	Ordnance Survey map scale 1:2500 of Gordon Gill and Ramshaw, 1853.	Pages 94/95

Chapter 9

53.	Patrick Mattimoe.	Page 99.
54.	Ramshaw School photograph c.1890.	Page 101.

Chapter 10

55.	Bowes Close, Ramshaw.	Page 103.
56.	Hannah Donlen in Galway.	Page 104.
57.	John Mattimoe, Hannah Donlen and son Stephen.	Page 105.
58.	Thomas Mattimoe with his family, October 1887.	Pages 106/107.
59.	Patrick Mattimoe, Mary Jane Rutter and children Stephen and Jane.	Page 109.
60.	Ordnance Survey map scale 1:2500 of Gordon Gill and Ramshaw, 1897.	Pages 110/111.
61.	John Mattimoe, Hannah Donlen and children.	Page 113.
62.	Ramshaw School photograph, 1893.	Page 115.
63.	Annie Mattimoe.	Page 118.

Chapter 11

64.	John Hannon christening group.	Page 121.
65.	Peter Mattimoe outside the Bridge Inn, Ramshaw.	Page 122.
66.	Molly Mattimoe.	Page 123.
67.	Stationmaster, Evenwood.	Page 124.
68.	Evenwood Prize Silver Band.	Page 125
69.	Ambulance Group outside Bridge Inn, Ramshaw, 1909.	Page 126.
70.	Molly Mattimoe.	Page 128.
71.	John Mattimoe's son, Thomas.	Page 129.

List of Photographs, Maps and Illustrations ix

72.	Patrick Mattimoe.	Page 130.
73.	Mary Ann Rutter.	Page 130.
74.	Ramshaw School photograph c.1905.	Page 131.
75.	Eldon Lane Colliery.	Page 132.
76.	John Mattimoe's family with Martin Donnelly	Page 133.
77.	Hannah Donlen's sister, Mrs Foley taken in Pittsburgh, USA.	Page 134.
78.	Molly Mattimoe and Willy Gray.	Page 135.
79.	Elizabeth Haigh with daughter, Jennifer, and mother, Mary Purtill.	Page 136.
80.	Willy Gray, Thomas Hannon and Frank Mattimoe.	Page 137.

Chapter 12

81.	Gordon Lane, Ramshaw.	Page 139.
82.	Roll of honour from St. Joseph's Catholic congregation, Coundon.	Pages 140/141.
83.	Route of Zeppelin L16 on the night of 5th/6th April 1916.	Page 143.
84.	Zeppelin L12.	Page 144.
85.	Stephen and Frank Mattimoe on military training.	Page 14

Chapter 13

86.	Frank Austin Mattimoe in army uniform.	Page 149.
87.	Frank Mattimoe's tour of duty on the Western Front.	Pages 152/153.
88.	Soldiers of the Yorks and Lancs Regiment repairing damage to their trenches.	Page 154.
89.	Horseback wrestling at an Army Horse Show.	Page 156.
90.	British troops and tanks at the battle for St. Quentin, September 1918.	Page 157.
91.	Trench map of the area where Frank Mattimoe fought and died.	Page 158.

Chapter 14

92.	Ordnance Survey map of Ramshaw, 1921.	Pages 162/163.
93.	Memory card for Elizabeth Ellen Hannon.	Page 164.
94.	Mary and Kitty Hannon.	Page 165.
95.	Randolph Colliery, Evenwood.	Page 167.
96.	Tommy Mattimoe on work camp.	Page 169.
97.	Railey Fell Colliery, Ramshaw, taken in the 1930's.	Page 172.
98.	Photograph of unknown group of Evenwood and Ramshaw old folk.	Page 175.
99.	Railey Fell incline engine house.	Page 176.

Chapter 15

100.	Great Uncle Martin.	Page 181.
101.	Great Uncle Martin in Special Officer uniform outside a New York bank.	Page 182.
102.	Thomas Mattimoe's youngest daughter, Julia.	Page 183.
103.	Police Sergeant Stephen Mattimoe on duty.	Page 184.
104.	Stephen Mattimoe with nieces Mary, Betty and Monica.	Page 185.
105.	Leo Mattimoe's wife Ginny Haws.	Page 186.
106.	Leo and Ginny's children Katie and John.	Page 186.
107.	Frank Mattimoe's wife Nellie Welsh.	Page 187.
108.	PC Frank Mattimoe.	Page 187.
109.	Willy and Molly Gray with their first three children, Jack, Laurie and Mary.	Page 189.
110.	Nora and Mary Gray August 1922.	Page 190.

111.	Grave of Peter Gray, Mary Gray and James Gray.	Page 191.
112.	Grave of John Mattimoe.	Page 191.
113.	Plan of Bishop Auckland Cemetery.	Page 191.

Chapter 16

114.	Stephen and Mary Ellen's family.	Page 194.
115.	"Miner's Bath" by J. J. Greenwell.	Page 196.
116.	Fire place in Miner's terrace.	Page 197.

Chapter 17

117.	Bridge Inn, Ramshaw.	Page 199.
118.	Peter Mattimoe in later life.	Page 200.
119.	Esther Mattimoe.	Page 201.
120.	Ordnance Survey map scale 1:2500 of Ramshaw, 1939.	Pages 202/203.

Chapter 18

121.	John Hannon.	Page 206.
122.	Jane Peacock nee Mattimoe.	Page 207.
123.	Joe Peacock.	Page 207.
124.	An agitated Joe Peacock appeared at the top of the stairs.	Page 208.
125.	Mr Quadrini was found sheltering under a hedge.	Page 209.
126.	Annie Hannon's brother, Frank Mattimoe.	Page 211.
127.	Sally Hannon.	Page 212.
128.	Frank Hannon.	Page 213.
129.	Class 6, Ramshaw School in 1920.	Page 214.
130.	Class 1, Ramshaw School in 1920.	Page 214.
131.	Ramshaw School Cookery Class c.1920.	Page 215.
132.	Nora Hannon on holiday in Ireland.	Page 215.
133.	Nora Hannon and Leslie Finlay on their wedding day.	Page 216.
134.	Leslie Finlay with model steam railway engine which he built.	Page 216.
135.	Nora, Sally and Leslie on holiday in Ireland.	Page 217.

Chapter 19

136	Aerial view of Gordon Gill.	Page 219.

Colour Plates

Plate 1. Kilmactranny Roman Catholic Church, Co. Sligo.
St Teresa's Roman Catholic Church, Carrigeenroe, Co. Sligo.

Plate 2. Benbulben, Co. Sligo.
Knockarea, Co. Sligo.
The old coach road leading down to Boyle from the Curlew Mountains.

Plate 3. Briecklieve Mountains, Co. Sligo.
Looking toward Coolboy from the Bricklieve Mountains, Co. Sligo

Plate 4. Parkes Castle on the banks of Lough Gill, Co.Leitrim.
Boyle, Co. Sligo.

Plate 5. Remains of Crannog, Cavetown Lough, Co. Roscommon.
Mount Irwin Friary near Gorteen, Co. Sligo.
Tractors, Co. Sligo.
Stack of peat blocks.
Abandoned cottage Co. Sligo.

Plate 6. Thomas Mattimoe's cottage, Carrigeenroe, Co. Sligo.
Lough Key, Co. Sligo.

Plate 7. 'An Irish Emigrant Arriving at Liverpool' by Robert Erskine, 1871.

Plates 8/9. Ordnance Survey map of the Bishop Auckland area, Co. Durham, 1945.

Plate 10. Bridge Street, Bishop Auckland, Co. Durham.
Viaduct, Bishop Auckland, Co. Durham.
Newton Cap Bridge, Bishop Auckland, Co. Durham.

Plate 11. Railey Fell, Co. Durham.
'Little Ireland' Gordon Gill, Ramshaw, Co. Durham

Plate 12. 'Going Home', Ralph Hedley, 1889

Plate 13. St. Wilfred's Roman Catholic Church, Bishop Auckland, Co. Durham.

Plate 14. Gordon Lane, Ramshaw, Co. Durham.
Jane Peacock's house, Gordon Bank Top, Ramshaw, Co. Durham.

Plate 15. Tom Mattimoe's card from the Western Front to his father, John.
Frank Mattimoe's grave, Trefcon Military Cemetery, France.
Trefcon Military Cemetery, France.

Plate 16. Richard Terrace, Coronation, Bishop Auckland, Co. Durham.
Coronation School, Bishop Auckland, Co. Durham.

1 Tragedy for the young Gray Family

We were a large family. My mother had four sisters and two brothers. A brother and sister remained single but the other five had thirteen children between them. Perhaps it was the predominance of sisters or the closeness brought about by the loss of their parents at a young age but my Aunts, Uncles and their children were very close.

The family home was in Bushey, Hertfordshire which had first been occupied by my widowed grandmother Molly Gray and her seven children soon after they moved from Coronation near Bishop Auckland, County Durham in the early 1930's.

Molly had brought her young family south some six years after the death of her husband, Willy Gray, in a mining accident at Eldon Colliery. Willy was a deputy-overman at the colliery. It was the job of the Pit Deputies to inspect the workings to ensure they were safe before the men entered. On one such inspection on 22nd April 1927 Willy, whilst working with three other Deputies, was killed by a fall of stone. He was buried in Bishop Auckland Cemetery.

Molly was only 32 years old when she lost her husband. Her young family were John "Jack" aged 12, Mary aged 11, William "Laurie" aged 9, Nora aged 7, Monica aged 5, Margaret "Peggy" aged 3 and Betty, my mother, who was 16 months old. Molly received a small amount of compensation which provided an income of three pounds five shillings per week.

Life in Coronation

Bringing up seven young children on a small weekly income was hard but the children had a very happy childhood. Molly was a good cook and kept the family supplied with home-made bread, pies and buns, and always made a Christmas cake for her brother, Frank's family at Chester-le-Street. She was also a good dressmaker and usually made the younger members of the family dresses and skirts out of a few yards of material, not to mention knitted jumpers that were always on the go.

The houses in Richard Terrace, where they lived had small back yards each with an outdoor ash closet but to the front was an access footpath the other side of which were gardens belonging to the houses. The garden was the reason Molly had chosen the house. At the end of the gardens was a narrow footbridge gave access to fields through which ran a small stream or beck. The beck and the countryside were a natural draw for the children and they spent much time playing outside, sometimes arriving home somewhat wet and bedraggled after falling in the beck.

The family were brought up to be well-behaved and polite. One of their cousins remembers that, following a visit to Auntie Molly's, her father turned to his chidren and said, in a way only a genial father with five lively young children could, "Why can't you be as well behaved as those children, and them with no father?" Despite setting such a shining example they had their differences and were not always as compliant to their mother's wishes as she would have liked. One such incident occurred when a travelling photographer called at the house to take a picture of the children when my mother, then aged about three, refused to participate. Fortunately a picture taken when she was about one year old does include her, though even then her expression shows a marked reluctance to participate.

Fig. 1

The arrival of a travelling photographer at the terraces of Coronation prompted my Grandmother, Molly, to fetch the children indoors, dress them in their best clothes, polish their shoes and brush their hair. They were then stood dutifully outside the house. Laurie, Jack, Mary and Nora at the back, Monica, my mother Betty and Peggy in the front. The five eldest children treated the event with gravitas but Peggy and Betty give the impression that they had been posed somewhat against their will. The photo was taken in 1927 shortly after the tragic death of their father in a pit accident. Several copies were obtained to be proudly sent to Molly's brothers, and perhaps to her Aunts in America. This particular copy had been given to Molly's brother Frank and came into my mother's possession seventy years after it was taken.

The move to Bushey

The 1930's were a time of economic hardship in County Durham and Molly was determined that her boys would not work down the mines. There were various Government training schemes at that time and in 1932 Laurie joined one such scheme to train as an electrician and left Coronation for Bushey, Hertfordshire. Jack joined the same scheme to train as a gentlemens hairdresser. When they completed their training the rest of the family moved to Bushey, initially in Roseberry Road, before moving after a year into Chiltern Avenue, destined to become the home of the extended family for the next sixty years.

Betty, the youngest, only returned to County Durham once in her childhood, with her mother at the beginning of September 1939. This visit was to be cut short by the announcement of the outbreak of the Second World War. A few months after the abortive trip north Molly Gray, who had not been in good health for some time, died on 28th December 1939 and was buried in the graveyard of Bushey Church. Betty was not to visit County Durham again until the 1960's when we passed through on holiday and met Betty's Uncle Leo and his family.

Following the death of their mother the young family all pulled together and each played their part selflessly in the running of the home. One clear example of this was the money tin. Every member of the

Fig. 2

Molly Gray and her daughter Monica walking in the Rose Garden at Bushey. This picture was taken in the Summer of 1939. Molly and her family loved Bushey and the photograph shows by their dress that the family were now comfortably off as the eldest children were working. The families happiness was soon to be shattered by the death of their mother only a few months after this photograph was taken.

family who was working put their entire wages into this tin. Money was drawn out to meet the household bills and individuals could draw out money for personal spending in agreement with the others. There was never a dispute over this cooperative pooling of income.

Seven young people living together in one house generated occasional frustrations though these were of a minor nature. For example when it was fashionable for young women to wear hooded scarves the two brothers despaired of finding a scarf which had not been folded lengthways and sewn down one side by their sisters to emulate that fashion.

Despite the dominance of its neighbouring Watford, Bushey still retains some of the village atmosphere that was very much in evidence when the Gray family first moved there. Right up until the 1960's there was a farm at the end of Chiltern Avenue and I remember staying with my Auntie Nora and visiting the old farm with my cousins Michael and Graham to watch the cows being milked.

In my childhood visits to my Aunts and Uncles were frequent, particularly to Auntie Nora and her family living in Chiltern Avenue. They were all fascinating people to me. Uncle Jack, who married Connie, was the eldest in the family and had consequently become the father figure for his younger brothers and sisters. He had a piano which, if we were lucky he could be persuaded to play. Auntie Mary worked as a waitress in a restaurant above the shops in the High Street, Watford, providing a good excuse to have tea and cakes served by my Auntie in her black and white uniform complete with hat whilst she

Fig. 3

This photo of Molly taken in the garden of Chiltern Avenue, Bushey. The glorious summers of this period justified the investment in the fashionable deckchair. The reverse of the photo contained the short message to her brother Frank and his wife, Nellie.

What do you think of this. I don't look bad after the weeks of illness I have had. Laurie insisted upon taking me. I am trying to knit. I took the glasses off, as I hate them. Just for the time I took them off. Laurie has a mania for Photo's. Jack is pipes and different tobaccos, also ties. I think everybody has a craze for something. Molly

and Mum caught up on all the news. Uncle Laurie, who was very easy going and remained single though very close to his sister Nora and her family. Auntie Nora, who married Geoff, was always pleased to see visitors, who were frequent to Chiltern Avenue, so we often met other Aunts, Uncles and cousins on our visits. Auntie Nora also followed the tradition brought with the family from Co. Durham of ensuring that all visitors were given something to eat and drink. Dear sweet Auntie Monica who remained single but loved all her nieces and nephews and never forgot their birthdays, nor in later life, those of their children. Auntie Peggy, who married Dave, was another home where you were sure of a warm welcome with the added bonus that Uncle Dave, who had a lovely sense of humour, would always make me laugh.

Catching the Family History Bug

Whenever my mother and my Aunts got together there was always plenty to talk about. I was always content to sit and listen particularly when they talked about their times in Co. Durham, the relations they left behind and their Irish ancestors. Molly's maiden name was Mattimoe and her mother's maiden name was Donlen. If I was very lucky Auntie Nora would reach up to the top cupboard to the left of the fireplace in the dining room and fetch down the old family photo album and letters. Here were Victorian photos of the Mattimoes and the Donlens together with the Hannons who had married into the family. There were also Grays and Haighs from my Grandfather's family, plus many other unknown relatives, family friends and even priests.

Family lore was that the Mattimoes came from Co. Roscommon, and the Donlens from Co. Galway. In a shrinking world where virtually any exotic location is only a package holiday away the romance of Ireland still exerts a strong emotional pull, even on those several generations on from those who first left the Old Country. I was not immune to that pull and willingly succumbed and immersed myself in the family's story. The family were full of colourful characters such as Great Uncle Martin, 6' 7 ½" (2.02 m) tall who emigrated to USA in 1912 and widowed Great Aunt Jane who everyone seems to remember. Consequently I decided to trace the family tree.

In the early 1980's I had a job which frequently took me to meetings in London. By carefully scheduling these meetings to start at 10.30am I was able to travel to London early and spend a frantic, if exhausting, hour at St. Catherine's House scanning the large, heavy indexes of births deaths and marriages for entries relating to my ancestors. After the meeting I would occasionally find time to visit the Public Record Office, then in Chancery Lane, to use their limited resources to search the censuses, tracking down where the Mattimoes lived, in small hamlet known as Gordon Gill near Evenwood in Co. Durham. The census also indicated that it was my great great grandfather, Thomas Mattimoe who brought his young family from Ireland. Who was Thomas? When did he leave Ireland? What was his life like in Ireland? How did their life change on reaching England? So many questions to be answered.

Fig. 4

The author standing outside the front door of the Gray family house in Chiltern Avenue, Bushey. Contrary to the pose the front door was rarely used. All visiting family and friends arrived at the side door which led into the small kitchen where everyone gathered to stand and chat, often blocking the doorway into the hall. I have memories of multiple conversations taking place as children ran to and from the garden squeezing past Aunts and Uncles whilst the family cat slept peacefully in front of the small coal burning stove. Auntie Nora in my memories is always at the far end of the kitchen by the sink and cooker, preparing the next meal or washing up after the last but central to all the discussions.

Little Ireland

In the mid 1980's I took my family to Bishop Auckland where, by prior arrangement with Father Cunningham, I was able read the register of St. Wilfred's Roman Catholic Church on an unseasonably wet August afternoon, fortified by the tea and chocolate biscuits kindly provided by Father Cunningham, and found many entries for my mothers family and our ancestors. At this time the Roman Catholic Church cared for all its registers, though many of the older registers have since been handed over to the local County record Offices to be cared for and preserved, in the process enabling easier access by family historians. Father Cunningham's help was typical of the helpful response I have received from Parish Priests in my quest to uncover the story of my ancestors.

On that visit I was also keen to locate Gordon Gill. The Gill was not easy to find, so I drew up next to an old lady who was walking down the hill from Evenwood towards the village of Ramshaw, just the other side of the River Gaunless. I asked if she knew how I could get to Gordon Gill which she readily explained and then when I told her my ancestors, the Mattimoes, had lived there she said "Oh yes, a lot of Irish families used to live in the Gill. The Mattimoes, the Hannons and others. It used to be known as *'Little Ireland'*. The name stuck in my mind and spurred me on to more research. Sure enough there were a group of Irish families who settled in the Gill from the late 1850's onward. Some were related before arriving whilst others forged new links through marriage. All were strong followers of the Roman Catholic faith and remained so, the records of the surrounding churches being rich in references to the families. This at a time when Methodism was the growing religion amongst mining families.

On that visit I met Lucy Hannon who had married my Great Grandfather Mattimoe's nephew. At that time I was only interested in tracing and learning about my direct ancestors and ignored the families of their brothers and sisters. This narrow view resulted in my failure to ask Lucy about other members of the wider family of whom several older members, who would have known my Great Grandparents and even Great Great Grandfather, were at that time still alive. I returned home pleased with the progress I had made but sadly unaware of the opportunity I had missed.

Fig. 5

Willy Gray's grave in Bishop Auckland Cemetery is in the section reserved for Roman Catholic burials. The small headstone is made from granite with lead lettering. The funeral was well attended by family, friends, workmates, representatives of the Deputies Association and the Colliery. The family still have copies of the correspondence written by Molly's brother Stephen to those who had expressed sympathy to Molly and her young family. These well written letters give testament to the fond, high esteem in which Willy was held by all who knew him.

There was then a gap of some years until the 1990's when my mother found and met her cousins Anne and Ronnie, the daughters of her Uncle Frank.

My mother had not seen her father's grave since visits made to it as a child with her mother, walking from Coronation, through Bracks Wood and over the bridge spanning the river Gaunless to the cemetery grounds. Determined to find the grave again and, having tracked down the date of her father's accident through a press cutting from the Auckland Chronicle of the time, plus help from the official at the Council Offices, she was able to locate the area of the grave. The grass was long and covered the small headstone and it seemed initially as though the grave would not be found. On the point of giving up my mother sensed that she should turn back to an area she had already checked. On return she went straight to her father's grave and found the headstone, its lettering obscured by moss and algae. Was it her father calling her back to his grave? Each person will have their own view but my mother was convinced that it was not chance that drew her back.

The next major breakthrough came in September 2002 when my parents, on holiday in Scarborough, drove up to and visited the Bridge Inn, Ramshaw, a public house associated with the Mattimoe family in the early years of the 20th century. Initially the visit appeared not to further investigations but a helpful person suggested they leave their name and telephone number in case any one who could help popped in. They returned home from their holiday not expecting to hear anything more and were therefore elated when my mother's second cousin, Angela, rang and made contact. From that time, with Angela's invaluable help, we have met many people who have been most helpful in providing new information. Angela has also contributed greatly by drawing on her own seemingly limitless memory of interesting facts and stories about the family. Gradually the pictures in the old family album not only acquired names but came to life as details of their way of life and their personal joys, tragedies and incidents both amusing and tragic emerged.

This book is the story of the Irish families of **'Little Ireland'**, how they came to be in Gordon Gill and how they lived during the period from their arrival to the 1930's. Fortunately they were families who took pleasure in having their "likenesses" taken and their descendants have found similar fascination in their story so many copies of such photographs have been passed down and kindly loaned to me in order to illustrate the story. The word story is carefully chosen, not to indicate that what follows is a work of fiction built loosely round few facts but rather to emphasis that it is a depiction of the lives of a group of families who as newcomers to the area played a full role in their community, whilst enjoying life and trying to lead good lives, strengthened by their religion, despite experiencing more than their fair share of personal tragedy.

My ancestors and their families were unique but their experiences were shared by others in similar circumstances. Not surprisingly where hardships were nationwide the solutions people sought became distilled into a few stark options. In Ireland the solution for many was to emigrate to England, Scotland, Canada or America. The outline story of the families of this book were acted out by many thousands of other families who found themselves in similar situations. I hope that those reading this book whose families left Ireland for England in the second half of the nineteenth century may, through the lives of those it describes, gain a better understanding of how their ancestors lived in those traumatic days and became integrated into their new homeland. I also hope it rekindles that love of Ireland which seems to lie in the heart of those whose forebears were born there and perhaps encourage a visit to that beautiful country and welcoming people.

2 Connaught's History

This chapter draws on the comprehensive and authoritative research on the history of Moylurg undertaken by Col. Cyril Mattimoe and documented in his book 'North Roscommon – its people and past'.

The early story of the Mattimoes is the story of Connaught, the province in the northwest of Ireland comprise of counties Galway, Mayo, Sligo, Roscommon and Leitrim. Within this province the kingship of Moylurg was the home of the families who would combine through marriage to produce the ancestors of the Mattimoes.

The Early History of Moylurg

The ancient Irish kingship of Moylurg stretched from Kilronan Mountain in Co. Sligo, southwest through Co. Roscommon enclosing Lough Key, Boyle town and the plains of Boyle then on past the eastern shore of Lough Gara to the border with Co. Galway. The northern half of Moylurg has been the heartland of the Mattimoes since at least the 17th century.

Mans early occupation of Moylurg is marked by the remains of ancient megalithic tombs and barrows, dating from 3000 BC There is a megalithic cemetery and the remains of a prehistoric village at Carrowkeel on the top of the Bricklieve Mountains to the west of Lough Arrow. Remains of Crannogs have been identified. These man-made islands in the Loughs, which date from 2000 BC through to early Christian times, accommodated timber and thatched dwellings and were linked to the shore by raised timber causeways. All that remains of these settlements now are small, low, stony islands often with trees growing where the houses would have stood. Evidence of Crannogs has also been found in lakes of the Scottish Highlands showing the links between the Celtic peoples of the north western edge of Europe. The Celtic Irish also left behind evidence of their craftsmanship in the form of beautiful, distinctively decorated jewellery and weaponry using designs that remain as desirable today as they were when first crafted over two thousand years ago.

Then, at around the time of the birth of Christ, a new group of settlers arrived in Ireland, the Gaels, who were to have a profound impact upon the country giving it a language which was spoken by the vast majority of the population for nearly 2,000 years and through which the rich tradition of poetry, stories, legends and music was passed down through successive generations.

The next wave of incomers to Ireland, the Romans, established a base at Dublin, primarily for trade. It seems likely that these trading links extended to smaller outposts along the major rivers. However they did not govern or colonise Ireland as they did Britain. Hence they had no need to improve communication routes through the building of roads, thus leaving the tribal pattern of the country, and most certainly Connaught, undisturbed. They did leave their alphabet which the Irish used to write both latin and Gaelic documents.

The Vikings, who began their raids at the end of the 8th century, did have an impact on Ireland. This time the invaders did not content themselves with attacks on the east of the country at such places as Dublin and Wexford but also raided the West. The Vikings were a feature of Irish life for three hundred

Connaught's History 9

Fig. 6   A megalithic passage tomb on the top of the Bricklieve Mountains at Carrowkeel near Castlebaldwin in Co. Sligo. There are several such impressive tombs. They are in a stunning location with views across to Lough Arrow and Lough Key and beyond to the Kilronan Mountain's.

Fig. 7   An authentic reconstruction of a crannog at The Scottish Crannog Centre, Loch Tay, Perthshire.

years and through most of this period contact between the Gaelic natives and the Norwegian invaders, and subsequent settlers, was of a violent, hostile nature. In 1014 Brian Boru, then High King of Ireland, defeated an army of Norsemen from Dublin at the battle of Clontarf. In a pattern that was to be repeated through the centuries the 'foreign' forces were supported by a number of Irish Chieftains, in this instance from Leinster. Vikings did settle in Ireland and were absorbed into the population with perhaps evidence of their distant genes still showing themselves through the occasional beautiful red-haired child with which families in the West of Ireland are blessed with.

From the 5th to the 16th century most of the population of Moylurg lived in raths. These consisted of single storey mud, wattle and thatched buildings within a circular protective bank. Some raths had two such protective rings whilst those occupied by a King had three rings. Evidence of these can be found at Tara, Co. Meath, home of the pagan Gaelic High Kings.

From a later period, sites of castles such as Ballinafad, plus mottes and moated houses bear witness to the continuing strategic importance of the area through the ages. The influence of the areas early Christian past can be found in the remains of simple stone monasteries, and their occupants response to the Viking invaders by the remains of the tall round towers used to keep watch for signs of the invaders and, with their high entrance door, provide protection during such raids.

Fig. 14 Approximate boundaries of the ancient kingship of Moylurg based on research by Col. Cyril Mattimoe

Sweat Houses

One other type of building whose remains have survived in the landscape is the 'sweat house' used in the treatment of bronchial illnesses, including pleurisy, and rheumatism. They were low, beehive shaped buildings constructed from stone walls and turf roofs leaving an enclosed area which would be heated by either lighting a fire or by placing tight bundles of rushes which had been steeped in boiling water. A bowl of water containing herbs would be placed in the sweat house during the heating process. When the temperature was sufficient the ashes or the bundles of reeds were dragged out and the patient placed inside naked on a bed of straw. The house was closed up with sods leaving just enough of an opening to allow sufficient air for the patient to breathe. The patient would then 'sweat out' their illness removing the sweat with a trowel. It is said that the patient could remain in the sweat house for up to three days. Sweat houses were usually constructed near to a stream so that the patient could be plunged into cold water on removal from the heat.

Sweat houses were in use up until a hundred years ago and the first recorded references to them are from medieval times though it seems certain that they were in use before that. There is speculation about their origins. They could possibly have been introduced by the Romans but the process seems to link more to the Scandinavian sauna therefore could have been a Viking introduction. They are unique to this part of Ireland.

Fig. 9 Round tower at Killala, Co. Sligo.

Fig.10
A sweat house, a form of ancient sauna almost unique to the area surrounding the borders of Co. Sligo and Co. Leitrim. This one is near Drumkeeran, Co. Leitrim. Despite its apparent age and long disuse the inside of the sweat house was sound and dry.

The Clans of Connaught

The people of Connaught were organised in tribes of which, over time, the Ui Neill became paramount. One branch of this tribe was the Ui Briuin Ai, descendants of Brian King of Connaught who was killed in 405 AD. A sub- branch, the Sil Murray, descended from Indrechtaigh Mac Muireadhaigh, established itself in Moylurg and included the O'Conors, MacDermots, MacManuses, O'Brenans, MacGeraghtys and, eventually, the Mattimoes.

Most of the population of Moylurg lived on the flatter, richer land south of the River Boyle. The northern part, including the future parishes of Kilmactranny, Kilronan and Ardcarne, the future stronghold of the Mattimoes, was heavily wooded and occupied by the MacDermot Roes who were known as the Lords of the Woods.

The land provided the small population of the area, which was probably less than 2,000, with an ample and varied diet comprising beef, pork, mutton, dairy products, cereal grains and vegetables plus fish from the many lakes and rivers. Herbs were used for flavouring as well as for medicinal purposes. With a sparse population and the boundaries of each tribes land or tuath well known there was no reason for fencing the land and it remained thus until the 17th century. This 'open plan' living had its downside as it facilitated the cattle raids which each tribe seemed to both inflict on, and suffer from, its neighbours. Perhaps due to the threat of raids the roads remained basic with the limited aim of facilitating travel within and not between tuaths. The bogs and mountains similarly provided a degree of protection from raids.

The Arrival of Christianity

Christianity came to Moylurg in the 5th century with the visits of St. Patrick. He established churches including one at Aughanagh, the parish where 1,400 years later Thomas Mattimoe was to be christened, and a nunnery at Kilaraght. A stone at St. Patrick's well in Boyle is said to bear the imprint of the Saint's knee. His success in converting the local population to Christianity was not without mishap. At Boyle the horses of his party were stolen in two separate incidents and the Saint was thrown into the river from his chariot whilst negotiating a crossing. The incidents did nothing for the Saints humour as he cursed both the local population and the river itself, though was persuaded to mollify his reaction.

Over the centuries the religious life of Moylurg was enhanced by others following in the footsteps of St. Patrick; St. Columcille (Assylinn) and St. Beoaidg (Ardcarne), 6th century; Augustinians (Elphin and Ardcarne) and Cistercians (Boyle Abbey), 12th century; Premonstratension or white Canons (Trinity Island, Lough Key), 13th century; Dominican Friars 14th century; Franciscan Third Order Regular (Knockvicar), 15th and 16th centuries.

Fig. 11   Celtic cross at Drumcliff, Co. Sligo.

Fig. 12 Ballindoon Friary on the eastern shore of Lough Arrow was founded in 1507 under the patronage of the MacDonagh's. The Priory and its lands were confiscated after Henry VIII's suppression of the monasteries but the friars continued to live nearby. The last friar was Father Michael Reynolds O.P. who was the parish priest for Aughanagh (Ballinafad) and died some time between 1785 and 1789. As such he would have counted several Mattimoe families amongst his parishioners including the grandfather of Thomas Mattimoe. The Priory is now a peaceful, romantic ruin surrounded by a small cemetery. Burials have taken place within the ruins themselves including several MacDonaghs showing a continuing link between the family and the priory. A unique feature of the church is the triple-arched screen across the centre of the church, its upper floor only accessible from an external stair.

The Kings of Moylurg

Mulrooney, son of Teig of the Towers, the King of Connaught, became King of Moylurg in 956. He became known as Mulrooney Mor, the Great Mulrooney, in recognition of his abilities. His descendants, the MacDermot's ruled Moylurg for six hundred years little troubled by either the Vikings or the Normans.

Dermot was an illustrious descendant of Mulrooney Mor who lived in the 12th century. It was in recognition of his kingship skills that the family took his name thus becoming the MacDermots. The MacDermot Kings had their official residence on The Rock, a small island in Lough Key whose ancient Irish name was Carraig MacDermot. The MacDermots were known through the centuries for their generous hospitality and The Rock was the scene of many lavish parties complete with sumptuous spreads and entertainment. Visitors would never be turned away and the door of the King's house was never locked.

The strength of the MacDermots largely protected the population of Moylurg from attacks by their neighbours but they had to endure natural disasters in particular harsh Winters. In early 1115 snow and storms caused widespread damage to buildings, loss of livestock and resultant famine for the population. Around this time one hundred and forty seven guests at one of the MacDermots entertainments were killed when The Rock was struck by lightning.

It should not be assumed though that this was a settled period. Succession to the kingship of Moylurg was not secured from father to son but rather by the Brehon code which dictated that the King be elected by the elite. This, combined with the gavelkind rule which on the death of a landholder split his land amongst his family members, prevented dominance of any one family but led to much internal strife which regularly spilled over into inter-tribal skirmishes. The latter were often little more then an excuse for some local 'cattle rustling' or collection of 'rent arrears' and as such were generally short lived with little loss of life.

This way of life led local chieftains to strengthen their position by hiring Scottish mercenaries from the late 13th century to complement their forces. These mercenaries, known as Gallowglass, were well trained, fierce fighting men who, unlike the Gaelic fighters of the time, had the advantage of armoured breastplates and helmets, and wielded a long-handled, double edged axe with deadly affect. The success of the Gallowglass led to a home-grown freelance mercenary force, the Bonnaght.

In the 1500's a third group of mercenaries, the Albanagh, arrived from Scotland. Unlike the Gallowglass who often stayed, married and integrated into the community, the Albanagh either moved on to be hired by others or roamed locally carrying out raids for their own benefit before returning to Scotland only to return in greater numbers the following year. The troublesome Albanagh were finally, if brutally, despatched by the forces of Sir John Bingham who had chased them from Keadue and massacred them, men, women and children, on the banks of the river Moy.

Teig of the Towers had another son, Conor, who became King of Connaught and was ancestor to all the O'Conor Kings of Connaught.

Whilst these events were happening in Moylurg the Normans had conquered England, allocated the land to Barons loyal to the Norman King and established a strong system of government. Ireland appears to have remained unconcerned about the developments affecting their larger neighbour. Similarly the Normans appeared not too interested in Ireland. This was to change and it was the Irish who instigated this change.

Fig. 13 Gallowglass

The High King of Ireland Unwittingly Provokes Norman Colonisation

During the first half of the 12th century the O'Conor King of Connaught, Turlough Mor and subsequently his son Rory, were absorbed in their own ultimately successful endeavours to become High Kings of Ireland. In this they were supported by the then King of Moylurg, Dermot, and his fighting men. Dermot was appointed Chief Marshal to Turlough Mor thus becoming his right-hand man. Fortunately much of the fighting took place outside Moylurg so it was a peaceful time for those who stayed at home and

Fig. 8 Ballinafad Castle, Co. Sligo, positioned strategically between the Curlew Mountains and the southern tip of Lough Arrow.

benefited from association with the successful Turlough Mor. The fighting was sporadic, casualties light and those involved were compensated by a the share of booty from successful expeditions. Turlough's tactic of divide and conquer amongst the other Kings had limited success requiring him to return to each province to reinforce his position through military strength. Thirty five such expeditions were required in his thirty seven year reign the length and breadth of the country.

One of Turlough's supporters, Dermot McMurrough, King of Leinster, was a violent, vicious man who made many enemies. When Turlough died his son, Rory became, what was to prove to be the last, High King of Ireland. Rory, who did not possess the qualities of his father, was supported by Dermot McMurrough's enemies and together they moved against the King of Leinster. In 1170 Dermot McMurrough, sought help from Strongbow, the Norman Earl of Pembroke. The superior military capabilities of Strongbow's forces, in particular their armour and archers were what Dermot desired and in return Strongbow saw an opportunity to expand his power and his wealth in Ireland which he achieved by marrying Dermot's daughter and succeeding to the title of King of Leinster on Dermot's death.

Not that Strongbow had things all his own way. In 1174 Rory O'Conor force's, supported by many men from Roscommon, attacked his forces and inflicted an overwhelming defeat on them at Thurles. This was Rory O'Conor's last major success. He later suffered defeat in Co. Donegal and many noble

Irish men were lost. In 1188 the Normans threatened Moylurg and attempted to attack from the direction of the Curlew Mountains. The pass through these mountains is deceptive. It is not flanked by high bluffs and crags but by true Irish bog. The Normans, like others who would take the similar route in future centuries to march into Moylurg, underestimated the danger. When the forces of the Connaught chieftains, including MacDermot, ambushed the Normans the mounted armoured knights floundered in the bog and were defeated and Moylurg was saved. However the Irish were to find, not for the last time, that short-term gain by the use of outsiders was to provide a long-term problem.

In England Henry II grew concerned at the developments in Ireland, in particular the growing power of Strongbow, and acted to restore his authority by installing Lords loyal to himself throughout much of Ireland. As was to happen many times in history these newcomers were soon seduced by Ireland and, after the initial land grab established their position, married into Irish families and adopted Irish customs and practices, including inter-tribal raiding and fighting. They even spoke Gaelic rather than their native French.

Consequently the Norman invasion had relatively little long term impact on Ireland other than the area around Dublin, known as The Pale, where English rule was maintained. 'Beyond The Pale' the rest of the country, and certainly Connaught, remained to the Normans awkward and independent.

Changing fortunes for the Inhabitants of Moylurg

Moylurg was not so fortunate in the 13th and 14th centuries being plundered ten times or more following disputes primarily concerning the Kingship of Connaught. These must have been dark days for the population to live through, full of uncertainty, fear and hardship.

The 15th century was a more settled period, however the hardship of civil strife was replaced with hardship brought about by severe winters, floods, droughts and plagues. As natural disasters subsided the Kings of Moylurg resumed their inter-tribal feuding, though without the success of their forebears. Eventually, disputes for the kingship of Moylurg resulted in regicide leading to an attack on Moylurg by the O'Donnell's from Donegal who tried to advance through the Curlew pass in 1497 and were defeated but not beaten. Two years later they chose to attack via Knockvicar and were more successful leading to a peace agreement with the MacDermots.

In the mid 16th century Rory, one of the strongest MacDermot kings, attacked The Rock and imprisoned the then king, in effect assuming that role himself. Under his kingship Moylurg became strong again and held sway over a large area beyond its boundaries receiving tribute in the prime currency of the time, cattle, from the neighbouring chieftains. Rory strengthened his forces with Gallowglass and other mercenaries and his raiding parties developed into an annual event with establishment of Summer camps in mid-Roscommon which provided bases from which to sally forth and extract tribute from the surrounding area. These camps were not purely military, they also provided entertainment in the form of poets, musicians and minstrels. The entertainment proved so diverting on one occasion that the camp was attacked and Rory captured. He secured his release, no doubt by payment of some form of ransom, as ten years later he was reported back in the area with a Summer camp.

Rory remained a strong king dying in 1568 at the grand old age, for those times, of eighty. As so often happens after a long period under a strong leader, an unsettled period followed and Rory's successor, Turlough, was to be the last King of Moylurg. This period also coincided with the English finally deciding to take the long ignored Connaught in hand.

Fig. 15 Boyle Abbey. Given to Sir John King in 1602 who was 'disappointed' in its condition as it was a ruin by that date.

The Elizabethan Wars

Perhaps ignored is too strong a word but Connaught had been left to its own devices, though Irish Kings and Chieftains continued to request help from English forces under the pretext of assisting the Crown when the true reason was often the settling of local scores.

Henry VIII was the first English monarch to tire of an increasingly rebellious Ireland. He attempted to bring the country and its Lords to heel in one stroke by confiscating all the land and re-granting it on a basis that ensured allegiance to the Crown. However it was left to his daughter Elizabeth I to turn this theoretical control into reality.

After a few false starts the first major step in weakening the powers of the local Chieftains ironically involved not a single blow being exchanged and was welcomed by many of the Chieftains. This 'Trojan Horse' was the Compossicion of Connaught of 1585 under which the often abused Brehon Law of Coigne and Livery was commuted to a rent payment. This law allowed the local Chieftains to billet soldiers, often mercenaries, with the local people. The change appeared to suit the Chieftains though in practice led to the weakening of their military strength leaving Connaught more susceptible to further English influence and control. The MacDermots of Moylurg were willing signatories to this change. The more sinister aspect of the Agreement was the failure of local Freeholders to register ownership of their land,

> ### The Lovers of Trinity Island
>
> During the Battle of the Curlews in 1599 when the Irish forces of the McDermots and O'Rourkes inflicted a defeat upon the English Army, Tomas Laidir Costello saved the life of Turlough, son of Brian Og MacDermot. In gratitude the MacDermots invited Tomas to The Rock. The Costello's were a similar warring family to the MacDermots and this invite appeared to put past difficulties between the families to one side. This was not to be and tragedy followed.
>
> Tomas met and fell in love with Una Bhan MacDermot, daughter of Brian but he would not countenance a marriage between them. Some time later a feast was held by the MacDermots and Tomas was amongst those nobles invited. During the feast Una was invited to toast the man she wished to marry and raised her glass to Tomas, much to the anger of her father who slapped her face. Una fled to her room and was inconsolable. Tomas stormed out. Una pined for Tomas and became very weak. Eventually Tomas returned and Una held his hand and slept properly for the first time since the fateful feast.
>
> That evening Tomas left the Castle in Lough Key and swore that if he reached the shore without hearing from Una he would never return. Her messenger arrived just as he reached dry land but his pride would not let him go back on his pledge to himself so he returned home.
>
> Una never recovered and when she died was buried on Trinity Island in Lough Key.
>
> Tomas never forgave himself and would swim out to Trinity Island every night to sit by Una's grave. On a stormy night he drowned and his body was buried next to Una. Two trees grew from the graves and entwined together.
>
> Many generations later, long after the Macdermots had been replaced by the King family, and Lord Lorton's Rockingham estate encompassed The Rock, Trinity Island and the surrounding land, his forester cut down the two trees by mistake. Lord Lorton is reputed to have been appalled at the loss and said he would rather have lost the whole of Rockingham estate than those two trees.

instead allowing an Over-lord to sign on their behalf. Thus at a stroke, or rather without a stroke, reducing themselves to tenants.

The arrival in 1584 of Sir Charles Bingham as Governor of Connaught heralded a more direct and brutal tightening of the English Crown's hold on the province. Bingham was cruel and ruthless and during his term ordered the hanging of many, both guilty and innocent, including Cathal MacDermot, son of Turlough, King of Moylurg. Bingham's representative in Boyle was Green O'Moyle who claimed to be descended from the O'Mulloys of Offaly though doubt has been cast on this claim. He gained the confidence of local Chieftains despite his dubious pedigree and his own brutal approach to his role. He hanged three innocent men at Knockvicar and over the border in Mayo hanged thirteen landowners who were in search of their cattle that had been stolen. His son fought against Cromwell and many of his descendants are buried at Ardcarne.

The attack by the Spanish Armada in 1585, like many threats from the continental mainland over the centuries, led England to strengthen its military hold on Ireland which it perceived, not without just cause, as its vulnerable western flank. Military forces were based at Boyle Abbey, Tulsk Abbey, and Ballymote whilst a 'great fortress' was built at Tintagh on the neck of land between Lough Arrow and Lough Key.

Fig. 16

This illustration, taken from the penny illutrated magazines of the early 20th century, depicts the ruins of the church on Trinity Island in Lough Key. The beautifilly carved limestone slab was not originally in the window but had been placed there for effect. The carving was still in the window bay sixty years ago but has long since been removed and has now disappeared without trace.

Connaught was not easily to be brought to heel. The Nine Year War began in 1593 with a rebellion against the English led by Hugh Maguire, Lord of Fermanagh. After marching through Moylurg, which he plundered, his forces met those of Bingham, almost by accident, and the resulting skirmish was inconclusive. From that time an Ulster Chieftain, Hugh O'Donnell known as Red Hugh, took up the fight against the English in Connaught. Fortunately for Moylurg its Lord was Conor Oge of Aghacarra who supported the O'Donnells so for the remainder of the war it saw many comings and goings of military forces but was spared further plundering. The local populace would have been required to feed the armies as they passed through but the forces were relatively small being geared to the hit and run tactics favoured by Red Hugh.

The first incursion by Red Hugh and his forces was March 1595 on their way to plunder the area west of Tulsk occupied by many English colonists. The campaign was very successful both in its military objective and in the amount of booty carried away. Red Hugh also managed to elude Bingham's army and return safely.

Red Hugh attempted to repeat his success a mere six weeks later returning to attack the garrison in Boyle Abbey. The measure of his confidence can be judged by the route he took through Carrigeenroe, past the fort at Tintagh and on past Ballinafad Castle to Boyle. The objective appeared not to be to oust the English forces from the Abbey but rather to make off with their sizeable herd of cattle. The small garrison refused to come out and fight, so Red Hugh contented himself with a circuitous return journey through Co. Longford which provided sufficient opportunity for acquiring additional booty.

Red Hugh was dominant in Connaught and appointed Chieftains loyal to him including Conor McDermot of Aghacarra, son of Teig the brother of Turlough the last King of Moylurg.

Red Hugh's success was Bingham's loss and in 1596 he was replaced by Sir Conyers Clifford. The new Governor with his superior numbers failed to prevent Red Hugh's attacks and in the following year the area south of Elphin was again pillaged by the Irish forces.

Whilst Red Hugh was an undoubted thorn in the side of the English their main protagonist was Hugh O'Neill, Earl of Tyrone, who had been appointed to that position by Elizabeth I and had spent time at her court. His undoubted feeling of loyalty to the Queen conflicted with the desire to maintain freedom of action on his estates in Ireland where his descent from the Ui Nialls, the clan of the High Kings of Ireland, reinforced his independent view. He joined forces with Red Hugh to repel a concerted attack by the English and in 1598 defeated them at Yellow Ford, a few miles north of Armagh.

Following on from this the MacDonagh's, one of Red Hugh's supporters, recovered their castle at Ballymote from the English. Red Hugh took a liking to it and persuaded the MacDonagh's to part with it for the bargain price of £400 plus 300 cows and it became his headquarters.

The Battle of the Curlews

Red Hugh went from strength to strength and was soon plundering as far away as Co.'s Mayo, Galway and Clare against Chieftains who sided with the English Queen.

In response to requests from her Governor Queen Elizabeth sent the Earl of Essex and a large army to Ireland to finally sort out the dissident Irish Lords and their forces. Essex was to prove as inept in his tactics as those who preceded him. On arrival he learnt that their Irish ally O'Connor Sligo was besieged by Red Hugh's forces at Collooney. After some ineffectual manoeuvring of his forces, which only succeeded in giving Red Hugh more time to secure the port of Sligo and the pass through the Curlew Mountains, Essex decided that Clifford should take a force of 1,500 foot and 200 horse from his base in Athlone and march to Colooney to raise the siege.

On arrival at Boyle on 15th August 1599 he was told the pass over the Curlews was unoccupied and, well aware of it as a danger point, decided not to rest his weary forces but to continue the march through the mountains.

Clifford had been misinformed. The pass over the Curlews was occupied by Conor MacDermot with 300 men. The MacDermots and the men of Moylurg had never been beaten in defence of the pass.

The vanguard of Clifford's forces, some 400 shot and 200 pike, were ambushed as they made their way through the pass. They responded but the Irish quickly withdrew drawing their foe into the bogs surrounding the pass. The Irish repeatedly attacked in similar manner until the English forces ran out of shot. By this time O'Connor's forces had been reinforced by Brian O'Rourke and 500 men. Feeling defenceless and out manoeuvred the English vanguard retreated in disarray. In doing so they alarmed the main body of Clifford's forces which also turned tail and ran pursued by the Irish. Clifford endeavoured to stop the rout but was killed before having any effect. The English cavalry were in Boyle and about to make their way up to the pass when they saw the foot soldiers running down from the mountain towards them. The cavalry chose to take a different route to engage the Irish. They had initial success but the soft ground hampered the horses and several chased the Irish into the bog never to be seen again. Despite this they were able to provide support until the infantry withdrew. The battle had lasted two hours but the English were beaten and retired to recover at Boyle Abbey before returning to Athlone. News of the English defeat led O'Conor Sligo to surrender at Colooney.

A magnificent statue of a mounted Gaelic Warrior towers over the road that leads from Boyle toward Sligo with his back to Lough Key and his face turned toward the pass over the Curlew Mountains where the forces of Conor MacDermot and Brian O'Rourke defeated the English army of Sir Clifford Conyers, Governor of Connaught.

The Flight of the Earls

The long feared Spanish involvement in Ireland became reality when a fleet landed at Kinsale in 1601. This force was besieged by the forces of Mountjoy, Elizabeth's Deputy, and in response Hugh O'Neill and his ally Red Hugh marched their armies south to relieve the Spanish forces. In the event the armies of O'Neill and O'Donnell, more used to fighting in the woods and bogs of the north, were defeated and fled north. The tide had turned in the English Queen's favour.

Fig. 17 This statue of a Gaelic Warrior stands above the Sligo road with his back to Lough Key and facing the Curlew Mountains where in 1598 the combined Irish forces of the MacDermots and the O'Rourkes inflicted a heavy defeat upon the English army led by Sir Clifford Conyers

The reign of the Gaelic Chieftains in Connaught was at an end. Conor MacDermot won one further battle in the Curlews but surrendered in 1603 and was dead within a year. Similarly Brian O'Rourke surrendered a year later and died shortly afterward.

Despite the defeats and losses he had inflicted upon the English Hugh O'Neill was pardoned, though not all his old adversaries were in agreement with this response. Subsequently rumours circulated about his involvement in further Spanish plots against England. Hugh O'Neill appeared to conclude that such rumours jeopardised his personal safety therefore in 1607 he set sail for France from Rathmullen, Co. Donegal with the Earl of Tyrconnell, Rory the heir of Hugh O'Donnell and many other loyal Irish Chieftains, an event subsequently referred to as the Flight of the Earls.

The departure of the two Earls left a power void in Ulster and led to significant developments which would have repercussions in Ireland to this day. In 1610 settlers were encouraged to take up opportunities in Ulster, opportunities created by dispossessing the Irish who lived there. This plantation process, unlike those previously was well funded and consequently more successful. Of more significance to the future history of Ireland another plantation of Scottish settlers had begun four years earlier. They were Presbyterians who, like the Irish had endured religious persecution in their home land, and came with strong resolve knowing the antagonism they would meet from the native Irish. They also possessed a strong scepticism in regard to help they could expect from an English Monarch or Parliament in time of need. The strong feeling of self reliance both in terms of the need to maintain their position and to

Department of Irish Folklore, University College, Dublin

Fig. 18   Suppression of the Roman Catholic Church led to the holding of Mass in remote locations away from the Authorities, Landlords and their supporters. Many such 'Mass Rocks' existed and local people can still direct the visitor to them. Often they were sites which already had a religious connection such as the site of an abandoned friary or a holy well. This photograph is of a well attended Mass at Milford. The open shelter covers the Mass Rock.

practice their religion resisted the natural process of integration and assimilation which had occurred with previous groups of incomers

Following the demise of the Irish Chieftains the English were slow to fill the void. Moylurg became lawless for a period with marauding bands a threat to life and property. In 1607 Sir John King started building his castle in Boyle and with it laid the foundations for the town that was to grow around it.

Religious pressure increased on the Roman Catholic majority. Their Priests were ordered to leave the country and they themselves were coerced into attending the Church of Ireland with risk of a fine for defaulters. The Roman Catholic churches were confiscated and given to the Church of Ireland. From that point Catholics had to attend mass in the open air. Traditional places of worship evolved, often referred to as Mass rocks located in remote parts of the countryside to avoid attracting the attention of the Authorities or the English landlords.

Changing Fortunes of English Kings Affect Moylurg

With the rise to the English throne of James I the rights of the Irish in Moylurg to their own land suffered another serious setback. The new King needed to bolster his finances and agreed to grant title of land to every Freeholder in Ireland. Just as in the Compossicion Grants a number of the Freeholders in Moylurg agreed to register collectively believing presumably that the 'word is my bond' approach of the Brehon Code still applied. The Brehon Code did not apply in London.

Finally in 1635 Thomas Wentworth, Earl of Strafford, the representative of another cash strapped King, Charles I, travelled to Boyle to carry out an Inquisition into land title. Regardless of his terms of reference Wentworth's own agenda was to maximise benefit for the King. Land whose title was in any way defective was defaulted to ownership of the King.

To Hell or Connaught

The next period of turmoil was a by-product of England's own internal disruption. The English Civil War of 1642-45 was a battle between the supporters of the Monarchy and the supporters of Parliament but had religious differences at its heart. In Ireland it was a conflict between Catholic and Protestant but at its heart was a battle for the return of confiscated lands and for freedom from English control. By this time only 59% of the land in Ireland was in Catholic hands but far worse was to come.

In 1641 there was a Catholic uprising and Protestant Settlements were attacked. Most attacks occurred in Ulster but incidents occurred throughout Ireland. Atrocities were committed, some of which would be remembered long by supporters of the Orange Order. In addition Royalist Armies were in Ireland. Once Oliver Cromwell had secured England from Charles I he turned his attention to Ireland, landing in August 1649. His actions were decisive and brutal with atrocities committed against the Irish Catholic population. The outcome was a victory for Cromwell and his followers and defeat for the Catholic population who suffered further confiscation of their lands and banishment to the lands west of the Shannon, or in the words of Cromwell "To hell or Connaught". A number of Irish families from east of the Shannon who had lost their land were 'transplanted' to the surrounding area of Boyle and given land confiscated from local families who had supported the Royalist cause.

Cromwell's soldiers and supporters benefited from the confiscated lands and whilst this was meant to involve land East of the Shannon it appears that some land in the area between Lough Gara, Lough Arrow and Lough Key was also confiscated for distribution to Cromwell's followers.

The Flight of the Wild Geese

The restoration of the Monarchy in the form of the Catholic Charles II did not bring the Irish Catholics the hoped for restoration of confiscated lands. His successor James II gave further hope but these were dashed when civil war broke out between the supporters of the King and those of his son-in-law the Protestant William of Orange. This war lasted three and a half years and affected the local population when in September 1689 the force of raw Irish forces occupying Boyle were surprised by the the seasoned Protestant troops of Colonel Lloyd arriving through the Curlew pass. Lloyd cut off the escape route from the town and in a short, sharp encounter three hundred Irishmen were killed.

The armies loyal to James II were beaten at the Battle of the Boyne and at Aughrim in 1690. The following year the Irish armies formally surrendered and their Commander with thousands of his troops were allowed to take exile in France to serve in the army of Louis XIV, and became known as the Wild Geese.

The Penal Laws

Following the coronation of William III the Penal Laws were enacted in 1695 which severely restricted the freedom of Roman Catholics. Whilst they were still allowed to practice their religion restrictions were placed upon their clergy and only those serving as parish priests were allowed to remain in the country. Catholics were not allowed to vote or stand for Parliament. They were not allowed to serve in government, practice law or serve in the Army. Critically to the economic well being of the Catholic majority, and thus ultimately Ireland itself, they were not allowed to buy land and on their death had to divide their land equally amongst all their children unless one son professed to be Protestant in which case he inherited the whole estate. Consequently the amount of land held by Catholics which had dwindled to 22% following Cromwell and then to 14% by the time of the Penal Laws subsequently reduced to a mere 7% by 1714.

The pressure on the Catholic gentry saw many of the sons of MacDermots, MacDonaghs, O'Connors and others follow the path of the Wild Geese and leave for France to serve the Republican Army. During the period 1690 to 1770 forty-two MacDonaghs served as Officers in the Regiment of Dillon, Earl of Roscommon.

Moran is a name associated with North Roscommon and South Sligo. In future years Morans and Mattimoes married in Ireland then at the end of the 19th century one of our Mattimoes was to marry a woman who had links with the Moran family of Bishop Auckland. It is interesting to note that a Jacque O'Moran, is the only Irishman whose name appears on the Arc de Triumphe. Sadly Jacque was to surrender his life to the guillotine during the French Revolution.

Connaught's History 25

Fig. 19   Map of the part of Co. Sligo and Co. Roscommon referred to in this book. The maps are from the 'Atlas comprising the counties of Ireland and a general map of the kingdom' by Samuel Lewis, 1837

3   Gaelic Roots

Col. Mattimoe undertook much research into the origins of the name Mattimoe and its relationship to the name Milmo. His first paper on the subject was completed in 1957 and he continued to research the name writing his final paper on the subject forty years later. In researching my ancestors I have frequently found myself following in Col. Mattimoe's footsteps and often so close behind that those I met spoke about him as if they had been talking to him yesterday. It is with deep regret that I did not meet him before he died.

His final paper acknowledged the assistance he received on the subject from the very able researcher Terry Arthur of Tyne and Wear whose Milmo/Mattimoe ancestors left Co. Sligo for England in the mid 1800's. I was fortunate to meet Terry Arthur at Co. Durham Record Office. By a million to one chance I happened to sit at the adjacent microfilm reader to that he was using. Conversations at such times are rare but I happened to be reading the records of St. Wilfred's Roman Catholic Church, Bishop Auckland which Terry was also keen to use. I explained why I was interested in the records and we discovered we were both researching the same family. Since then Terry has been helpful to me in my research for which I am very grateful.

Origins of the name Milmo

There is strong evidence that Mattimoe is synonymous with Milmo though the reverse is not true. Wolfe in his Irish Names and Surnames states that Milmo, Milmoe, O'Molmoy and O'Mulmoy were all derived from the Gaelic *O Maolmuaidh*. Edward MacLysaght in his book More Irish Families agreed with Wolfe in regard to Milmo adding that they were thus descended from a minor sept of the Silmurray located in Co. Roscommon. Knox in his book History of Mayo stated that there was a tribe known as **Ui Fiacrach Muaidh** who held land on the northern border of Co., Mayo and Co. Sligo until the 6th century providing many of the Kings of Connaught. In Chronicum Scotorum there is mention of Domnall son of the king Maelmuaidh in 945 who held lands in Co. Sligo. . The Annals of the Four Masters state that in 1016 Ceallach Hua Mael Midhe the Provost of Drumrath died. Drumrath was five miles from Boyle. O'Hart in his Irish Pedigrees states that Milmo derives from Mael na mBo, 49th King of Leinster and Grandfather of Dermot MacMurrough who brought the Normans to Ireland and died in 1016.

Milmo is clearly an ancient Sligo name. It has many variations resulting from Anglicisation of the Gaelic name by the English from Elizabethan times onward and the poor literacy of the native population which led to phonetic spelling of names introducing further variations including Wilmo, Wullamoe and Mullamoe.

Origins of the name Mattimoe

Mattimoe is a relatively new name and for generations was restricted to a narrow area on the borders of Co. Sligo and Co. Roscommon stretching from south of Collooney in Co. Sligo across the border to Boyle in Co. Roscommon. This area is still the Irish heartland for those of this unusual name. From the middle of the 18th century through to the middle of the 19th century three genealogical sources give a snapshot of the distribution of the Mattimoe name which taken together with the Roman Catholic registers of the parishes encompassing this area enable the history of the Mattimoes to be partially unravelled and some theories developed as to their origins. These three sources are the Census of the Diocese of Elphin taken in 1749, the Tithe Applotment records of 1823-38 and the Griffith's Valuation 1857/58.

In the Census of Elphin there were twelve Mattimoe families living in this area plus four Mullimoe families. It seems probable that there were also Mattimoe families living just outside the boundaries of the diocese at Lissaneena to the north and at Kilmactranny to the east as both these areas were well represented by families of that name by the time of the Tithe Applotment Survey. The absence of any reference to the name outside this area in the two surveys of the early 19th century suggest strongly that these were the only Mattimoe families excluded from the Census of Elphin. We will discuss in detail the distribution of the families in the three sources later in but first we will consider the strong clues they provide to the origin of the name.

The Census of Elphin points to three stages of development of the family. Coolboy to the west of Castlebaldwin has the strongest representation of Mattimoe families and, judging by the ages of the children appears to contain the most senior representative of that name thus pointing to this being the point of origin for the Mattimoe families in Co. Sligo. Lissaneena, north of Coolboy and Bricklieve to the south appear to hold families representing the first wave of expansion. Those further south in Ardcarne are young families who appear to be tenants of Lord King, who also owned land near Coolboy, and thus may have obtained their tenancies by that route. A similar migration route may explain families moving to Kilmactranny. The land of these new tenancies was not as good but it provided the best route at that time for the sons of Mattimoe families to become self sufficient whilst leaving the main family farms intact and as such represented the second wave of expansion for the Mattimoe family. It seems therefore that the Mattimoes had been in Co. Sligo for at least three or four generations by the time of the Census of Elphin. This would put the date of their arrival to 1650-1675 at the latest and possibly up to fifty years earlier.

The Tithe Applotment Survey charts the next wave of expansion developing from the stronghold in Coolboy where the landholdings continued to be significant and in the areas of Ardcarne, Boyle and Kilmactranny where farms had become fragmented and small reflecting the smaller tenancies that would have been awarded when Mattimoes moved there from Coolboy. Significantly all the Mattimoe families in Coolboy and the surrounding area changed their name to Milmo during the eighty years following the census of Elphin. Col. Mattimoe suggests this might have been as a result of marriage to a female member of the Milmo family and retaining her name for the family rather than that of the husband. This does not appear to account for the widespread change of name. Clearly all the Mattimoe families in the area felt comfortable with the change indicating that the two names where already regarded as synonymous to the extent of virtually being an alias and that the name change may have been made by an administrator without causing concern to the families. Somewhat contrarily the Mullamoes in Ardcarne appear to have changed their name to Mattimoe.

Whilst the name changes held for the next twenty years and are recorded as such in the Griffith's Valuation the families seemed comfortable with using either Mattimoe or Milmo. At Lissaneena in the 1850's Darby Milmo was referred to as Mattimoe when he gave land to enable the construction of a church in the area. His son Patrick retained the name Milmo when he emigrated to Mexico in 1857 to live with the family of a rich uncle in Mexico becoming Don Patricio Milmo, amassing a colossal fortune and marrying the daughter of the celebrated Mexican statesman, Gen. Vidaurri who "taking sides with the Emperor Maximillion shared that Emperor's unhappy fate". Don Patricio did not forget his roots and "during the late famine in Ireland the said Patrick Milmoe sent a handsome donation to the Priests of his native county for distribution to the distressed".

28 Little Ireland

the mattimoe homeland

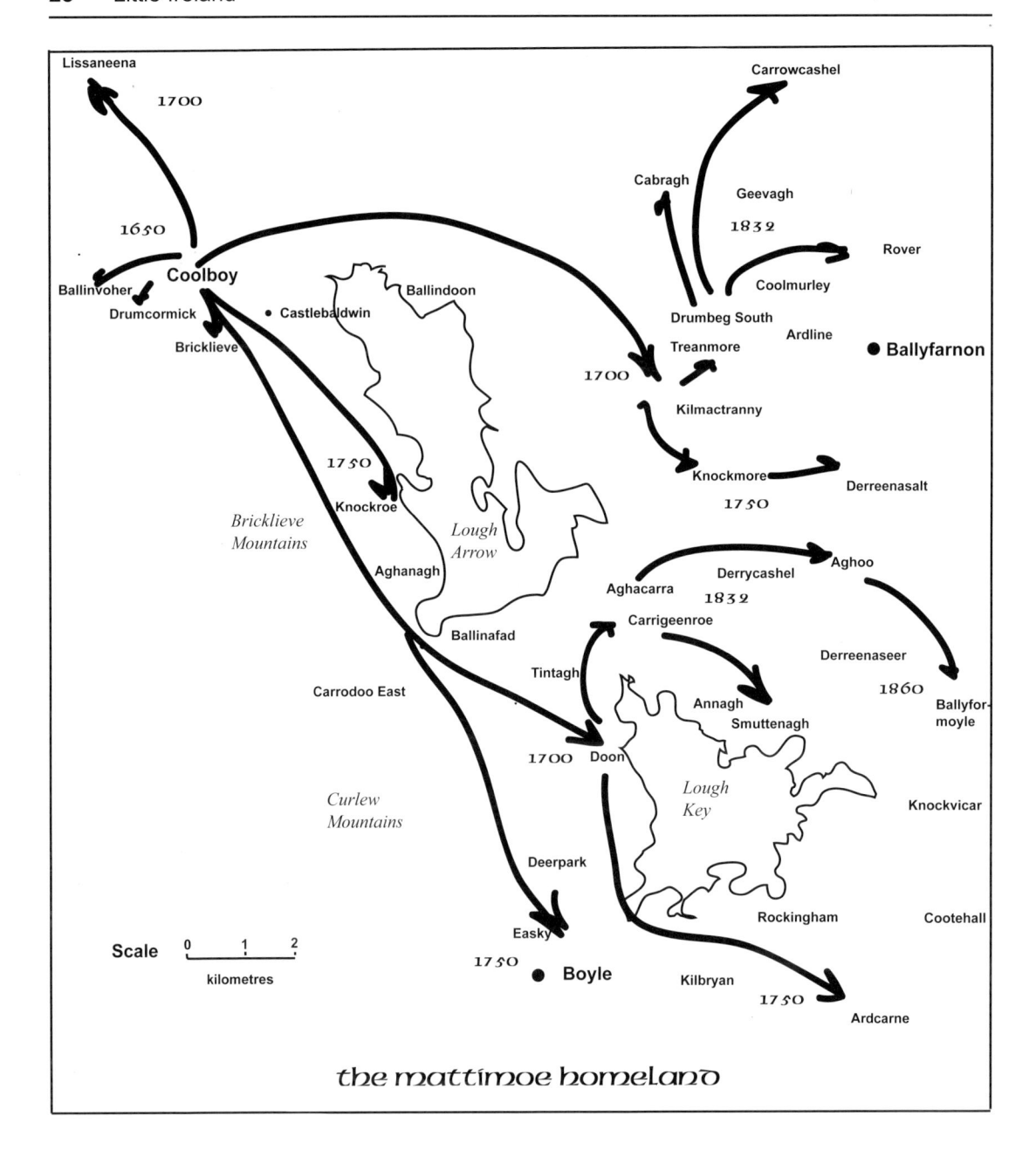

Fig. 20 This map of an area less than 12x12 miles (20x20 kms) encompasses the land on which the Mattimos lived since the earliest records available. It seems most likely that the first Mattimoes lived in the townland of Coolboy arriving between the end of the 16th and first half of the 17th centuries. From here they spread south to the banks of Lough Arrow, Lough Key and Boyle. The Tithe Applotment of the 1830's and the Griffith's Valuation of the 1860's chart the spread of the families south and east. The Roman Catholic Church records detail the next wave of expansion. Despite this growth and spread this small area of Ireland on the borders of Co. Sligo and Co. Roscommon remains the heartland of those who bear the name Mattimoe.

By the time of the Griffith's Valuation further rapid expansion and consequent fragmentation of holdings had taken place in Ardcarne and Kilmactranny. The names seemed settled but well into the 20th century Milmo families in the area of Coolboy readily acknowledged that they were synonymous with Mattimoe as did the Mattimoes in Kilmactranny and Ardcarne.

It seems therefore that Mattimoes first appeared in Co. Sligo under that name during the early or middle part of the 17th century. So where did they come from? There seem to be two possible theories, one reasoned by Col. Mattimoe based on available facts the other relying more on family lore.

Emigrants from the Pale

A strong possibility is that the name appeared in Co. Sligo when those of that name moved there from elsewhere in Ireland. Such a move would have taken place between the late 16th and late 17th centuries. Cromwell banished a number of Irish families to Co.. Sligo in the mid 17th century but none had a name similar to Mattimoe.

In his research Col. Mattimoe identified a number of people of similar name to Mattimoe who lived in the area surrounding Dublin known as the Pale during the 17th century. A James Mathmore is recorded in the parish records of St. Michael's, Sarah Martimore is recorded in those of SS Peter and Kevin in 1682, Ann Martimore is recorded in the parish of SS Marie Luke, Catherine and Werburg in 1723 and John Massimore in the same parish in 1749.

These individuals could have been descended from English colonisers. Rainey in his English surnames states that Mattimoe is an English surname. A William Matheumogh is listed in the Derbyshire Survey Rolls 1327, Ann Mattimore appears in the Greenwich Pipe Rolls of 1619 and a Mary Mattimore married a Thomas Kidget in St. James Church, Dukes Place, London in May 1691. Interestingly many Mattimoes have become Mattimores a generation or two after moving to England and the USA, we will come across two such instances later in this book.

Significantly around 1670 Lord Carlingford was granted a large estate of 11,000 acres near Ballymote from Charles II and was keen to find good tenants. It is known he brought some from the Pale. Could the Mattimoes have been amongst them? It is very tempting to see this link. The Mattimoes were Roman Catholic as was Lord Carlingford and such a move would place the Mattimoes in the right place and right time to fit in with later developments. The similarity of the name to the traditional Milmo of that area of Co. Sligo would encourage the newcomers to adopt the more Irish, less English Milmo as an alias.

The Family Lore Theory

In his original paper on The Origin of the Name Mattimoe Col. Mattimoe states that it was family lore that the "first Mattimoe was an Army Officer". Pa Mattimoe of Doon, where Mattimoes have lived for 250 years since expanding from their Coolboy origins, told me that it was family lore in his branch of the family that the first Mattimoe was a Frenchman or possibly a Spaniard shipwrecked at Killala Bay on the north coast of Co. Sligo. Who could this have been? The Mattimoes were established in Ireland before the French landed at Killala bay in 1798 so he could not have been a refugee from General Humbert's force. Prior to this French fishing boats were common off the Sligo coast. One of these could have come to grief and the survivors washed up on the coast. It would explain the presumed nationality but not the army link.

The Spanish Armada

During 1587/88 Philip II of Spain had assembled an armada of 130 vessels with the intent of uplifting a Spanish Army from Flanders to Margate before attacking the English Navy. The army would march on London thus removing the threat Queen Elizabeth, her armies and fleet presented to Spain. Assembling and equipping an armada of that size took time and suffered a setback when the man in charge died at a crucial time. Medina Sidonia a reluctant replacement completed the job and the fleet, laden with 19,000 soldiers, 10,000 sailors, plus administrators to run the conquered England, equipment and supplies set sail from Lisbon at the end of May 1588.

The exceptionally bad weather, which was to bring the disaster to the Armada, first struck as the galleons and accompanying hulks left port. A storm blew them south and the ships were at sea a month without making significant progress. This forced them to put in to Corunna close to the north western tip of Spain to regroup, undertake repairs and re-stock.

The armada set sail again on 21st July and by the end of the month was sailing up the English Channel. The English fleet intercepted them and their smaller, more manoeuvrable craft harried the Spanish fleet, attacking stragglers, waiting for the right opportunity to attack selected ships including that of Medina Sidonia himself. The Armada maintained formation and its objective ignoring the English fleet which presented no great threat. They anchored in Calais roads but again the weather turned against them. The English launched burning fire-ships against the Spanish galleons which inflicted little direct damage but broke up the Spanish formation. They re-grouped but the wind caused them to drift toward the Dutch coast but eventually the fleets engaged in a fierce sea battle which lasted nine hours and only broke off when the English fleet ran out of ammunition. Much damage was inflicted upon the Spanish vessels and the English expected the damaged ships to be wrecked on the Dutch coast but the wind changed and the badly damaged Armada was able to sail northward.

The attack plan was, like the Spanish fleet, in tatters. Medina Sidonia had no option but to implement the disaster plan which involved sailing the remaining 105 vessels around Scotland, Ireland and back to Spain. In the event only 65 ships would return to Spain.

Exceptionally fierce storms hit the Armada, dispersed the vessels and brought many to grief. A total of 28 vessels were lost off the Irish coast with terrible loss of life. There were many acts of outstanding bravery by Spanish captains and their crews who went to the assistance of ships in distress. Many of those brave rescue attempts led to the loss of the rescuing ship and its crew.

Several Spanish ships came to grief on the Co. Sligo coast. In one incident three ships were lost off Streedagh a few miles to the north of Sligo. The ships had 204 crew and 744 soldiers on board but this number was probably swollen by crew and soldiers rescued from other ships which had perished. Of the probable 1,200 men on board the three ships only 300 hundred survived. Following the disaster the coast was strewn with bodies. The wrecks here, as elsewhere, provided a one off opportunity for the Irish clans of this coast. The ships, where accessible from land or sea, were stripped of all items of value or use. Timber and canvas were valuable commodities in the west of Ireland. Furniture from captain's cabins adorned many a Chieftains castle. The bodies of sailors and soldiers were stripped. Gold coins had been sewn into many uniforms to provide protection in battle and security in the event the armada had been successful. In the event the weight of the coins contributed to the number of drownings.

Thousands of Spanish soldiers and sailors drowned and hundreds of others were slaughtered by English troops garrisoned near the Irish coast. They were buried by the Irish clansmen in mass graves with the rites of the Roman Catholic Church.

An Armada Survivor

The major disaster on the north Sligo coast during this period was the catastrophe that befell the Spanish Armada. After its encounter with the British Navy off Gravelines on the Flanders coast the Armada had invoked its emergency plan to sail up the North Sea, round the Scottish and Irish coasts back to Spain. These ships, many designed for the calmer waters of the Mediterranean and since modified by the addition of several additional poop decks at the stern to hold the soldiers of the intended invading army, were to encounter unusually fierce storms off Ireland. Twenty eight ships were to come to grief on the Irish coast.

Those soldiers and sailors who managed to get to shore safely faced English troops garrisoned on or near the coast. Little mercy was shown to these survivors by the English. Some of the Irish were just as ruthless but most assisted the survivors whilst securing their share of the salvage from the wrecks and the dead. Many of the survivors were helped to escape to Scotland, where they were eventually repatriated to Spain, whilst a few stayed with their rescuers, married and raised families.

The San Esteban

A Spanish galleon was wrecked on the Co. Mayo coast near Killala Bay. On September 20th the San Esteban, a Biscayan ship from the Guipuzcoa Squadron, went down off the White Strand. She was a large vessel of 736 tons carrying 246 men and 26 guns from the port of Corunna. Less than forty survived the shipwreck. They were apprehended by English soldiers from the nearby garrisons, some dying in the process. Those who were captured were later hung in a mass execution. Could the first Mattimoe have been a survivor from this wreck of the San Esteban and escaped capture by the English with help from the local Irish clansmen and women? It is possible though unlikely. However the image of a Frenchman or Spaniard being washed ashore on Co. Mayo and nursed back to health by Irishmen, his fellow Roman Catholics, before making his way inland eventually finding a home in Co. Sligo is a beguiling one and not dissimilar to the fate of some of the Armada survivors. Certainly the name Mattimoe is not unknown in Spain. A mayor of Marbella was once a Mattimoe.

A Mattimoe Army Officer

If Col. Mattimoe's piece of 'family lore' is true it points to a time when an organised army or its representatives were present in Co. Sligo.

The earliest period where someone can claim to have been an Officer was in the time of Queen Elizabeth I. English troops were garrisoned in Connaught during Elizabethan times and an Officer could have put down roots in Co. Sligo. This was an unsettled time and an English Officer would have been at risk beyond the safety of the garrison perimeter. The English had strengthened their hold on Connaught after the Flight of the Earls and this could have provided sufficient security for an Officer in Elizabeth's army to stay on and put down roots in Co. Sligo although there were better opportunities for such a move in Ulster at that time.

The next period where an Army Officer could have participated was Cromwell's brutal conquest in the 1640's. Some of Cromwell's soldiers certainly did acquire land as part of their reward or in lieu of wages owed by Cromwell's Army. A hundred years after Cromwell the records show that Mattimoes were Roman Catholics indicating a rapid assimilation into that religion if the Officer had served in Cromwell's Puritan Army. Such assimilation had happened in an equally short time with other waves of settlers so this in itself does not discount the possibility of a Cromwellian being the first Mattimoe.

The final possibility would be an Officer fighting in the conflict between the forces of James II and William of Orange in 1688/89. The fact that all Mattimoes were professed Catholics fifty years later would require an even faster assimilation into the local religion than it would for one of Cromwell's followers. However Col. Mattimoe does mention meeting a Dutchman by the name of Van Mattimoe.

Census of Elphin

In 1749 the Protestant Bishop of Elphin, Bishop Synge, ordered a census to be taken of the diocese of Elphin which stretches through most of Co. Roscommon north through Co. Sligo to the coast. In doing so it encompassed the north and central part of Moylurg, the Mattimoe heartland.

Fortunately the census has survived. It lists the head of each household in the Church of Ireland parishes of the diocese giving their religion, occupation and the townland in which they lived. In the census Protestants were sometimes identified as 'reformists' whilst Catholics were identified as 'papist' or 'popish'. The number, sex, religion and age (under or over 14) of children in each family were recorded together with the number, sex and religion of servants.

Townlands are not related to towns or other urban development but are in fact the smallest civil unit of land in Ireland. All of Ireland is divided into townlands, an ancient division of land dating back to the Middle Ages, and they vary in size from one to several thousand acres. Townlands are referred to in the census of Elphin, the Tithe Applotment survey of 1832 and the Griffith's Valuation of 1864. Townlands are also mentioned in the Roman Catholic registers of births and marriages during the second half of the 19th century. For example the registers for Ardcarne identify the townland of those married from the 1860's and those baptised from the 1870's. Identifying the townland where an ancestor resided can help corroborate details of family ties gleaned from other available sources and can, importantly, enable the family historian to locate the area, if not the actual location where their ancestors lived bringing its own sense of excitement and identification with the past.

Whether the results of the census were to the Bishop's liking is not recorded but they were unlikely to be a surprise to him. The population was 90% Roman Catholic with some Church of Ireland parishes not recording a single Protestant family. The only areas which went against this trend were in the south of the diocese, the rich farmlands of Co. Roscommon and the towns, but even here Protestant families rarely exceeded thirty per cent of the overall population. The exception was Boyle, the only town of any size between Roscommon and Sligo, which had a population of whom over 50% were Protestant. Boyle was the market town for the overwhelmingly Catholic population of farmers, cottiers, farmworkers, servants and labourers of the surrounding area, many of whom lived on the poorer land to the north of the town.

Mattimoe families in the Census of Elphin

Tantalisingly the families listed in the Census of Elphin are at least a generation short of providing links with the surviving Roman Catholic parish registers but the census provides interesting information regarding the distribution of surnames.

In the case of the Mattimoes it identifies only twelve families of that name all of whom lived within a narrow strip just ten miles long to the west of Lough Arrow and Lough Key to Boyle. All were Roman Catholic and ten were identified as farmers. Details are given in Appendix A

Travelling north to south along that strip in 1749 we would have first encountered six Mattimoe families farming on adjacent plots in the townland of Coolboy and a further family in the adjacent townland of Bricklieve. One family in Coolboy, that of Mark Mattimoe, employed three servants indicating that his farm was at least twenty acres. The close proximity of these families to each other points to a strong family bond between them. Some could have been Mark's sons, whilst those with older children could possibly have been Mark's brothers. Coolboy and Bricklieve are in the Church of Ireland parish of Drumcollum. This parish had a surprisingly high proportion of Protestants, some 25%, but the families in those townlands where the Mattimoes lived were all Catholic.

Moving south we would have detoured close to the shore of Lough Arrow to the townland of Knockroe where Thadius Mattimoe lived and farmed with his young family. Further south we would have crossed the narrow strip of land separating Lough Arrow and Lough Key and on the western shore of the latter, in the townland of Doon where Mattimoe families still live today, we would have found the young families of farmers Michael and James Mattimoe. Continuing our journey to Boyle we would have met the remaining two Mattimoe families. Luke was a shop owner, one of only four in that town, and John was a pump owner. Again they appear young men as their children are all under 14.

Given the geographic area covered by the diocese of Elphin and the continuing affinity those of the Mattimoe family continued to show in records during the following 120 years it seems likely that these twelve families were the only ones of that name in Ireland at that time. It is possible that a handful of families may have been overlooked on the western side of Lough Arrow, close to the Kilronan Mountains where several families were recorded some eighty years later. This might have been because they lived just over the border in the diocese of Achonry or that the census enumerator, simply overlooked them.

There were other families of a similar name recorded in the census. In the townland of Coonhibir to the east of Lough Key, a future Mattimoe stronghold, there were four cottier families with the name Mullimoe. A labourer's family in distant Sligo town had the name Mulloremoe.

The Census of Elphin, unlike the later Tithe Applotment Survey and Griffith's Valuation listed all households including labourers who formed a significant proportion of the population. The fact all Mattimoes were classed as farmers indicates that they were descended from a family who had a significant landholding in the 17th century.

Agrarian Unrest

The second half of the 18th century saw a growth in agrarian unrest through the formation of secret societies such as the Defenders and the Whiteboys which provided the only outlet open to a people suffering injustice and living in poverty who had been excluded by the Penal Laws from participating in the legal and political systems of their country. The activities of these groups were directed at local issues, primarily tenancies and rents, but the Protestant landowners were also agitating for change. They wanted more self-government for Ireland.

A concerned British Government responded with legislation dismantling much of the old Penal Laws. Importantly by 1782 Roman Catholics could purchase and bequeath land on the same basis as Protestants. This on its own would not have made much difference to the landless Catholic majority but it in 1793 the Catholic Relief Act enfranchised 40/- freeholders. By the 1820's there were some 85,000 Catholics eligible to vote who were to prove a potent electoral force. For many in Ireland, both Catholic and Protestant, these changes were not enough.

By 1793 the Defenders had strong support in the parishes of Ardcarne, Cootehall and Keadue in the border area of Co.'s Roscommon and Sligo. They were led locally by John MacDermot who was, unusually, a Catholic member of the gentry. Matters came to a head when Lord Lorton, the major landowner of the area, called in the dragoons to deal with a gathering of the Defenders at nearby Kilronan. The gathering was probably to protest at rent increases, one of the prime reasons for action by the Defenders. The confrontation turned into a minor skirmish but in the actions that followed John MacDermot was arrested and subsequently tried, found guilty and hanged on Kilmainham Green, Dublin in front of a huge crowd.

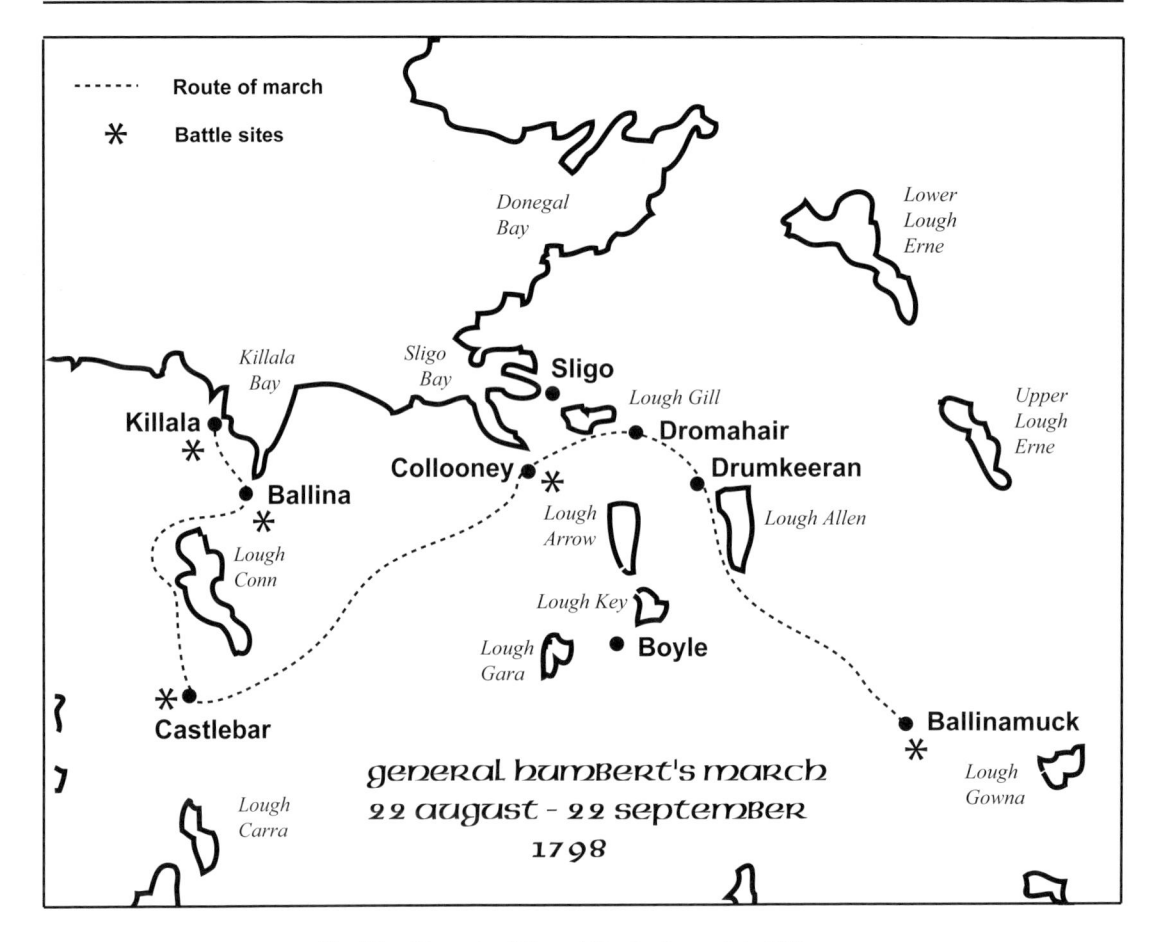

Fig. 21   The route of General Humbert's march in 1798.

Rebellion in Ireland

This was a period of revolution. The American War of Independence had taken place in 1776 then in 1789 the French Revolution took place. In Ireland the Society of United Irishman was formed, primarily by Presbyterians and eventually led by a Protestant Wolfe Tone, which aimed to unite Protestants and Catholics to bring about an Irish Republic. No doubt spurred on by the revolutions elsewhere it became a secret society and in due course enlisted the help of the French. In 1796 a substantial fleet of thirty five French ships carrying thousands of French Republican troops sailed into Bantry Bay. Bad weather intervened and the ships could not berth to land the troops. Wolfe Tone could only look on from the deck of one of the ships and ponder on the opportunity lost.

Unrest continued involving the Defenders. The English responded by sending in the army who conducted a brutal suppression of the rebellion and brought with them the wooden triangle on which guilty and innocent alike were mercilessly flogged to extract information. Half-hanging and the pitch-cap were other methods used to achieve the same end.

French Soldiers March Through Connaught

Finally in March 1798 there was rebellion with most of the action taking place in Leinster and Ulster. The rebellion was crushed by the British Army then Connaught, whose population had not embraced the Society of United Irishmen, became the centre of activity when in August of that year a French force of 1,000 men under General Humbert landed at Killala Bay on the north coast of Co. Sligo. After some initial military success, but having failed to stir the men of Connaught to rise in his support and lacking the expected French reinforcements (their fleet had been intercepted and captured at sea) Humbert marched his troops across Connaught. They marched down the western side of Lough Allen from Drumkeeran and camped close to the southern tip of the Lough and it is here that local folklore gives a different nuance to the generally accepted historical view of General Humbert's campaign.

In the 1930's a Mrs Gaffney of Arigna, Co. Sligo related how the French Army were betrayed by a local man who stole the chains from the French wagons as they camped next to Lough Allen. Despite the apparent indifference of the men of Connaught to the French invasion the local women showed no such reticence and came to the aid of the French, plaiting their blankets and quilts making rope to replace the stolen chains. The help was to be of no avail. Upon reaching Ballinamuck, Co. Longford, Humbert's force of, by then, 850 troops, were confronted by the 10,000 troops of Lord Cornwallis, the new Lord Lieutenant of Ireland and surrendered. The history books record the confrontation as a minor skirmish but the story passed down locally talks of an awful battle at Ballintra bridge beside Lough Allen following which a lot of French soldiers were buried beside the road to Drumkeeran.

Whilst the arrival of the French had bypassed the farms of the Mattimoes the families might have witnessed the panicked evacuation of Boyle by those who thought the French planned to attack the town. They might then have witnessed the passage of troops through the town on their way to intercept General Humbert's forces. Finally, after General Humbert's surrender, they might have seen some of the French prisoners and their Officers on their way to Boyle from the battle site.

The French soldiers were deported back to France but the Irish captured in the battle and those subsequently tracked down in Connaught and suspected of involvement were hanged.

Wolfe Tone had been on the intercepted French fleet and was taken to Dublin, tried and condemned to hang but committed suicide before the sentence could be carried out.

Three French ships containing 2,000 troops dropped anchor in Killala Bay a month after the battle at Ballinamuck but learning the outcome of that battle the ships weighed anchor and returned to France.

What of the man who according to the local story betrayed the French and thus, in Mrs Gaffney's overly optimistic view of events, prevented the French from freeing Ireland? He brought shame, disgrace and persecution on his family's name. Even when descendants of the family went to Scotland to work in the mines it is alleged they were singled out and "pillared" to the roof of the pit which involved trapping a mans hands between a pit prop and the roof so that the pressure on the victims hands increased. The persecution was so strong it is said descendants were forced to change their name.

The Act of Union

Having restored its control over Ireland militarily the British Government decided a united Government was in its best interests and by the Act of Union in 1800 abolished the Irish Parliament and from that time Ireland was governed from London. Far from 'bringing Ireland into the fold' those representing Ireland, themselves part of a Protestant minority in their own country, became a political minority at Westminster submerged by the issues which were deemed of importance to mainland Britain. The resultant remoteness of government was to have catastrophic consequences for Ireland forty five years later during the Famine.

4 Early Nineteenth Century Connaught

We resume the story of our Mattimoes in the early decades of the 19th century. Ireland was predominantly an agricultural economy, particularly so in Connaught. These were not the rich farmlands familiar of Leinster in the Irish midlands. The land here is heavy and damp. The wet winters which affect this part of Ireland leave the soil cold in the Spring leading to a shorter growing season than the areas further south. Barley and oats would have been the only cereal crops grown at that time. Even today in the area between Boyle, Ballymote and the land surrounding the shores of Lough Arrow and Lough Key there is no sign of arable farming. The small farms are dedicated to the raising of beef cattle mostly in herds of no more than forty beasts. The land rises gently from the edge of the Loughs to rolling hills that meet the Curlew Mountains in the west and the Kilronan Mountains in the east. The flat land south of Boyle toward Roscommon, known as the Plains of Boyle gradually becomes more productive for cereal crops.

Ireland had seen a dramatic growth in its population from 900,000 in 1659, 2,500,000 in 1767 to 5,000,000 by 1801 and in the 1830's was close to the peak of 8,000,000. Until 1815 high produce prices had enabled this growth to be accommodated through employment on the land. The vast bulk of the population were cottiers and labourers. The former were tenants of small tracts of land who paid their rent partly in labour and partly in sale or surrender of a portion of their crop. Those on larger plots would have sufficient land to raise chickens and a pig. The landless labourers led a more precarious existence under the "conacre" system whereby they leased a plot of land for a year growing a crop which was then sold to pay the rent. Failure of a crop would leave the labourer destitute. These two groups were wholly reliant on the potato as the prime source of nourishment as it was the only crop which could be grown with sufficient yield to feed a family from the ever smaller plots they came to occupy. The potato was not a crop that could be stored for long periods so the Summer months were a time of hunger even in the best years.

The hungry Summer months could tempt the poorest in the Roman Catholic community to convert, albeit temporarily, to the Protestant faith in return for food. In 1855 the Priest at Ardcarne felt moved to enter in the Church Register, amongst the baptisms, a poem on the subject written in 1822 when a partial failure of the potato crop led to severe food shortages in some areas. It demonstrated that the practice of tempting converts with food, prevalent during the Famine, was not unknown twenty years before that terrible event.

Continued Agrarian Unrest

The deep seated cause of unrest in Ireland continued to be land and specifically the relationship between landlord and tenant. The Defenders seem to have been a spent force locally after the arrest of John MacDermot but their place was taken first by the Whiteboys in 1806 and then by the Ribbon-men. This latter group acquired their name through their habit of wearing white ribbons in their hair. Unlike their predecessors the Ribbon-men took action not only against landowners but also those Catholic tenant farmers who benefited by expanding their holdings at the expense of evicted neighbours. Punishments

Poem from the Roman Catholic Parish Register of Ardcarne

A Satire composed in the year 1822 by Thomas Barlow of Mount Prospect upon a few Roman Catholics who during the Hard Summer of [that] year went to Ardcarne Church and feigned to conform to Protestantism for "Belly" sake

You will soon hear of Join to the Parson come on
Your Reverence I'll worke here on Monday
If you allow me a trifle of Meal
I will come up to Church every Sunday

I am hungry and poor as I stand at your Door
And any Trade w'ont afford me support, Sir,
My Scissors, and Thimble, and Lapboard I'll part
and here to your Church I'll resort Sir.

The next come was Barney his tongue sweet with Blarney,
Your Reverence I hope w'ont reject me,
I'll be true to your cause and your Protestant Laws
If from hunger y'll say y'll protect me.

Yes my friend Barney, that's my delight
For all such good Food as I am able,
Whenever you call, y'll find in the Hall,
Strong Stirabout laid at the table.

Next Larry come in with his faultering Tongue,
Me will go with the rest without doubt, Sir,
I have not a tack of a Coat to my Back-
Nor a morsel to put in my mouth, Sir,

Now let us three for ever agree
Our hearts and our minds in one union
We never will fail while you give us the Meal
W'll forsake our Priest, Creed, and Communion

involved spoiling of crops, maiming of stock animals and, in extreme cases, physical violence such as 'carding' which involved flailing of the back or breast with the metal studded brush used to tease out wool fleece prior to spinning.

The fall in produce prices encouraged landowners to change usage of the land from tillage to sheep grazing reducing the demand for labour causing unemployment amongst the labouring class and the eviction of cottiers. In a related cause and consequence this change led to an increase in sheep-stealing.

Courtesy of the National Library of Ireland

Fig. 22 Labourer's cottage, Gweedore, Co. Donegal. This one-roomed cabin with its single small window was typical of the basic accommodation occupied by the landless families.

Insurrection Act

The disturbances in Ireland led the British Government to introduce a number of measures to curtail such activities. This culminated in the Insurrection Act of 1822 which prohibited the taking of unlawful oaths, a feature of the agrarian rebel groups, and a curfew order which required people to be in their homes after sunset. This last requirement reflected the fact that many attacks on people and property took place at night. Those found guilty of offences under this Act could be sentenced to transportation or hanging.

The Boyle editions of the Roscommon and Leitrim Gazette recorded details of continuing problems and the fate of those who were convicted of offences under the Act. Occasionally the 'outrage' seemed minor as when Colonel Terrence found five of his sheep had been shorn during the night. More seriously ricks were set alight and houses were burnt. Frequent mention was made of the conviction and subsequent hanging or transportation of those caught for these crimes at the Assizes locally and in neighbouring Counties.

Under the Act local men 'being found out of their premises' were committing a crime. In August 1822 two brothers John and Robert Doyle were found guilty of being absent from their house at night when found returning to their home from different directions. They were convicted and sentenced to immediate transportation. This would have been for a period of seven years.

Attacks continued and the paper reported two such incidents in April 1826. The first was on the dwelling of William Keaney whose farm was attacked and robbed. In an indication of the violence of the time the paper reported that one of the intruders had fired a blank cartridge into the mouth of the farmer.

Not surprisingly this incident had left the farmer in a severe state of shock. The second attack was by a group of men on the farm of John Walsh. The door of the farm was broken and the windows smashed. A shot was fired into the room where the family slept. No one was injured in this attack which the farmer attributed to an attempt by the attackers to be offered potato gardens at a 'certain rate'.

The continued unrest led Lord Lorton, the major landowner of the area, to place a letter in the paper telling his tenants to ignore those who were trying to 'lead them astray'.

Tithe Applotment Survey

Our next snapshot of the Mattimoe families dates from this period of unrest and is provided by the Tithe Applotment Books. Tithes, payable to the Church of Ireland were deeply unpopular with the Catholic majority. The Composition Act 1823 replaced payment of tithes in kind by a financial payment. A valuation of all the land was conducted between 1823 and 1838 and provides an analysis of those who either owned or leased land in the years leading up to the Famine.

Because its intent was to assess the value of the land it excluded a substantial part of the population who were classed as labourers in the Census of Elphin sixty years earlier. It was also not comprehensive in regard to land. For example in Munster grass land was excluded but potato patches were included thus the tithe payment fell hardest on the poor in that province.

The valuation is organised by townland, within Union by County. It lists the Occupiers of the land, their immediate lessor, a description of the land, the size of the holding and its value. There was little consistency in the way the valuation was undertaken. Some valuations divided the land into five quality categories whilst others divided it according to a description. Bog and moor did not attract a tithe commutation payment nor did rocky land or mountainside.

Mattimoes in the Tithe Applotment

The valuation shows that the Mattimoes had thrived and expanded since 1749. Details are given in Appendix A. Oddly the area surrounding Coolboy, the stronghold of the Mattimoes in that census, does not record a single family of that name. Instead these Mattimoe families appear to have changed their name to Milmoe. Three Milmoe families were farming between fifteen and twenty acres each in Coolboy. Eight other Milmoe families farmed in nearby townlands each holding between eight and eleven acres. It should be noted that an Irish acre of 7,840 sq. yds. was significantly larger than an English acre of 4,840 sq. yds.

The Mattimoe stronghold had now become Kilmactranny to the east of Lough Arrow. Their sudden appearance in this area may be misleading. Whilst none were mentioned in the Census of Elphin, Kilmactranny is on the far eastern edge of that diocese and the Mattimoes might have either lived just over the border into the next diocese or simply not been counted. Whatever the reason, by the time of the Tithe Applotment survey there were sixteen Mattimoe families farming in that civil parish, each holding between one and fourteen acres. The description of the land shows that their holdings included a large proportion of the less productive moor and upland.

The next Mattimoe stronghold was the adjacent parish of Ardcarne. There were six families in the townland of Aughoo each with three acre holdings indicating perhaps a division of a fathers land amongst his sons. A further five families had holdings of between two and five acres in other townlands of the parish.

The next parish, Boyle, continued to list Mattimoe families, five in the townland of Doon, where their ancestors had lived for at least ninety years, three in Aghacarra where the Thomas Mattimoe of this book was to farm, and one family in Deerpark.

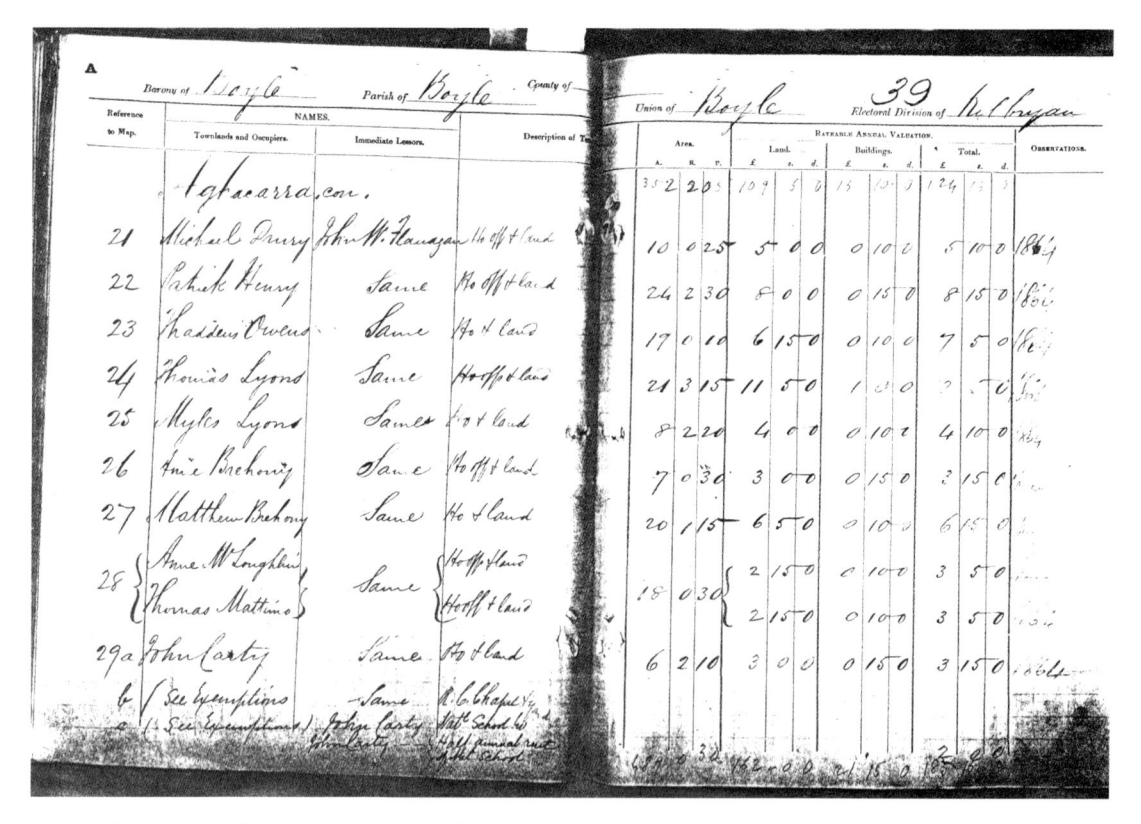

Fig. 23 (above) The above entry in the Griffith's Valuation lists Thomas Mattimo(e) farming in Aghacarra jointly with Anne McLoughlin. The Valuation was a living document and the 'cancelled' books show that Thomas Mattimoe gave up the holding in 1867 the year we find him registering the birth of his son, Peter in Bishop Auckland, Co. Durham.

Fig. 24 (next page) This map identifies the location of the farm (28) at Carrigeenroe just north of Lough Key. The Roman Catholic Church and National school are shown on the opposite side of the crossroads, just south of farm 29.

Most of the Mattimoe families were small farmers whose living would not have been easy but was significantly better than the precarious existence of the cottiers. The exception to this were the families in Coolboy and Kilmactranny whose holdings in excess of fifteen acres put them in the top twenty percent of the population. It seems probable that by this time there would have been as many tradesmen and shopkeeper Mattimoes families in these parishes as those engaged in farming.

The distribution of the different quality land illustrates how the Catholic farmers had been squeezed out of the better land. By way of example the following table shows the distribution of land in each category held by the Mattimoes in the parish of Ardcarne and compares it to the similar distribution of land in Lord Lorton's Rockingham estate and the total in that parish.

Name	Category 1	Category 2	Category 3	Category 4	Category 5
Mattimoe families	0	20	17	13	0
Rockingham	485	142	101	42	24
Ardcarne (total)	2211	2182	2312	1118	525

Early Nineteenth Century Connaught

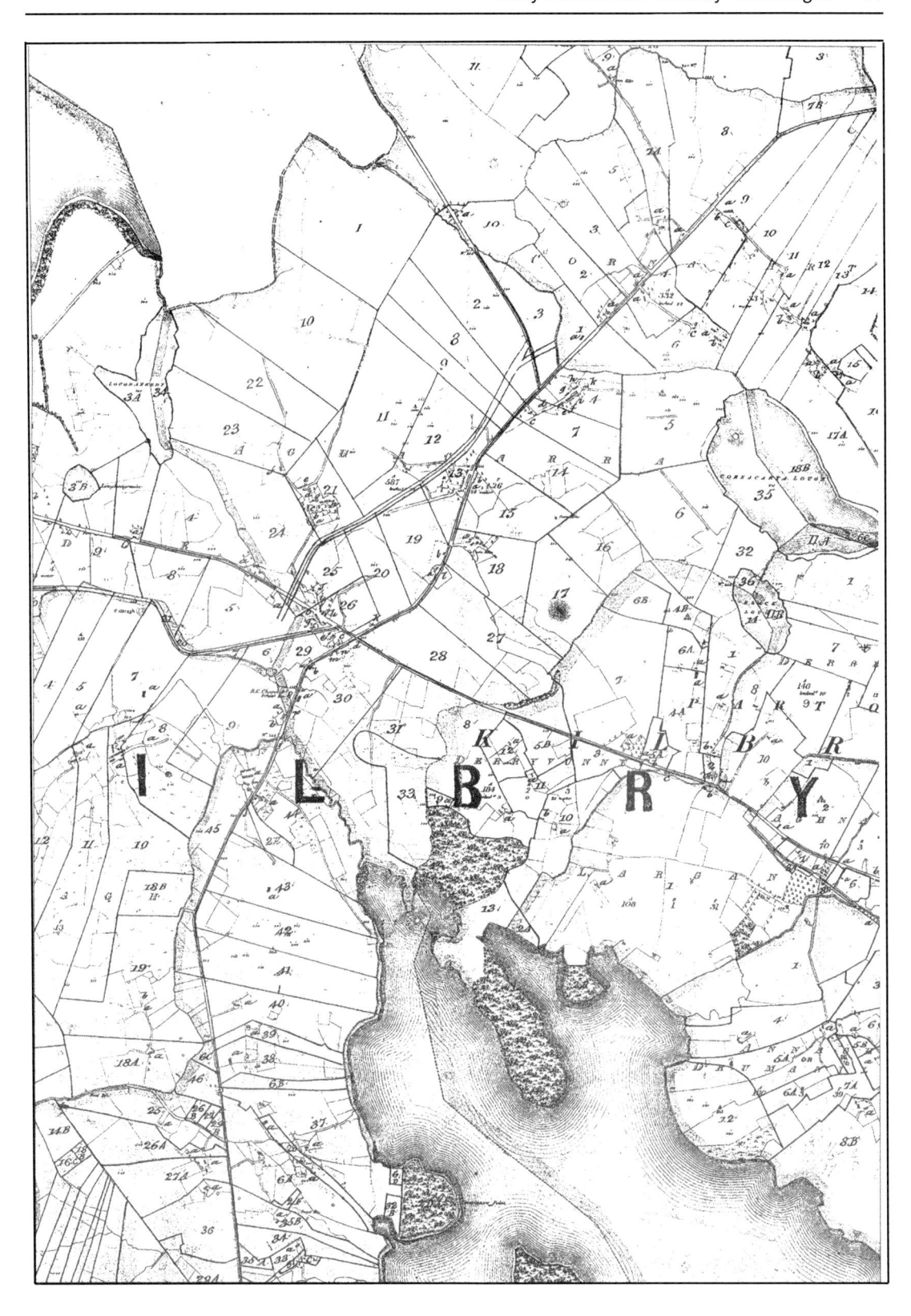

Lord Lorton

Viscount Lord Lorton, the owner of the Boyle and Rockingham estates from 1799 until his death in 1854, was a member of the wealthy King family. His ancestor was Sir John King of Yorkshire who arrived in Ireland to play his part in subduing the population on behalf of Queen Elizabeth I and was rewarded with the lease to the Abbey lands of Boyle in 1603. He then received grant of the lands of Rockingham from James I in 1617. These lands had been the traditional home of the MacDermots, the Kings of Moylurg for centuries. Over the generations the King family prospered through marriage and conquest assembling an estate which became one of the largest in Ireland. Sir John's son, Edward, was drowned returning to Ireland from King's College, Cambridge and was immortalised in Milton's poem Lycidas. On Sir John's death his son, John, succeeded him but led a troubled life. He married Margaret O'Kane, a maid in his father's house. He converted to Catholicism and was disowned by his family until James II restored his position. His restoration was to be short-lived as he sided with the Jacobites and lost everything when they were defeated but later an agreement was reached with the Crown and he received his grandmother's estate at Mitchelstown. His uncle's sons retained the Boyle and Rockingham estates.

One son, Sir Henry King, built the King House in Boyle in the 1730's which, following the move of the family to Rockingham some sixty years later, was destined to become the Headquarters of the Connaught Rangers. Sir Henry married Isabella daughter of Edward Wingfield of Powerscourt, Co. Wicklow.

Viscount Lord Lorton's grandfather was Edward King of Rockingham born in 1724 the second son of Sir Henry King. He became Baron Kingscourt on the death of his brother. In May 1752 he married the illegitimate daughter of Thomas Caulfield and Peggy Jordan. On his death Thomas left his daughter £10,000 a considerable sum at that time equivalent to £500,000 today.

Viscount Lord Lorton's father, Robert King, was born 1754, educated at Eton and was styled Viscount Kingsborough 1768-1797, was Member of Parliament for Co. Cork 1783-1797 and Governor of Co. Cork in 1789 and Co. Roscommon in 1797. He married Caroline Fitzgerald when he was only fifteen and Caroline was sixteen. They had a child one year later. Caroline inherited the estate of Mitchelstown thus reuniting the estates of Robert's great grandfather. He died in 1799 at Mitchelstown. Caroline, who had separated from her husband some years before his death died at Roehampton, Surrey in 1823 aged sixty eight and was buried in Putney churchyard.

Viscount Lord Lorton was born Robert Edward King on 12th August 1773 in Berkeley Square, London. He was educated at Eton and Oxford and entered the Army in 1792 and distinguished himself in Martinique, St. Lucia and Guadalupe. He was wounded at Point-a-Petre in May 1808. In 1813 he was promoted to Lt. General and full General in 1830. He was Member of Parliament for Jamestown 1796-1797 and for Boyle 1798-1800.

In 1798 he was accused, along with his father, of the murder of Col. Henry Gerald Fitzgerald, an illegitimate son of his mother's brother, who it was said "with circumstances that were peculiarly dishonourable had seduced" his sister, Mary. Viscount Lord Lorton, then Col. King challenged Col. Fitzgerald to a duel to redeem his sister's honour. In the event six shots were fired but neither protagonist was hit. Mary subsequently eloped with Col. Fitzgerald who was already married with two children. Lord Lorton, his father, Viscount Kingsborough assisted by a groom caught up with Col. Fitzgerald at an inn and confronted him in his room. In the scuffle that ensued Col. Fitzgerald allegedly drew a pistol at which point Viscount Kingsborough took out his pistol and shot Col. Fitzgerald inflicting a mortal wound. Lord Lorton and his father were tried and acquitted of the murder, Lord Lorton at Cork Assizes and his father, a few months before his death, by his peers in the House of Lords . Mary withdrew from society and later married a clergyman with whom she shared a long and happy life.

On 9th December 1799 Lord Lorton married his cousin Frances the daughter of Laurence Parsons 1st Earl of Rosse and Jane the daughter of Edward King the 1st Earl of Kingston. In 1810 he commissioned John Nash to build a 'classical mansion with a dome and ionic colonnade' at Rockingham to replace that built by his ancestor which itself had replaced that of Brian MacDermott. His wife Frances died at Rockingham on 7th October 1841. Lord Lorton died at Boyle on 24th November 1854 in his eighty-second year.

Courtesy of the National Library of Ireland

Figure 7 Rockingham House seen from Lough Key. Designed and built for Lord Lorton by John Nash in 1810. It was struck by fire in May 1863 but was rebuilt. In 1957 it was again destroyed by fire and the ruins eventually demolished. The Harman King family later left the Rockingham demesne to the public which today forms Forest Park.

A Mattimoe Funeral

Graphic evidence that not all Mattimoes were farmers was provided by the following report which appeared in the Boyle edition of the Roscommon and Leitrim Gazette in early February 1826.

'On Monday last this town was put into a strange state of alarm in consequence of a disagreement that arose between two parties who assembled at the house of Mr Mattimoe a thatcher who had departed this life concerning the ground wherein he should be interred. The funeral procession moved on from Boherbue (the place where the poor man died) within a mile of this town, until it arrived at the turn leading from the end of the Fair Green towards Kilmactranny burying-ground, where some of the deceased's family had been before interred. Here they made a halt and manifested symptoms of a quarrel; one party wishing to have him interred at Assylyn - the other at Kilmactranny; and had it not been for the interference and prompt vigilance of Captain C. Robertson, who, through his well known humanity attended the procession to the burying-ground and caused them to desist, riot and imminent danger would have ensued.'

Courtesy of the National Library of Ireland

Fig. 26 Evicted family of nine surrounded by their meagre belongings. The turf roofed, two roomed cabin had provided inadequate accommodation but they now faced a period of life in the open with no shelter. Families who took in those who had been evicted often risked being evicted themselves for their humanity.

The paper, somewhat sanctimoniously, criticised those involved being astonished at

> 'such rude conduct … at a time when feelings of a divine nature should be cherished in their bosoms, and when they should recollect that themselves (Heavens knows how soon) may be reduced to a "clod of earth"'.

On a more practical note, given the two to three days of a traditional Irish 'lying in' and wake, it seems strange that the dispute should have arisen at such a late stage in the proceedings. One wonders in which burial ground the grave had been prepared, or perhaps one had been prepared in each burial ground.

Catholic Emancipation

Despite the setback of the Act of Union the early decades of the 19th century saw constant agitation by Irish activists for greater political representation by the Catholic majority. Most notable amongst these was Daniel O'Connell, a charismatic man and able orator who was a trained lawyer. He was descended from a wealthy Catholic family of Co. Kerry which had managed to survive the Penal Law years with its wealth not only in tact but increased.

The Roman Catholic Church had also survived the Penal Law years and began to grow in strength. It had embarked upon an ambitious programme of church building. The priesthood had expanded with young politicised priests drawn largely from the families of tradesmen and tenant farmers and trained at the new seminaries established in Ireland.

In this heightened political atmosphere the radical organisation, the Catholic Association, was formed to achieve Catholic emancipation but more significantly to achieve Catholic representation at Westminster. Daniel O'Connell became its leader and through his ideas and oratory quickly broadened out its appeal to the mass of Catholic Irishmen. The Association levied a penny a month subscription from these 'associate' members creating a substantial fighting fund. In 1826 this fund, and the support of those Catholic freeholders who now had the vote succeeded in electing pro-emancipation candidates to Westminster. Then in 1828 Daniel O'Connell himself was elected to a constituency in Co. Clare. Being a Catholic and refusing to take the oath which involved denying his faith he was prevented from taking his seat in Parliament. The Wellington/Peel Government fearing the unrest that would follow if he was excluded, and despite having been elected on an anti-emancipation mandate, backed down and the Catholic Emancipation Act was passed in 1829 allowing Catholics to sit at Westminster and hold any public office except Regent, Lord Chancellor of England or Ireland and Lord Lieutenant of Ireland. George IV, himself vehemently anti-Catholic emancipation, initially refused to sign the Act but Wellington and Peel persisted and the Act entered the statute book.

The political price for this victory was the raising of the 40/- rule for eligibility to vote to £10, thus reducing the Catholic electorate from approximately 100,000 to 16,000. Despite this setback a significant breakthrough had been made. Those of the Catholic majority could now represent their fellows in Parliament and importantly the Catholic majority had learnt that direct action could bring about change.

Daniel O'Connell was an Irish hero. He held mass open air meetings where his oratory rang out leaving a lasting impression on all those who heard him. In October 1845, as the potato blight struck marking the start of the Famine, O'Connell stayed a night at Boyle with the Parish Priest on his way to one such rally in Sligo and he was to be cheered by crowds along the route. On leaving Boyle the next morning his carriage was towed to the top of the Curlew Pass by a willing gang of men followed by the town's folk and led by the town band. I like to think the Mattimoes, Gaffneys and other Irish families of this book participated in that rousing send off. O'Connell received a similar enthusiastic escort on his return journey from Sligo.

Clearances

Despite the improvement in political rights the daily life of the majority was a precarious existence squeezed between the demands of their landlords and the natural harshness of scraping a living from ever smaller plots of land. Cottiers suffered most. They leased their land from others who themselves were major tenants of the landowners. These middle men were most often Catholics who had gradually benefited from the relaxation in the Penal Laws but were equally as ruthless in their dealings with the cottiers as the landowners had been. The division between the landed and the landless could no longer be equated with a division along sectarian lines.

Landowners themselves continued to play an oppressive role on the disadvantaged. Their desire to change land use from tillage to sheep grazing requiring less labour led to increased rents for small farmers which they could not afford. This often resulted in evictions enabling the landowners to consolidate farms making them more suitable for sheep farming. In the implementation of evictions the landowners drew on the assistance of the Volunteers, a local armed force drawn solely from the Protestant population and originally established to 'fill in' the role undertaken by the British Army units withdrawn from Ireland to fight in the American War of Independence.

The major landowner in the area of Co. Roscommon surrounding Boyle, Lord Lorton, owned 4,000 acres locally including Rockingham on the southern shore of Lough Key. In addition he owned land in Co. Longford. Lord Lorton was not one of the hard pressed landowners to whom non-payment of rent threatened bankruptcy. Despite his financial strength he carried out clearances of some 128 tenants, approximately 500 people, half of which were in the parish of Aughanagh. One of the reasons for the scale of clearances in this area may have been that it was an alleged hotbed of troublemakers.

Fig. 27 An Irish farmer.

Department of Irish Folklore, University College, Dublin

Mending Fences

The passing of the Catholic Emancipation Act gave hope to the Catholic population but Lord Lorton's tenants, being practical farmers, realised such change would be slow and in the meantime needed to repair the relationship with their landlord who remained very much in control of their fortunes. Consequently in January 1830 a "numerous and respectable" meeting of the Catholic tenants of the Boyle and Rockingham estates was held in the Chapel of Boyle. We can only guess how many of these tenants had been directly involved in any of the activities of the societies such as the Defenders, White-boys and Ribbon-men or had harboured or turned a blind-eye to others who were involved. However at the meeting no hint of rebel sympathies was evident. A number of resolutions were passed which, even allowing for the formal style of writing of the time, were couched in very obsequious terms. The local edition of the Roscommon and Leitrim Gazette which had reported "agrarian outrages" for the previous seven years and whose readership was drawn from the better off Protestant professional and landowning sections of the local population, relished printing the detail of the meeting virtually verbatim. The following is an example of one resolution.

> '... if political events over which we exercise no control had hitherto in any degree marred our better feelings and more kindly recollection we now gladly seize the opportunity of tendering to our Noble and benevolent Landlord the humble but sincere tribute of our gratitude ...'

One of the resolutions was to request publication of an open letter to Lord Lorton, a request the paper, unsurprisingly, readily acted upon. Extracts from the letter are as follows.

> 'We the Roman Catholic Tenantry of the Boyle and Rockingham Estates beg to tender to your Lordship our unfeigned attachment and respect. We have long experienced your Paternal solicitude as a resident Landlord – We know, and have profited of your beneficence in the distribution and reduction of your property – and have grown up into prosperity and comfort under your benign influence of the system which you so underratingly pursued – that of giving back through extensive employment, with a humane and munificent hand, the wealth derived from your large possession.
>
> Gratitude, my Lord, would at all times demand this humble but honest tribute to your benevolence. And now at the dawn of a new social and political era it is fitting we think, this respectfully, to re-assure you of the deep feeling which we entertain of your past kindness and of the high estimate which we cherish of your Lordship .... Angry times my Lord have just gone by: The agitation and excitement ... attendant upon great political struggles have at length subsided. We freely own that our own passions too were aroused in the storm. We felt, what we believe to be inseparable from human nature, an impatience of unmerited degradation and hurried along by the vehemence of our emotions, we forgot perhaps for a time the most sacred ties of private life as well as the choicest bonds of social unions. But a gracious Sovereign and wise Legislature have stayed this headlong course. In the pain we have looked ... with regret upon the untoward events of angry passions which the conflict had necessarily engendered and are moved ... to resuscitate the reciprocity of feeling between man and man which alone can render society sense and happiness.'

The letter recognises that Lord Lorton was not one of the absent landlords whose remoteness from their estates led to a detachment from the plight of their tenants. The extent to which the writers and supporters of the letter genuinely harboured the view of their landlord expressed in the letter is a matter for conjecture. It is easier to see irony in the reference to 'a gracious Sovereign' who in the event was a very reluctant signatory to the Catholic Emancipation Act.

The Roscommon and Leitrim Gazette published a reply to the tenants' letter from Lord Lorton in the same issue. In the tone of a headmaster addressing a group of errant schoolboys who had been disrespectful during assembly but were now contrite he wrote as follows.

> 'I feel happy in receiving the ... address and resolution [from the] Roman Catholic Tenantry of the Boyle and Rockingham Estates.
> Perfectly agreeing in the sentiments and expressions so strongly marked as to the relative duties of Landlord and Tenant which I trust may never be interfered with again either by man or any Political event, I shall look forward with a degree of confidence to the re-establishment of that compact which ought never, in the slightest degree to have been broken in upon ...'

Looking back it is possible to understand the concerns of the tenants to re-establish a good relationship with their landlord in those uncertain times but an unknown poet of the time took a more cynical view which was shared by the Parish Priest who twenty five years later in 1855, a few months after the death of Lord Lorton, felt drawn to enter the untitled poem from the anonymous bard into the baptisms and marriages register of Ardcarne. The Priest re-enforced the message of the poem by introducing it with an attack both on "the late Lord Lorton for his anti Catholic practices and propensities and at the sorry and subservient and crouching and adulatory and serf-like professions shamefully put forth to appease his Lordship ... by the Roman Catholic Tenants at a meeting held in the Court House at Boyle in the year 1830."

The implication in verses 1 and 2 is that the Catholic tenants of Lord Lorton were under threat of being evicted if they did not agree to the terms of their leases and would be replaced by Protestant tenants.

References in verse 3 to Cromwell refer back bitterly to his confiscation of land in this area some one hundred and eighty years earlier.

National schools had begun to be built by Government but verse 5 illustrates the distrust of these institutions and consequent non attendance by the children of the Catholic majority.

Verse 6 refers to the Catholic Association, led by Daniel O'Connell, which was set up to achieve Catholic emancipation. It was notable for the penny a week contribution its members paid to provide a fighting fund. Protestants responded by setting up Brunswick Clubs for those who agitated against Catholic emancipation.

The sarcastic reference in verse 7 to King George IV reflects the fact that the King had to be pressurised by Wellington and Peel to sign the Catholic Emancipation Act though they themselves had been elected the previous year vowing to resist Catholic emancipation.

Verse 8 refers to transportation to the penal colony in Tasmania which was the sentence handed down to many of those of the secret agrarian societies such as the Defenders, Whiteboys and Ribbon-men who were arrested and convicted. The penal colony in Tasmania was one of the harshest, brutal regimes and did not need the additional horror of imaginary cannibals.

The bibles referred to in verse 11 were provided by various Protestant groups to Catholics to encourage them to convert to Protestantism known as proselytism.

As indicated in verse 12 landlords were changing from tillage to sheep-farming which required less labour leading to evictions. The reference to books implies that Lord Lorton's anti-Catholic actions extended to the destruction of Catholic religious books which his supporters were able to find.

Verse 13 makes a further reference to Brunswick Clubs indicating that one had been set up in Boyle. Protestant missionary bible societies also distributed religious tracts with the aim converting Catholics to Protestantism. The Religious Tract Book Society alone distributed some 4,400,000 tracts.

1
Great Lord accept this our petition
Pity the pitiful condition
Of tenants who your Highness greet
And in submission due and meet
Just throw themselves down at your feet

2
Ocon! We are told 'tis your behest
No Papist on your land shall rest
That all Craw Thumping Folk must fly
To make room for your Coplony
Of Protestants and Penwry

3
That Catholics must quit the sod
Which their forefathers proudly trod
'Ere Cromwell and his Rebel Crew
Robbed many a Loyal man and True
To fill the Fobs of Rapps like you

4
Dread Sir withdraw this rash Command
As we can pay, Lease us the Land
There's Lloyds example in your Eyes
With strangers do not colonise
Nor solvent Popish Serfs despise

5
Alas we were such wicked elves
We ventured to think for ourselves
We should have been submissive Fools
Have sent our children to your schools
And not be independent fools

6
And when the Club met in our town
To keep your Lordship's Blue Corps down
To our Clergy straight we went
And paid the association Rent
To Dan our "Penny Pittance Sent"

7
When Royal George struck off our chains
We cared to bless him for his pains
Blessed Wellington, and Bob Peel too
Blessed Brougham, and the Patriot Crew
Who laughed at Eldon, Fudge and you

8
We dared to think you mad in fact
When you'd receive the Traitor Act"
By which your Cronies would command
The Papists to Van Diemen's Land
And Cannibals with flesh be crammed

9
We have done these and other things
To vex the best of Lords and Kings
Our misdeeds we will long deplore
And if you rub out the Old Score
Dear Master we will sin no more

10
Let us now pass without reproach
We'll swear young Bob ne'er Drove a Coach
Tho' wags may sneer and say in grief
We'll prove, He quite a Solon is,
His ugly mug Apollo's Phiz.

11
We'll ne'er, Great Lord, presume again
To think – to speak – to act like men
We'll read our Bibles night and day
Nor heed what Commentators say
No matter tho' we go astray"

12
Grant huit New Leases to us all
We'll bless you and your Lordly Hale
We'll praise Lough Key with lambs so fair
Praise all the horrid fishes Tare
That read the Books you fling on them

13
Give back the farm to Chairman Phil
And to us all your tenants Stile
We'll dress up Bill from top to toe,
To Brunswick meetings we will go,
Like Mac your friend from Silver Row

14
Your Liberal mind shall be your Boast
The Glorious Memory our toast,
We'll give our Spawn each bible tract,
Vote for the Insurrection Act
And swear your knob-ship is not cracked

5   Hard Times

Pre-Famine Connaught

By 1841 the population of Connaught, excluding towns, was 386 per square mile. The nearest town to the Mattimoes was Boyle and this had a population of less than 5,000 at that time. The Catholic majority, some 96% of the population of Connaught were small tenant farmers, cottiers and labourers working on land owned by, often absentee, landlords. The bulk of the small farmers farmed plots of less than five acres and cottiers farmed plots of ¼ acre.

A Government report in 1836 reported that some 585,000 labourers upon whom some 1,800,000 others were dependant, were unemployed for thirty weeks of the year. Many planted their plot then left the family to tend it whilst they travelled to Scotland and England to find seasonal work.

Many sought to escape this hardship through emigration. In the period 1831-1841 400,000 Irishmen emigrated to the USA and Canada whilst 100,000 crossed the Irish Sea to England and Scotland.

Housing conditions in Ireland reflected the harsh times. In 1841 forty percent of the houses consisted of one room with a bare earth floor and sods of earth covered with thatch for a roof. Many had no window or chimney. Furniture was usually limited to a table and stool with a straw bed. Cooking utensils were similarly basic. A further thirty seven percent of the homes had between two and four rooms.

Diet for the cottiers and labourers would have consisted primarily of the potato supplemented by buttermilk. A working man would eat a staggering 14lb of potatoes a day. Meat would have been a very rare treat. Despite, or perhaps due to, this diet Irishmen were amongst the strongest in Europe. Clothing for the poorest was little more than rags with women and children going shoeless. Small farmers were able to clothe themselves decently though such clothing was made to last.

The only luxuries within the reach of most of the population were tobacco and drink. The latter took the form of beer, whisky and the illicitly distilled poteen. Drink was consumed in large quantities both on special occasions and often when there were not.

Whilst drink may have helped bring relief from the hardship of life in Ireland in the years which led up to the Famine the Irish also knew how to enjoy themselves through music using song, the fiddle and the uillean pipes which would be heard at weddings, wakes and fairs. Dancing would also be an essential ingredient to such gatherings. Fairs provided the opportunity to watch entertainers such as jugglers.

Sport was limited but hurling was very popular as were tests of strength and skill such as weightlifting and bowls.

Connaught had a significant proportion of Irish-speakers but by the 1830's English was increasingly the preferred language spoken by the majority.

The worst years of religious oppression were passing but the persecution of priests leading to the holding of Mass in remote outdoor locations known as Mass Rocks would still have been a vivid memory for the Roman Catholic majority of that time.

Education for the children of the rural Catholic majority was at best to elementary level and for most of the period in question was through the "hedge-school". These got their name from the habit of holding classes outdoors in good weather. In the winter a local farmer would be prevailed upon to allow the use

Department of Irish Folklore, University College, Dublin

Fig. 28 'Lazy beds' was the disparaging term given to the manner of growing potatoes in long narrow raised beds. Soil was dug from either side of the bed and placed in the middle. A layer of manure was placed on top in which the tubers were planted before another layer of soil was added. The resultant raised beds provided a free draining rich sandwich in which the tubers could develop.

of a barn or outbuilding. These schools concentrated on the three R's. The schoolmasters of the "hedge-schools" were encouraged to teach their charges English. The Government funded National schools and Charity funded elementary schools were provided particularly from the 1830's onward but the Roman Catholic majority feared, often justifiably, an underlying agenda of religious conversion. School hours would have accommodated the need for the children to work on their parents land and the demands of religious education.

A Childhood In Ireland

Thomas Mattimoe was born in 1833. It is almost certain that he named his children according to the traditional precedent in Ireland whereby the first son was named after his paternal grandfather; the first daughter after her maternal grandmother; the second son after his maternal grandfather; the second daughter after her paternal grandmother; the third son after his father; the third daughter after her mother;

the fourth son after his father's eldest brother; the fourth daughter after her mother's eldest sister. The system was liable to break down if more than one relation had a given name and can be misleading if the death of a child is not detected but it appears to have been applied by Thomas for at least five of his children as follows.

> First son Patrick after Thomas's father
> Second son John after Thomas's wife's father
> First daughter Mary after Thomas's wife's mother
> Third son Thomas after Thomas himself
> Second daughter Ann after Thomas's mother

Interestingly Thomas's second son John seems to have followed the naming precedent for his own eldest three sons.

It seems, therefore, that our Thomas was the son of Patrick Mattimoe and Ann McLoughlin and was christened in the parish of Aughanagh (Ballinafad) on 5 February 1833. There was a Pat Mattimoe farming in the townland of Aghacarra within that parish at the time of the Tithe Applotment in 1833.

The countryside surrounding Lough Key and Lough Arrow remains as beautiful today as it must have been when Thomas was born. The waters of the Loughs are still and peaceful. The gentle indentations of their shores provide ever changing views from the promontories and bays across the waters to distant wooded islands such as Castle Island, Trinity Island and Hermit Island in Lough Key and Annaghgowla Island and Inishmore in Lough Arrow some of which played their part in Connaught's history and now rest easy in their tranquil setting. The low marshy edges of the Loughs are softened by long grass and reeds bend gently in the breeze before the land rises gradually to low rolling hills with a distant backdrop of grander summits. Today, north of Boyle there are still no towns or villages of any size. Human habitation is spread thinly in single dwellings in keeping with its history of small scale farming. Derelict properties are frequent, hinting at a higher population in the past though it seems certain that this beautiful area has always been sparsely populated.

Into this rural environment Thomas was born. He had an elder brother Patrick christened 2 November 1831 and a younger sister Mary born 25 January 1835. It is possible that the Grandparents of Thomas were Matthew Mattimoe and Mary McDonagh. Matthew died at Aughanagh in September 1842 having reached the impressive, for those times, age of eighty years.

The Mattimoe family lived in a single storey, thatched, four room cottage with a chimney. Furniture would have been basic. They would have grown potatoes as their mainstay plus vegetables, fruit and perhaps some oats and barley. Livestock would have been an assortment of geese, chickens, ducks and turkeys and a few pigs, cows and sheep. The size of the farm and the variety of crops would have provided the family with a simple diet, though better than that enjoyed by the majority, with wheaten bread, oatmeal and milk supplementing the basic potatoes and buttermilk. It seems certain that they spoke English at this time though would have retained knowledge of their native tongue.

Thomas could read and write and was probably taught at the National school which had been constructed next to the nearby Roman Catholic chapel. Its position next to the Church under the watchful eye of the Priest probably increased its acceptability to the Mattimoe family.

Play for the young Thomas and his brother, sister and friends centred on the simple pleasures afforded by the countryside and the nearby Loughs though they had to help out on their parent's farm particularly at times of peak activity such as planting and harvesting. The market at Boyle provided a special treat if they were able to accompany their father and mother to sell their surplus vegetables, butter, eggs and livestock. The town, with its population swelled by the farmers, tradesmen and entertainers, presented a colourful, bustling sight to the children. The inn's and alehouses would have been overflowing with those who had been successful in selling their produce and were anxious to both celebrate and refresh themselves before the long journey home.

Thomas Mattimoe's Irish Family

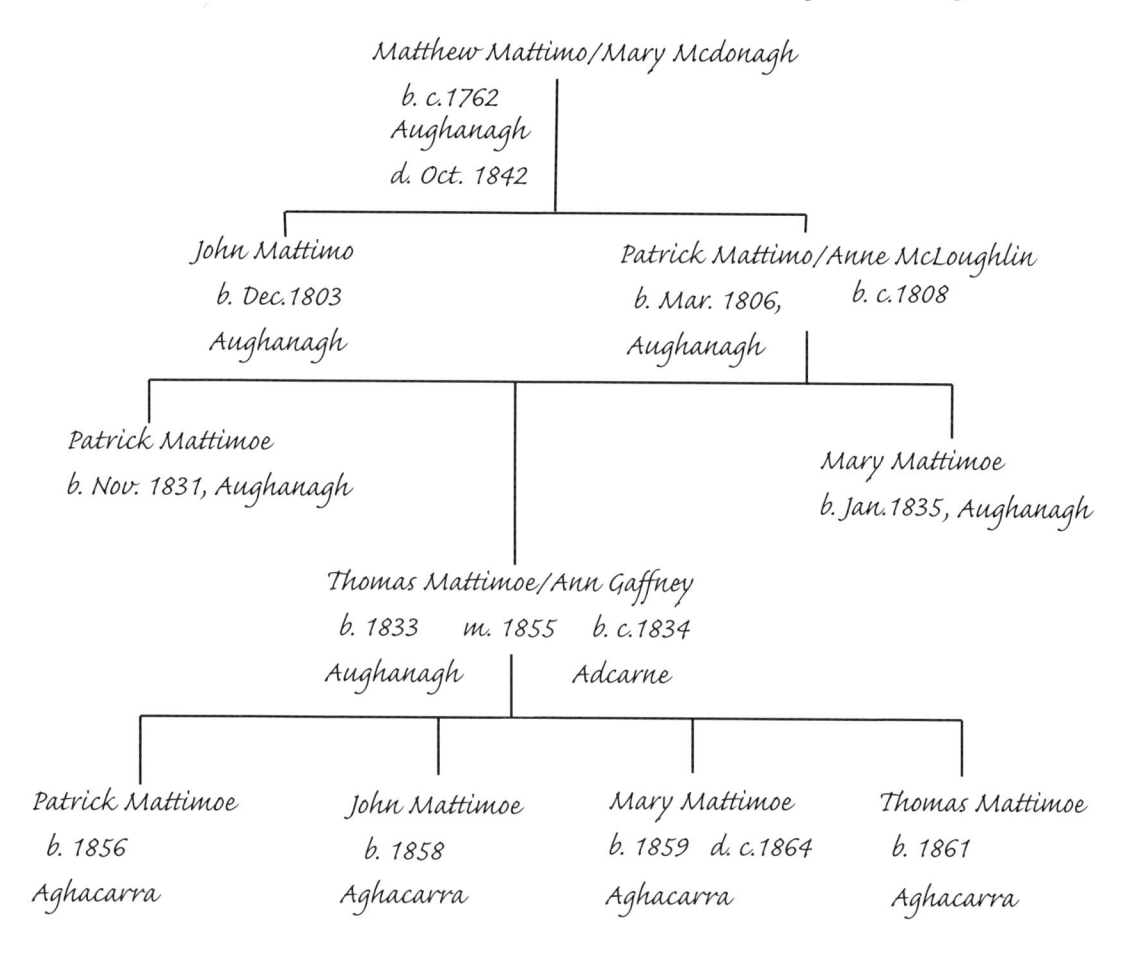

Matthew Mattimo / Mary Mcdonagh
b. c.1762
Aughanagh
d. Oct. 1842

- John Mattimo
  b. Dec. 1803
  Aughanagh

- Patrick Mattimo / Anne McLoughlin
  b. Mar. 1806,   b. c.1808
  Aughanagh

  - Patrick Mattimoe
    b. Nov. 1831, Aughanagh

  - Mary Mattimoe
    b. Jan. 1835, Aughanagh

  - Thomas Mattimoe / Ann Gaffney
    b. 1833   m. 1855   b. c.1834
    Aughanagh   Adcarne

    - Patrick Mattimoe
      b. 1856
      Aghacarra

    - John Mattimoe
      b. 1858
      Aghacarra

    - Mary Mattimoe
      b. 1859   d. c.1864
      Aghacarra

    - Thomas Mattimoe
      b. 1861
      Aghacarra

Fig. 29 A market scene in Ireland with women in shawls selling their wares and a bare foot boy, similar in appearance to young Thomas Mattimoe, looking curiously at the camera.

Faction Fighting

Faction fighting was one of the more unorthodox pastimes the young Thomas may have encountered. These mass brawls took place between certain families once a year, usually associated with public events such as fairs or race meetings where a good crowd of participants and spectators could be guaranteed. These activities certainly took place in Boyle as it was reported that Matt Ganly 'local giant and faction-fighter' had organised the triumphal towing of Daniel O'Connell's carriage to the top of the Curlew pass in October 1845.

There is no mention that the Mattimoes were involved in this disorderly behaviour but Gaffneys traditionally fought the Guihans and the McManus' each year at Keadue on 8th September, the day of St. Laisar, known as Pattern Day. These Gaffneys were allegedly descendants of those who had fought at Kinsale in 1599 and settled at Keadue on their return from that battle. They would start each years fight with the cry *"While Lasair is in Kilronan the Gaffneys will hold sway"*. It is not known how close, if at all, these Gaffneys were to the family of Thomas Mattimoe's future wife who lived in Ardcarne, some four miles from Keadue.

By a twist of fate the annual faction fight saved many of the Gaffney and McManus families. In 1798, when General Humbert led his men through Co. Sligo on his way to the encounter with Cornwallis's

Fig. 30 Irish farmer and his wife.

army, some of the Gaffney and McManus men, no doubt persuaded in part by the promise of food and uniform, joined with the French. The timing of the encounter turned out not to the liking of these new recruits. In an interesting assessment of priorities and loyalties the Gaffney and McManus contingent decided that family honour in the form of the time honoured tradition of faction fighting on Pattern Day had a stronger pull than the opportunity to inflict a bloody nose or worse on the English. Consequently they went to Laisar to fight each other thus missing the fateful battle at Ballinamuck and almost certain death.

Despite the tradition of faction fighting being linked, nefariously or otherwise, with the Gaelic tradition of the 'Cult of the Warrior' it was frowned upon by the Authorities and the magistrates would bring in police mounted on horseback to disperse such events. This tradition persisted and as late as February 1866 the Roscommon Herald was able to carry a report concerning the arrest and trial of a John Bermingham who, the previous May, had attempted to incite a faction fight amongst a large crowd of some eighteen hundred people gathered in Strokestown. He had attempted to start the fight by, in the tradition of such events, crying out his family name *"Bermingham"* whilst swinging a cudgel around his head. Despite the apparent overwhelming odds John was apprehended and the faction fight averted

Even allowing for the possibility of such exciting interludes Thomas's early life revolved around his family and their farm. The evenings were enlivened with music and story-telling. The love of singing, music and dancing gained by Thomas during his life in Ireland was passed to his children and from them to their children.

Thomas no doubt had a happy childhood however this was to be affected dramatically when he reached his teens by the horror of the Famine.

Orangeism in Boyle

Sectarian strife was not a feature of life in this part of Ireland apart from one brief period in the largely Protestant town of Boyle. The Memoirs of Skeffington-Gibbon states that "On the return of any popular candidate as well as on the festival days of Orangeism, the town and neighbourhood were convulsed in parading through the one street and fulsome lanes, displaying Orange Lilies and playing party tunes; and these Loyalists dressed in all the colours of a gloomy rainbow, the van generally led by the Rake-ems and Take-ems, when the Frys, Fawcetts and Phibbs were too genteel to join such ragamuffins ... If any ignorant rustic ... utter a sentence or even smile, they were knocked down, shot dead or sent to the horrible Bridewell, another Calcutta Black Hole called Boyle Jail as suspicious Papists". It was Lord Lorton who brought these disturbances to an end.

Molly Maguires

The Famine began in the Autumn of 1845. The potato crop had failed several times within living memory but such failures had been localised and rarely in consecutive years. They had brought hunger and deaths from starvation but assistance from the British Government had helped the population through to the next harvest. The significance of the failure in the late Summer of 1845 was not fully appreciated.

The local issue receiving prominence in the Boyle edition of the Roscommon and Leitrim Gazette during the late Summer of 1845 through to the Spring of 1846 was the Molly Maguires. These were a group concerned to protect the position of the labourers and cottiers against the oppression of the landlords and British Government. They took direct action against landowners and any tradesman or farmer they perceived colluded with or benefited from their actions or those of the British Government.

They were well supported locally. There were reports of groups of 50-100 men gathered in fields between Ardcarne and Crossna. They were also well organised and disciplined. At Cootehall 50 men were reported exercising and marching in military formation.

Those whom the Molly Maguires considered to have acted individually or collectively against the majority received a warning notice to correct the matter. Written warnings were either sent directly to the person concerned or posted on trees for all to see. One received by a farmer demanded he give land and property to a widow whom the Molly Maguires considered had been unjustly deprived of these assets. A general notice stipulated a maximum price which could be charged for produce including the lumper potato upon which the majority depended.

Failure to heed the warnings led to direct action. Attacks against livestock were most common involving the maiming of cattle by cutting off their ears, killing of sheep leaving the carcasses in the field and mutilation of horses. A dog was hung belonging to someone who informed on local men. More serious offences in the eyes of the Molly Maguires brought greater retribution. A man from Knockadoo was beaten by three men from Boyle for agreeing to carry the luggage of the Army.

Activities of the Molly Maguires were generally in country areas away from the town of Boyle though in early 1846 it reported a worrying development when Molly Maguires had been seen at Doon, 2 ½ miles from Boyle, "a previously peaceable part of the country". Successes by the police in apprehending members of the Molly Maguires received prominent reporting in the local paper. When police at Frenchpark chased a gang of men who had attacked a gentleman shots were fired and they were chased into a bog escaping by jumping into a river. Later one man thought to belong to the gang was found drowned. The police claimed he had received a gunshot wound, though the manner of its reporting leads the reader to suspect this to be an embellishment by the police to enhance their part in the incident.

The activities of the Molly Maguires reduced when the extent of the disaster facing the majority became apparent.

Fig. 31 Group of barefoot Irish women

The Famine

In the autumn of 1845 a good potato harvest suddenly succumbed to blight, a disease imported from North America. The variety of potato most affected was the heavy cropping, late maturing "lumper" potato. Almost overnight the leaves and stems of the plants rotted whilst the firm white flesh of the tubers turned to a stinking black putrefying mess. The initial shock of the population turned to despair when it became known that the crop throughout the country had been destroyed and they faced the very real danger of starvation during that coming year. The potato crop was to fail through blight in the following two years bringing about the worst humanitarian disaster in Ireland's history. It is not for this book to debate the background to the disaster or the inadequacy of the response, of the Authorities both in Ireland and in England. Others have written and published comprehensive works on the subject some of which are detailed in the bibliography.

The Roscommon and Leitrim Gazette mentioned the crop failure in October 1845 but only expressed serious concern in August 1846 when that years crop failed completely. That month a peaceful protest by 500-1,000 people at the lack of food took place in Boyle. The protesters dispersed having made their point but no action was taken by the Authorities or Landowners to alleviate the situation. Consequently there was agitation for a rent strike which led Lord Lorton to write an open letter to his tenantry in October stating that he employed 200-300 people and had spent £300,000 in improvements to his estates then, without making any acknowledgement to the life threatening position in which many of his tenants then found themselves, he warned against a rent strike threatening troops. In an effort to appease his tenants, which could be taken to reflect the nature of his personal concern for the hardship his tenants were enduring, he mentioned the Government labour schemes which were planned to be established. In the event these were slow to materialise and inadequate in their operation. It does appear though that Lord Lorton had donated seed to his tenants though this would not have addressed their immediate needs.

The situation was already chronic however and in November 1846 the paper made the first references to people dying from starvation. In December a man from Arigna was reported to have dropped down dead from starvation whilst working. In that month 90 people died in Carrick-on-Shannon workhouse.

The impact of this disaster was most severe in Co. Galway and Co. Sligo with the impact not significantly less in neighbouring Co. Roscommon. In Co. Galway it was reported that "the population were like skeletons, the men stamped with the livid mark of hunger the children crying with pain – the women, in some of the cabins, too weak to stand".

Government Reaction

The British Government could not avoid being unaware of the humanitarian disaster unfolding in Ireland. Nicholas Cummins, a Justice of the Peace in Co. Cork, reported in a letter to the Duke of Wellington printed in The Times on Christmas Eve 1846.

> "Being aware that I would have to witness scenes of frightful hunger, I provided myself with as much bread as five men could carry, and on reaching the spot, I was surprised to find the wretched hamlet apparently deserted. I entered some of the hovels to ascertain the cause and the scenes that presented themselves were such as no tongue or pen can convey the slightest idea of. In the first six famished and ghastly skeletons, to all appearances dead, were huddled together in a corner on some filthy straw, their sole covering what seemed a ragged horse-cloth, their wretched legs hanging about, naked above the knees. I approached with horror, and found by a low moaning they were alive - they were in fever, four children, a woman and what had once been a man. It is impossible to go through the detail. Suffice it to say, that in a few minutes, I was surrounded by at least 200 such phantoms, such frightful spectres as no words can describe. By far the greatest number were delirious, either from famine or from fever. Their demoniac yells are still ringing in my ears and their horrible images are fixed upon my brain. ... In another case ... I found myself grasped by a woman with an infant just born in her arms and the remains of a filthy sack across her loins – the sole covering of herself and babe. The same morning the police opened a house on the adjoining lands, which was shut for many days and two frozen corpses were found, lying upon the mud floor, half devoured by the rats.
> A mother, herself in fever, was seen the same day to drag out the corpse of her child about 12, perfectly naked, and leave it half covered with stones."

The same edition of the paper reported the story of a man who had to leave his aged mother and younger brother, both ill with fever, to walk eight miles into the nearest town to beg for food. He obtained some charity but then died on the return journey. His body was conveyed to his home and one can only imagine the horror of the family to see the body knowing his loss meant certain death for themselves. Unusually the body was subject to an autopsy and his stomach contained only a few undigested turnips and stunted cabbage stalks, his only food for the previous few weeks. Similar horrific images were sadly commonplace throughout Connaught.

The British Government was ruled by the dogma of non-intervention and market forces. It had introduced a programme of public works though this was slow to be implemented and poorly executed.

Government stores in Sligo had substantial quantities of maize which it had refused to release, content to await the remedy of market forces whilst people died of starvation. Belatedly the Government agreed to release some stored corn onto the open market at the price which it had been purchased. Market forces, the virtues of which the Government was so keen to extol, immediately pushed up the price of the limited corn released to 33% above the Government sale price. Alongside comments on the price of corn the newspaper reported, without seeing any sad irony in the matter, that substantial amounts of wheat and oats had arrived at Liverpool from Ireland where the price of these cereals had tripled.

Frustratingly reports of ships arriving in Ireland from America "groaning with corn" were not translated into food on the table of the starving.

Deaths Widespread Around Boyle

In January 1847 the Roscommon and Leitrim Gazette reported "deaths from starvation general in every district within a 10-12 mile radius ... unnecessary to particularise them". Despite this it carried a report of a family in Foxford who were found living on the flesh of a dead diseased horse and another where a brother and sister were found dead having died several days before whilst the mother and another child were found dying. Elsewhere the body of a child was found under a few stones, the face and leg eaten by dogs. The Winter of 1846/47 was extremely harsh. In February local newspaper reported "Heavy fall of snow … frost. Cold has been intense."

The death rate increased to the extent that burying of the dead became a problem in itself. The cemetery at Assylin was forced to make an urgent appeal for soil to cover the dead there had been so many burials. The poor were often too weak to dig graves whilst others could only dig a foot down to bury their loved ones. Burial plots in cemeteries were limited. The body of a man who had entered an empty cottage and died was found by the Owner who put the body put in a sack and wheeled it to the cemetery where the Sexton refused permission for the man to be buried. Only members of that parish were allowed burial. The man buried the body in unconsecrated ground behind the police station. Coffins were in short supply and the local newspaper reported the use of coffins with hinged bottoms which allowed the body to be deposited in the grave and the coffin reused. In areas with the highest death rates fields were taken over as cemeteries which became known as 'Famine Graves'. There is one at Derreenagan less than two miles from where Thomas and his family lived. In the same area a woman is said to have single-handedly brought the body of her brother from Carrigeenroe to the cemetery at Kilmactranny, a distance of over two miles. Some remained unburied either because they died alone or for fear of infection. A body was found on the road between Kilmactranny and Ballyfarnon which had been partially eaten by dogs.

In March twenty people died in Boyle Workhouse, ten shortly after admission reflecting the view of the local population that the workhouse was really a place of last resort to be avoided if at all possible. The following month "a gentleman met a woman on the road leading a donkey, on which was placed, the dead body of her husband while she conveyed a dead child in her arms to the place of interment."

Despite reports of a good harvest in the Autumn of 1847 the situation did not improve in 1848 reflecting the fact that the destitute majority had been unable to plant a crop that Spring. In January the police made a grisly discovery when it was reported "a poor man in the mountainy district of Ballyfarnon, who had been out begging, was found ... at the side of a ditch, partly devoured by pigs". The following month at Greevagh a man died and lay undiscovered for seven days.

Between 1st January and 20th February 1848 400 people were buried at Assylin, 12 per day, 15 one Sunday. The newspaper reported "During the day a man was perceived approaching the graveyard – on his back was a coffin and in it the remains of his wife. The poor fellow travelled in this state nearly two miles and when descending the Green fainted under the load".

Breakdown of Law and Order

It was inevitable that the local newspaper began to report instances of sheep and cattle being killed and stolen. This was not the work of the Molly Maguires. This time the carcasses were not left to remind their owners of the need to treat tenants fairly. This time the animals were removed to feed starving families. Fortunately most were more careful than the man who, after a snowstorm that winter stole a cow, led it to his cottage where he butchered it leaving a clear trail from the field to the blood stained scene for the police to follow.

Robberies also increased and the mail coach was held up and robbed at Ardcarne. Two alleged Molly Maguires were captured at Leitrim and taken to Carrick-on-Shannon goal after they had broken in and attacked a farmer then beat him with intent to rob.

A young man broke a window after being refused entry to Boyle workhouse in the hope of being arrested and kept in goal.

The gentry and landowners became so concerned about their safety that in January 1848 Lord Lorton in an open letter printed in the local newspaper instructed his tenants to hand in all firearms or risk prosecution under the Whiteboys Act.

In November 1847 a convoy of eleven horses and carts laden with oatmeal was attacked at Collooney. This was not a well planned attack, probably executed by those to whom the sight of so much food was too great a temptation. Several of the wagons were hi-jacked but soon recovered with their cargo still intact.

Fig. 32 Old woman in traditional dress. Note the single storey, thatched cottages in the distance.

Civil unrest was surprisingly absent but in March 1848 notices put up in Boyle asking everyone to assemble in the town on St. Patrick's Day to be "informed of cruelties suffered under the British Government and compare to the 'glorious conduct of France'". An open letter published from Lord Lorton warning against attending this meeting and in the event the streets were deserted.

The Spread of Disease

Deaths from starvation were far exceeded during this period by those from typhus, relapsing fever, dropsy and cholera to which those weakened by hunger and drawn to live together by their destitution in overcrowded, insanitary conditions easily succumbed. Disease was also spread by those driven to roam the byways looking for work and through the overcrowded conditions in the recently constructed, but now overflowing, workhouses. In Boyle workhouse, where 700 desperate people were housed and women and children who had not eaten for forty eight hours waited outside, 343 died during the winter of 1846/47, 23 in one week, and many more died in Carrick-on-Shannon workhouse where 50 died in one week. By April dysentery and fever were widespread throughout the area surrounding Boyle.

In June at Slevenroe fifteen people died in three weeks from fever of whom three were not discovered for some while by which time they were so mutilated by dogs they could not be identified. Neighbours thought the family had left the country.

Church Reaction

The Roman Catholic Priesthood showed great dedication during the Famine. Many Roman Catholic priests, curates, religious brothers and nuns died from disease as a result of carrying out their duties. The need to give 'last rites' to the dying placed them at particular risk. Fr. Sweeney, a curate at Boyle died from disease contracted whilst carrying out his work. Church of Ireland Vicars and Quaker representatives who selflessly worked to help the suffering also succumbed in large numbers, though the work of these two groups was tarnished by evangelical Protestants whose food was provided to persuade the recipients, particularly children, to abandon their Roman Catholic faith. This callous opportunist practice, which became known as 'souperism', was rightly despised by the Roman Catholic population.

Landlord Reaction

Many Landlords sought to rid their land of tenants who could not afford to pay their rent by seeking tenders to transport them to Canada and America. The local newspaper was able to report that between October 1846 and September 1847 92,000 people had emigrated to Canada from Ireland. The newspaper also carried stories of the risks of this journey both in disease on what became known as the 'coffin ships' and through shipwreck as in June 1847 when the Carrick sailing to Quebec from Sligo sank off Cape Rosier with the loss of 119 of the 167 aboard.

The poorest also fell victim to landlords who, realising that rents would not be paid quickly, resorted to eviction. The number of evictions in Co. Roscommon rose from 230 in 1847 to 2,405 in 1848 and 3,643 in 1849. Those evicted had to resort to making a rough shelter to protect themselves from the elements and had lost all hope of being able to feed themselves.

In March 1847 Lord Lorton, to his credit, published an open letter in the local newspaper announcing he had taken notice, albeit belatedly, of the representations made to him by his tenantry and reduced rents on small plots by 50% and by 16% on larger plots.

Outdoor Relief

The British Government tried a number of schemes to alleviate the crisis but harboured an underlying suspicion that they were largely abused. Consequently each was quickly ceased as soon as there was a hint that the situation was improving. Unfortunately when these improvements were proved false the replacement schemes were slow to materialise.

By the Summer of 1847 the poor were able to claim 'outdoor relief'. This was to be paid for by a revised Poor Law rate. This was to prove an onerous burden on the small landowner as the new rate for Ballinafad, Boyle and Ardcarne was double that for Lord Lorton's richer land at Rockingham. Many farmers of holdings between eight and twenty five acres found the Poor Rates brought them to bankruptcy and abandoned their farms.

'Outdoor relief' was no easy option. It involved travelling to their nearest workhouse which could be miles away where they would then be assessed to see whether they were deserving of help. When granted, the relief was often inadequate for the needs of the recipients, added to which relief could be withdrawn at any time leaving the families destitute. Despite this, and in a reflection of the worsening position of the poor in 1848 the number receiving 'outdoor relief' grew substantially as can be seen from the following table.

	Ballinafad	Kilmactranny	Ardcarne	Rockingham	Boyle Union
March 1848	n/a	414	307	213	4,230
April 1848	300	400	500	340	7,092
May 1848	370	582	754	581	9,000
June 1848	650	784	1,236	612	14,480

A good harvest in 1848 did little to ease the suffering of the weakest and poorest. Failure of the crop the following year compounded their misery.

Population Change

The population of Ireland as a whole fell by two and a quarter million during the Famine with eight hundred thousand dying through the affects of the famine and the remainder emigrating to the USA, Canada and mainland Britain. Liverpool and Glasgow were the key points of entry into mainland Britain where at the peak some three thousand immigrants from Ireland arrived each day.

The Barony of Boyle lost 30% of its population to starvation, disease and emigration but losses were 38% in the north of the Barony where the Mattimoes lived. Thousands emigrated through the port of Sligo, 60,000 in 1847, though this was an avenue of escape not open to the penniless majority.

Some estimates of the population drop base the figure upon an estimated 'non-famine' population which assumes a rate of population growth seen during the years leading up to that terrible event. Examination of the Roman Catholic parish registers shows that marriages and baptisms virtually ceased during the Famine years. By "Black '47" when despair and hopelessness were felt throughout the area Madame MacDermot of Coolavin wrote *"There is nothing of a gay nature spoken of. Not one has married here since the potato failed"*. The register for Ardcarne records only six marriages in the eight months from September 1847 to May 1848.

Fig. 33 Eviction was usually followed by the destruction of the cottage to prevent it being reoccupied. The Department of Irish Folklore, University College, Dublin has many transcripts of stories handed down through the generations which describe evictions and the 'tumbling down' of the cottages, the families left to find shelter under bridges.

A Witness to the Famine

Thomas was twelve years old when the Famine began and spent his adolescent years living through it. He would have left school when the Famine was at its height and started work on the family farm. What dreadful experiences did he encounter? The bodies of wanderers who had succumbed to starvation or disease, lying unburied by the side of the road; the death of families he had known all his life; the emigration to America, Canada and mainland Britain of other families; hardship, hunger, disease and loss within his own family. We will never know. If only someone had said to him in later life *"What was it like in the Famine Grandda?"* and passed the information on to later generations. Perhaps like the memories of those who fought in and survived the Great War the pain and horror was too painful to recall and relate.

The Ardcarne, Aughanagh and Boyle, Roman Catholic parish registers of the time give an insight into the suffering of the local population and the Mattimoes in particular. The number of weddings and baptisms in each reduced dramatically during the Famine years.

Fig. 34 Eviction scene demonstrating that these events were often attended by police and troopers to ensure that the will of the landlord was enforced without public disturbance.

Courtesy of the National Library of Ireland

In Ardcarne in the years immediately prior to the Famine there were twelve young Mattimoe couples baptising children. Six of these families had one or more children before the Famine but none during or after that tragedy. A further four families baptised a single child during the Famine period but again none afterwards. Two families had children baptised before the Famine but then none until 1852/53.

In Aughanagh six families had children before the Famine. No children were baptised during the Famine and only one family is recorded as baptising a child after the Famine.

In Boyle nine families had children baptised in the years immediately prior to the Famine. Four families did not baptise another child after 1845. Two families registered a birth during the Famine, though these were conceived just prior to the Famine. One family did not baptise another child. Three families had children baptised before the Famine, none during then at least one in the years following.

Were the mothers too malnourished to conceive? Were babies stillborn or died? In those families where baptisms ceased had one or both the parents died? Did the Mattimoe families who disappeared from the registers perish or emigrate? We will never know, but it is an inescapable conclusion that the Mattimoe families, descendants of those twelve farming families recorded one hundred years before in the Census of Elphin, suffered terribly during the Famine.

Life after the Famine

Thomas survived the Famine but the structure of the rural economy had changed. The number of small farmers had reduced through death, emigration and eviction and as plots became vacant they were consolidated into larger holdings. Consequently in Ireland as a whole those farming plots of between one and five acres reduced from 310,000 (45%) to 88,000 (15.5%) whilst those with holdings of over fifteen acres increased from 128,000 (18.5%) to 290,000 (51%). It seems Thomas's family had survived with their holding intact but had not increased it significantly. Whilst many farms changed from mixed farming to livestock it seems that the Mattimoes in common with a lot of more traditional farmers on the poorer land of western Ireland continued to farm as before.

Griffith's Valuation

The Griffith's Valuation paints a picture of how the surviving Mattimoe farming families had been affected by the Famine and its aftermath. This valuation took place in Co.'s Roscommon and Sligo in 1857-58. The valuation was made to enable local taxation to be based on the productivity of the land and the potential rent of buildings.

The distribution of Mattimoe families, detailed in Appendix A, had changed little in the thirty years since the Tithe Applotment survey. The contiguous parishes of Boyle, Ardcarne and Kilmactranny still formed the strongholds of those with that name with families maintaining a presence in the townlands mentioned in that earlier survey. The description of 'gardens' given to some plots as gardens they were held by elderly or widowed people whose plot was sufficient to provide them with vegetables and poultry on which to live. Of the remaining farms held by Mattimoe families fourteen were larger than fifteen acres and most of the remainder were between five and fifteen acres indicating that they had generally not only been able to survive the Famine but to increase their holdings. The estate papers of Lord Lorton record evictions during the Famine years including at least two Mattimoe farmers however in each instance the farm had been sublet to others in whose name the farm was re-let. In one case this was to another Mattimoe. Therefore it seems that the evicted Mattimoes would not have been made homeless as a result of their landlord's action.

In summary The Griffith's Valuation lists forty two landholders with the name Matimo, Matimoe, Mattimo or Mattimoe. Of these a staggering thirty two lived within an area of only fifty square kilometres just to the east of Lough Arrow and to the north of Lough Key. The remaining ten families lived within an adjoining similar sized area just to the south of Lough Arrow and west of Lough Key which included the town of Boyle. That is not to say that there were no other Mattimoes living in Ireland. Griffith's Valuation only lists landholders. There may have been, and probably were, landless craftsmen and labourers of the name in Ireland, indeed the Roscommon Herald records details of a case at Boyle in April 1866 where a Mattimoe successfully sued another for £5 5s he was owed for work undertaken since the previous Christmas. However with forty two landholders of that name living so close together it argues strongly for a continuing close identity of the Mattimoes with this small part of Ireland. For the sake of completeness it has to be pointed out that a landholder with the name Mattymoe held land six kilometres north of Lough Arrow and probably had links with the Mattimoes to the south of him and that a Mattimore held land in adjacent Leitrim and may or may not be related. There was also a Thomas Mattimoe, though not the Thomas who is central to this story, living several miles to the west of Boyle across the border into Co. Sligo in Kilfree. Kilfree is in the same parish as Knocknaskeagh where a Matthew Hannon was then farming. Matthew was the father of Thomas Hannon who will enter this story in the 1890's.

The Milmoe's of Coolboy, who it seems safe to assume were distant relatives of the Mattimoes, had also survived the Famine and increased the size of their farms.

An Irish Wedding

Five years after the Famine and just before his twenty-second birthday Thomas married Ann Gaffney in Ardcarne, Co. Roscommon. Edward MacLysaght states that Gaffney is the anglicised name of four Gaelic names. The Gaffneys of this book are rooted firmly in Co. Roscommon, where the name is still common today, and on that basis would be descended from the Gaelic **Mac Carrghamna** family.

Prior to the Famine men had often married at a young age inheriting a portion of the family farm. This trend began to change in the lean years following Waterloo. The impact of the Famine hastened this change so it seems that the Mattimoe family, as in a number of areas, were sticking to tradition perhaps against the then current trends. Had Thomas's father died enabling the farm to be split amongst his sons? A Patrick Mattimoe was a witness to Thomas and Ann's wedding but this could have been Thomas's brother and not his father.

A copy of the record of Thomas and Ann's marriage in that parish on 22 January 1855 was kindly provided by the local priest who I inadvertently disturbed from his afternoon sleep. It is possible that the Priest of that time would have married Thomas and Ann in her parent's cottage as was the tradition but it seems more likely that the ceremony took place in Ardcarne Church. The church records show that there was another Mattimoe marriage on that same day, another Thomas Mattimoe marrying a Mary Mattimoe. It is impossible to determine whether the two Thomas's were closely related but it seems unlikely they close enough kin for the weddings to be celebrated jointly.

Fig. 35

This photograph shows a version of the strawboy dress. Often the headdress came further over the face to hide the identity of the wearer. The appearance of strawboys at a wedding was considered to bring good luck to the bride and groom. Strawboys were usually local young men who arrived at the wedding breakfast and danced furiously with the wedded couple before being rewarded with porter and leaving.

Department of Irish Folklore, University College, Dublin

Thomas and Ann's ceremony would most probably have taken place during the morning followed by the wedding breakfast of cabbage and bacon, washed down with porter. This would have been followed by drinking, music, singing and dancing. The bride and groom would have hoped for a visit from the Strawboys. These were local young lads, and occasionally a girl, who would dress in a suit of straw. Each lad would wrap straw or oats round their legs to make the trousers then make a long jacket from the same material. Finally they would fashion a pointed headdress, like a helmet, from straw which came down over the face obscuring their features. They would then arrive at the cottage where the celebrations were being held and call out the bride and groom. The strawboys would then dance wildly with the couple, sometimes a strawgirl providing the groom's partner. They would then release the newly weds and were rewarded with a gallon of porter. The strawboys were slightly unpredictable in their behaviour

Fig 36. The highly respected Uillean Piper, Stephen Ruane, 1852-1935, who lived in Co. Galway and played at all the local weddings.

but this seems due to youthful exuberance rather than any deliberate bad behaviour.

Once the celebrations had come to a natural end it was time for the "haulin' home". This was when the husband took his wife to their new home hauling the belongings she was to take to her new home. Sometimes this was the marital bed but could include other furniture and items. Often the celebrations did not finish until the early hours of the following morning so the new husband would call to collect his wife during the following week. By tradition, care had to be taken in choosing the day to collect the wife as it was said "Friday's flitting makes a long sitting".

Carrigeenroe

Following their marriage Thomas and Ann moved to Thomas's farm in Carrigeenroe by the old crossroads not far from the northeast shore of Lough Key. Thomas and Ann had four children in Ireland, Patrick born 1855/56, John born 1858, Mary, born 1859, and Thomas born 1861.

A new crossroads now carries traffic past Carrigeenroe but the old crossroads can still be seen four hundred yards to the west. The lane south from the old crossroads leads to Boyle via Doon, with views to the left across to Lough Key. It is now no more than a footpath but walking down that lane, trod some one hundred and fifty years earlier by my ancestor and his family as they took their beasts and produce to market gave me a very warm and happy feeling bringing me inextricably closer to them than any research or old photograph had achieved.

The area seems little changed from the days when the Mattimoes farmed the land. It remains beautiful and slightly wild. Even today making a living from farming appears difficult. Thomas farmed nine acres

Coal Mining at Arigna, Co. Roscommon

Kilronan Mountain, which cuts through the border between Co. Sligo and the northwestern tip of Co. Roscommon contains one of the few deposits of iron ore and coal in Ireland.

In 1621 Sir Charles Coote, soldier of fortune, was handsomely rewarded with land in Connaught. He established the ironworks in the mountains above Arigna. Initially charcoal was used for the smelting process but coal was found in very narrow seams of 18-24 inches (400-600 mm) making them amongst the narrowest in Western Europe. Drift mines were dug into the side of the hills to access the seams but the work to extract coal from the narrow seams was extremely arduous requiring the miners to work on their sides as they hewed the coal. Ventilation shafts were dug to allow the miners to work underground. The narrow coal seam did not produce gas therefore there was no need for the elaborate system of ventilation required in the deep rich coal seams of Co. Durham.

In 1788 the O'Reilly brothers established an ironworks at Arigna. Their allegiance was with Wolf Tone and a united Ireland. They dreamt of funding the struggle through the ironworks but it was not be, though the area did see disturbances. In 1793 Col. Tennison's mansion, aptly named Coalville, on the banks of Lough Meelagh, was attacked by Defenders and destroyed. Five years later General Humbert, his French troops and Irish sympathisers passed nearby on their way to defeat at Ballinamuck.

The ironworks were never very successful and closed in 1838. Coal mining continued sporadically through the Famine years and provided some local men with a stake to afford the crossing to Scotland and England together with a skill which was in great demand in those countries with the arrival of the steam age. No evidence has been found of direct recruitment of miners from Arigna and the surrounding towns of Ballyfarnon and Keadue during this period but it may have been a factor used by some local landlords to persuade tenants to leave and allow the holdings to be consolidated into more productive units.

Coal mining in the mountains above Arigna continued until 1990.

Fig. 37   Slag heaps above Arigna, Co. Roscommon in the late 19th century.

Fig. 38 This cottage in Carrigeenroe is close to Thomas Mattimoe's farm. His house would have been of the same design though with a thatched roof at that time. The cottage had three rooms with an extra room built on at the back. Two rooms had fireplaces. Opposite the land Thomas farmed is a cottage still owned by a Mattimoes but now derelict and totally overgrown.

alongside Anne McLoughlin who also had a holding of nine acres. We do not know who this woman was but she bore the same surname as Thomas's mother so could have been his Grandmother, Aunt or even cousin. It seems likely she was a widow and farmed the land in conjunction with Thomas.

A ruined cottage stands on the other side of the road from the land farmed by Thomas and may well have been his home. Today it is overgrown with ivy and elder, and has trees growing through its walls but it is stil possible to walk into the the three-roomed building. The front door provides access to the main room approximately 16' (5m) square. A simple planked door immediately to the left gives access to a similar sized room which would have been used for sleeping. Opposite the front door a further door gives acces to the fourth room of solid lean-to construction probably used for storing food, outdoor clothes and footwear. On the far wall of the main room is a fireplace served by a chimney which also serves the fireplace in the final room, most likely Thomas and Ann's bedroom. An old cottage two hundred yards further up the road to Carrigeenroe is of the same type but still in sound habitable condition though this now has a slate roof rather than its original thatch. Whilst many such old cottages still provide good, sound living accommodation, now with the benefit of modern services, the countryside of Sligo and Roscommon is still littered with the remains of abandoned cottages bearing witness to depopulation of the land during the past two hundred years, a process which continues today.

Thomas and Ann worshipped at nearby St.. Teresa's and sent their children to the adjacent National School. Despite the nearness of the school the eldest son Patrick did not learn to read and write before leaving Ireland, perhaps hampered by the need to help out on the family farm during the difficult times still being experienced by farmers in Ireland.

The Build up to Departure

It is clear that the Mattimoe's and other families who went to live in '*Little Ireland*' retained an undiminished love of the country they felt obliged to leave. So, having survived the Famine, what led them to depart the country of their birth?

It was probably a combination of reasons. The write-up's on Boyle market in the early 1860's indicate that good prices were being obtained for livestock, particularly cattle. In England at this time the national herd had been struck hard by rinderpest, or 'cattle plague' as it was normally referred, which may have led to higher prices for cattle in Boyle most of which would have been exported to England through Sligo. However bad weather during this period led to a run of poor harvests.

The winter of 1866/67 was harsh in Connaught. Lough Key froze sufficient to encourage people to skate on its surface. This led to tragedy in one case where a man fell through the ice and was dead by the time he was rescued and taken to the shore. The Spring was also hard with severe snow falls in March resulting in the loss of many young lambs. The bad weather continued through April. Was this a contributory factor in loosening Erin's hold on Thomas and his family.

Three Gaffney men were accused of murder that Spring though it seems they were not closely related to Thomas's wife Ann.

Personal tragedy had struck when Thomas and Ann's daughter Mary died some time before 1864. These difficulties may have led them to be susceptible to correspondence from Ann's brothers who had emigrated to Scotland during the Famine and were now living in '*Little Ireland*', Gordon Gill, Co. Durham. They would have written of the many opportunities and good money to be earned in the coal mines. Perhaps all these things and more conspired to loosen the hold Ireland had on Thomas and his family.

Fenian Unrest

The political situation was also uncertain. This was the period of 'fenianism'. Fenians, taken from the name of the ancient warrior protectors of Erin, were members of the political group in the USA which advocated establishment of an Irish Republic. They were Irishmen who had left Ireland during the Famine but retained a love of the country of their birth combined with a bitterness toward the British Government for its for its actions, or lack of them, during the Famine years. These Irishmen were prepared to back up their support with finance and, in some instances, direct action. The Fenian Brotherhood was formed and a force of some 85,000 men assembled including many veterans from the American Civil War.

Fenianism was not purely an American inspired reactionary movement. It had strong roots in Ireland. Fears of an Irish rebellion led to significant movements of troops to Ireland. The movement at short notice of Royal Artillery troops from Woolwich Barracks to Ireland led to rioting by Irishmen living in that part of London. In Ireland the Habeas Corpus Act was suspended to allow the Authorities to arrest and detain those they suspected of 'Fenianism'. A number of Irishmen who had returned to Roscommon from the USA were arrested and subsequently deported despite no evidence of their involvement in any clandestine activities. The American Fenian leadership did sail from New York in January 1867. A rebellion was planned but the organisation was betrayed by informants from within, leading to the discovery of guns and ammunition which were being smuggled into Ireland through Dublin.

Despite the setback the rebellion started in March 1867. It had some success capturing police barracks in various parts of the country but intended to concentrate on guerrilla action. In the event the rebellion failed when those involved were overwhelmed by the British Army.

Was Thomas's departure from Ireland linked to these events? The family certainly enjoyed singing Rebel songs but so did all those who left Ireland for England. There is no indication that Thomas's

Fig. 39 (above)   Sligo Harbour.   *Courtesy of the National Library of Ireland*

Fig. 40 (left)   Advertisement in the Roscommon & Leitrim Gazette, 1864

By permission of the British Library (1866 M10849)

love of Ireland ever translated into any form of direct action. Quite the contrary Thomas and his family were to become well respected and loved members of the Northern England community they were to join. Thomas's departure was just coincidence though the unrest may have been a factor.

Emigration, the way to a better Life

From the time of the Famine, emigration, whilst already a feature of Irish life in the decades preceding it, had become an accepted way of 'bettering' ones self. The growth of the railways from the late 1840's provided an extension from Longford through Boyle to Sligo. Whilst this development helped the trade by making it easier to export cattle it also provided a more ready route by which families could travel to Sligo, catch a steam packet to Liverpool and a new life. The sea crossing took two days and sailings were regularly advertised in the Boyle edition of the Roscommon and Leitrim Gazette.

The Griffith's Valuation provides the date when Thomas and his family emigrated to England. The Valuation was a living document and over the course of time was amended to reflect the changes taking place in tenure and ownership. In the revisions of 1871 the entries for Thomas Mattimoe and Ann McLoughlin are crossed through showing they had relinquished their tenancies in 1867. Both holdings had been combined as one and were being farmed by a John Bannon. Had Ann McLoughlin died loosening still further the hold of Ireland upon Thomas and his family and maybe providing additional funds to allow them to emigrate? We will never be sure. We do know however that by August 1867 Thomas and his family were living in Bishop Auckland, Co. Durham.

The Mattimoe Mug

We will never know the manner of their departure but it does not appear to conform to the generally held image of a barefoot family travelling with a few meagre belongings tied up in a cloth. One item gives the lie to this image is the "Mattimoe mug". This is the only surviving item which has been passed down through the family with a provenance that states that it came from Ireland. It is not a particularly valuable item. It is more likely to be an imported item from Germany than an early example of Balleek ware but it clearly remained important to the family through the generations and continues to be cherished. Was it one of a set given to the family as a leaving present by well-wishers? If so it implies that the family took a reasonable number of belongings with them including breakables.

Farewell to Erin

Leaving Ireland, the place of their birth, was a big step for the family. Today the availability of cheap flights, telephone and the Internet provides easy contact with anyone anywhere in the world and it is easy to forget that those leaving Ireland for England were leaving family and friends knowing they would never see them again. There was little prospect in the 1860's of returning to Ireland to visit once you had left. There would have been a farewell get together of friends and family but the imminent departure would have given the occasion some of the elements of a wake. Thomas and his family would have received a blessing from the Priest. It is possible that close members of the family travelled with them to Sligo to give them a tearful send off from the quayside.

One can only imagine the mixed feelings of sadness, trepidation and excitement felt by Thomas, Ann and their sons as the steamer sailed out of Sligo harbour leaving that beautiful green coast with its gently rolling hills dotted with thatched, grey stone cottages, and backdrop of distant purple mountains. Knocknarea to the left, its summit crowned with the ancient tomb of Queen Medb of Connaught who was killed in battle and, by legend, buried here in a standing position facing the sea ready to repel her seaborne enemies. Then gentle Benbulben to the right at whose base the peaceful church of Drumcliff nestles on an ancient monastic site and where, in this most beautiful of settings W. B. Yeats is buried. The boat would have passed Rosses Point and Coney Island, the latter destined to give its name to a far brasher island on the other side of the Atlantic, then out into clear water but probably remaining in view of Ireland until they passed through the channel running between Co. Antrim and the Mull of Kintyre.

The poem on the following page from the archives of the Department of Irish Folklore, University College Dublin, encapsulates the feelings of many who, like Thomas, were obliged to leave Ireland to seek a better life for their family but felt the emotional wrench of leaving the country of their birth. It illustrates a love of the country and knowledge of its history and folklore and provides a fitting conclusion to the story of our Mattimoe family in Ireland. The poem was collected by Brighid M. Ni Ghamhnain of Boyle in 1938 from Pat Feeney a 65 year old farmer living in the townland of Corrick, Ballinafad. He had heard it 40 years earlier from James Garly, then aged 90, living in that same townland. It seems likely it originates from the 1860's or a decade either side.

Boyle

Farewell to Boyle its lakes, and all
That spans my native town
Each crystal rill and tall fair hill
That looks so nimbly down
The schoolhouse o'er the river
Green Island and the mill
And your pleasant cot Frank Egan
Its plain I see you still
The cascade near outside the door
Where trout and salmon play
And every thrush upon its bush
Caroles its merry lay
No more we'll roam those flowery banks
Or birdnest in the dell
Or pluck the shamrock fresh and green
That blooms round Patrick's well
The old forge is extinguished
That once was all aglow
With loud and merry laughter
A curse on Erin's foe
They tumbled many a homestead
From Lough Gara to Lough Foyle
And you were no exception
My native town of Boyle

Farewell old Ruined Abbey
The pride of days gone by
Your old majestic walls
Were proud erect and high
There stands its lofty gables
Still battling with the years
From age to age, a living page
Of Ireland's faith and tears
The Noble river sweeps along
Parting silver spray
And from the old cross roads,
And Easkey bridge
Round Doon and fair Lough Ce
Fair crescent and old Abbey town
The echoes of Mockmoyne
And the clover fields of Felroy
That belongs to you Pat Coyne
From Easternsnow to Silverrow
And all round Knockadoo
Jail Flags, Cross Lane, Main Street and Drieu
I bid you all adieu

The leal and true are rapped in you
Like grim deaths icy call
And your glory too it yet illumes
The hills and dales round Boyle

Farewell Lough Gara many a day
I rambled by your shore
To watch the Boatmen set sail
And hear the waters roll
I praise thee in my Irish heart
Thy Billow lone and clear
And on thy shore there still remains
A name to Ireland dear
Wid sires of old neath green and gold
Led clansmen to the fight
And gave deep graves to foreign knaves
Who dared dispute their rights
To rule and live, to make and give
Our fathers on the soil
Pure Irish Laws within your Cause
Beannacht leath past days in Boyle

Farewell laughter, farewell to thee
And all these happy hours
I spent within your Castle shrine
And ivy covered bowers
The island where the lovers sleep
Where death could not divide
Where two weeping willow gently loops
O'er those graves, side by side
How lone today the castle walls
That oft stood wars rude shock
Boyle Annals tell where heroes fell
By sleeping hill and rock.
Manys the combat fierce and long
The MacDermotts proud and brave
Dealt blow by blow, with Erin's foe
Their father's home to save
Farewell to the old chapel
Where first I knelt to pray
When ere I think on thee,
Though my lot be what it may
Though driven from my native shore
In foreign lands to toil
But in foreign lands with upraised lauds
I'll pray success to Boyle.

6 Early Days in England

Arrival

Emigration to England for Thomas, his heavily pregnant wife Ann and their three young sons would not have been an easy task. After a 48 hour sea-crossing they arrived in Liverpool. This city had thrived on its maritime trade. It was the main port servicing the Americas and its docks full with craft of all sizes either unloading or preparing to sail. The dockside was crowded with dockers, traders, merchants and passengers. There were many Irish amongst the passengers many just arrived as they had whilst others were embarking for the USA and Canada. One can only imagine the worry and trepidation felt by the young Mattimoe family who had never encountered anything like the busy City. Did they find lodgings for that first night? Did they find a helping hand from a stranger or relying on the trust in strangers they had been used to in Ireland were they taken advantage of by those who could easily identify vulnerable newcomers. They did not linger but headed for Bishop Auckland at the earliest opportunity.

The next stage of their journey was probably by train as the network had expanded rapidly in the 42 years since the establishment of the Stockton and Darlington railway. It had reached Bishop Auckland in 1843 though a few changes would have been required to affect the journey from Liverpool to their new home town. It is probable they had the name and address of someone who would help them on arrival. This person would have been from the Irish area of the town where the inhabitants would have welcomed and helped the newcomers, no doubt as they themselves had been helped when they first arrived.

Bishop Auckland

Bishop Auckland had begun as a small settlement surrounding the Bishops Palace which the Bishops of Durham used as one of their residences. It remained a quiet town until the Industrial Revolution generated a need for coal to drive the iron works, factories and mills of the North of England. The railways provided the means by which the 'black gold' could be readily transported.

The Mattimoes arrived in Bishop Auckland at a time of major growth. The coal mines were providing employment not only in their own right but through the support industries and those providing services to the population which had grown dramatically from 2,180 in 1821 to 5,112 in 1851 and was to reach 10,112 by 1871.

Housing was not easy to come by for those new to the town. Many Irish emigrants had come to settle in Bishop Auckland during and since the 1840's, initially to escape the Famine, and had gathered together as those with a common background and culture will always tend to do. The areas these newcomers occupied were often in the poorest areas of the town which provided crowded and insanitary conditions. In 1852 a report by the Board of Health criticised overcrowding in the town, particularly amongst the Irish.

> "The cottages are mostly divided into separate tenements and amongst the Irish a single family rarely occupies more than one room. Indeed I have known as many as three or four

families crowded into a single room and without a bed, a chair or table. A few stones are put in a circle round the fire for seats, and straw or shavings will serve them to lie upon"

The groups of cottages and tenements each shared a common ashpit for the disposal of refuse and human waste. Open sewers ran through the cobbled streets. Water was from springs, wells and standpipes inadequate for the growing population leading to long queues. The diet of the Irish, in common with English unskilled workers, was mainly bread and potatoes. Thus their living conditions were no better than they experienced in Ireland before the Famine and, due to the crowded conditions far less sanitary.

The report by the Board of Health led to the establishment of a Local Board of Health which had recommended and overseen improvements in the town's public services including an improved water supply and a sewage system by the time Thomas and his family moved to the town. These changes eradicated the very worst of the unhealthy conditions but these benefits were not shared by all, particularly those new to the town arriving with little money and few belongings.

Irish families arriving in Bishop Auckland found their spiritual needs better catered for than their physical needs. A mission had been established in 1842 in a room lent for this purpose by a Mr Peacock. The influx of families from Ireland during the 1840's increased demand for a permanent place of worship for the growing Roman Catholic congregation and led to the construction of St. Wilfred's Church, on land given to the Church by a Mr Peacock containing one of the town wells. The presbytery was built over the well in 1869 which, though now heavily silted, still has drinkable water. St. Wilfred's was opened in October 1846 to seat 300. Irish workers continued to be drawn to the town by the mines and the nearby ironworks at Witton Park resulting in the church being enlarged in 1857 to accommodate 700. A school for the children of Roman Catholic families was built next to the Church in 1861.

Thomas and Ann attended St. Wilfred's and the names in the church marriage and baptism records clearly show that Irish immigrants formed the bulk of the congregation.

Poor Housing

The first record in Bishop Auckland of Thomas and his family is when Thomas registers the birth of his fourth son Peter in August 1867. They had not been long in the country. Thomas was working as a labourer and had found accommodation for his young family in Corn Close. This was part of a development of housing built in the 1850's. Though recently built they provided poor living conditions as can be seen from this quote from the Minute Book of the Local Board of Health, May 1855.

> "They had ascertained that there are 79 persons living in Mr Robert Grear's buildings in Corn Close who have no Privy accommodation whatever – Resolved that a proper notice be given to Mr Grear for the construction of 4 Privies and ashpits."

That October the Surveyor to the Board of health reported that

> "he had visited 4 cellar dwellings in Corn Close occupied by Joseph Barnard and John Newby and found them surrounded with water – Ordered that he inspect the premises again and report thereon at the next meeting."

A month later

> "The Clerk reported that he had again visited the cellar dwellings in Corn Place and considered that in the absence of drainage they would be liable to be flooded with water."

Finally in December, demonstrating the persistence and effectiveness of the Board of Health

> "The Surveyor reported that Robert Grear had constructed 4 Privies and Ashpits in connexion with his buildings in Corn Close to his satisfaction."

Whether these meagre improvements recommended by the Board of Health had been further enhanced by the time the Mattimoes moved there in the Summer of 1867 it seems certain that the living conditions with water obtained from a standpipe, no drainage to the properties and, at best, shared ash closets for toilets, would have been smelly and insanitary providing conditions much worse than they had left in Ireland.

It must have been with much relief that the family soon found improved accommodation in Bridge Street where we find them on the birth of their next son Stephen on Christmas Day 1869 by which time Thomas was working as a mason's labourer. In further evidence of the links between the Mattimoe family and the Gaffneys of Gordon Gill Michael and Ann Gaffney stood as godparents for Stephen when he was christened at St. Wilfred's in February the following year.

The terraces in Bridge Street appear to have been built on a piecemeal basis. Up until the 1890's there were large gaps between groups of houses since filled in by construction of similar properties. Bridge Street leads steeply down to the stretch of the River Wear between the Newton Cap Bridge and

Fig. 41

The oldest surviving, and perhaps the first, photograph of Thomas and Ann Mattimoe was taken around 1870 whilst living in Bishop Auckland or shortly after they had moved to Gordon Gill. In it Ann is well dressed in a fashionable, well fitting dress with a large brooch at the neck and a pair of pince nez. Thomas is dressed in a three piece suit. The sleeves on the jacket look rather too long, a fact the photographer disguised by carefully folding the excess material at the elbow. It is possible that Thomas may have 'borrowed' the outfit from the photographer for the occasion but Ann's would appear to be her own and indicative of a satisfactory standard of living. The studio setting with its painted backdrop of a window looking onto countryside and ornate brocaded chair with table and pile of books was typical of that time. Was the photograph taken in order that copies could be sent to family they had left behind in Ireland? If so it would have conveyed the impression that Thomas and Ann were making a success of their new life.

Fig. 42

This early photograph of Patrick Mattimoe, eldest son of Thomas and Ann, was probably taken around 1874 when he was eighteen years old. It is a 'tintype' where the image is captured on a thin piece of iron. The resultant image is often dark as in this case. The metal sheets were often used to capture multiple images which were then roughly cut into individual photographs. The resultant image was usually quite small but in this case the photograph measures 2 1/2 x 4 inches (6x10 cms).

the railway viaduct now converted to carry the traffic to and from Bishop Auckland. The soundly built houses are still occupied though some in the surrounding streets have been demolished.

Life in Bishop Auckland

The eldest son Patrick found work as he was by then too old to attend school. John and young Thomas attended the Roman Catholic school which had been built next to St. Wilfred's Church in Hexham Street, a short walk from the house in Bridge Street.

Thomas's three eldest boys, Patrick, John and Thomas must have enjoyed living near the river with its countryside just beyond. Other attractions for the boys included the thriving market which took place on a Thursday and the parkland and river of the nearby Bishops Palace.

Thomas no doubt enjoyed a drink from time to time with his friends and workmates at one of the many public houses in the town at that time. Perhaps the Maid of Erin in West Street near to the area occupied by many of the other Irish families would have been a favourite.

The Irish families in Bishop Auckland had a strong social bond through the Church and events organised for the congregation on its behalf. The women in the families cared for the children and the home and shared each others company during the day. In the evening visits from friends would be enlivened by stories and songs from the Old Country.

No doubt all the family would have enjoyed the annual flower show that took place in the grounds of

Little Ireland

By permission of Beamish the North of England Open Air Museum

Fig. 43   Bishop Auckland Market Place in the late 19th century. The town hall is to the left of the picture and in the distance beyond the market is the entrance to the grounds of the Bishop's Palace. Newgate Street with its shops led from the right foreground of this photograph. Both Corn Close and Bridge Street were a short walk from the Market Place.

the Bishop's Palace. The show enjoyed a run of glorious sunny weather in the years the Mattimoes lived in the town and during this period attracted crowds of up to twenty thousand people. The programme included not only flower and produce tents but dairy produce and animal classes such as rabbits, pigeons, poultry, sheep and dogs. There was a horse show and the crowds were entertained by bands, the Grenadier Guards and Life Guards being popular regulars at the show. The genteel atmosphere of the Bishops Palace gardens contrasted with the brasher entertainment on offer in the town described in the following extract from 'Bishop Auckland – 100 Years Ago' by Derek J Hebden.

> "The excitement of show day was not confined to the Bishop's Park. Bishop Auckland market place boasted shows of all descriptions. There were trumpets blaring, drums thumping, boxing booths, fat women, thin men, pigs with five legs, giants, dwarfs, acrobats, dancing bears, performing lops (fleas). Punch and Judy, Aunt Sallies, hobby horses and a new kind of entertainment in a ring of bone shaking bicycles propelled 'by great lads and men working for all they were worth to make the wheels go round'."

No doubt there would have been ample opportunity for the men to slake their thirst on these hot show days in one or more of the sixty or so public houses and inns Bishop Auckland possessed in those days.

Ann would have enjoyed the healthier living conditions provided by the house in Bridge Street but must have found the steep walk up to the town tiring particularly with two babies to take with her and two young boys to keep an eye on. The novelty and excitement of a busy town with bakers, butchers, grocers, hardware shops and confectioners, as well as drapers, dressmakers, milliners and shoemakers, and many more must have appealed to Ann as the family finances gradually improved. The town would have been particularly busy on market days, Thursday and Saturday the latter being popular with mining families from the town and the surrounding villages whose men folk only worked half a day on Saturdays.

Despite the improvement in their living conditions the lure of being closer to Ann's family, the improved employment opportunities and a more rural way of life was to draw Thomas and Ann with their growing family to look for an opportunity to move to Gordon Gill on the edge of Ramshaw.

7 Work in the Mines

The primary reason for families moving to Gordon Gill was for the men to find employment in the mines of Ramshaw and Evenwood. The pits were to provide work for the Mattimoe, Hannon, Gaffney, Cox and Tarbert families of '*Little Ireland*'. There were a range of jobs that men and boys could undertake and the members of these families were employed in most of them at one time or another. Women never worked down the mines in Co. Durham as it was viewed as bringing bad luck and the practice had been banned by law by the time the families of '*Little Ireland*' began work in the South Durham Coal Field. Boys generally did not start work underground until they were twelve though the censuses, if the details were recorded correctly, show that on occasions boys as young as ten were employed during the 1880's and 1890's.

Mining remained primarily a 'pick and shovel' activity for the period covered by this book. Miners dressed in loose jacket, vest, knee breeches (hoggins), over trousers (longuns), all made of flannel, long stockings, strong shoes and a thick leather cap. The workings were not cold and the work was arduous so miners stripped down to their vests and knee breeches to work. The whole shift was spent underground so miners took their 'bait' to sustain themselves. In the damp drift mines of Railey Fell, Ramshaw, this was jam and bread or sugar and bread. Anything else tasted bad when eaten underground. The bait was carried in a special metal box in which one half fitted snugly inside the other to create a good seal keeping the food untainted and protected from the rats which lived in the tunnels of the mine. The 'bait' would have been accompanied by a tin of cold water or tea.

The workings in Ramshaw were always wet and dirty. Miners would often wade through dirty water halfway up their knees and their clothing was always damp. This together with the unavoidable inhalation of coal dust led to many early deaths of miners from bronchitis. Added to these unhealthy conditions the informal arrangements for the men and boys to 'relieve' themselves were cited as one of the causes of outbreaks of typhoid in mining communities. There were no pithead baths. And the tin bath in front of the fire was the means by which miners cleaned themselves after a shift.

Working conditions were not only uncomfortable but dangerous. A major safety improvement was the introduction of the Davy lamp in 1816. This safety lamp used gauze to shield the flame of the lamp from the dangerous gases that occurred in the mine thus preventing the explosions and loss of life which occurred before its introduction. The disadvantage of the design was the limited amount of light from the flame, tempting miners to use the lamp 'open' when they thought there was no risk of explosion. This practice led to the locking of lamps which was the duty of the deputy over-man before allowing men into the workings.

Whilst the major disasters rightly grabbed the attention of the public and led to improved working practices most mining deaths and injuries resulted from incidents involving a single worker. Every edition of the local paper, The Auckland Chronicle, reported several such accidents in the South Durham Coalfield each week, most often involving hewers killed by falls of stone, but pony putters also suffered accidents in trying to control the ponies and their heavy loads in the confined space of the underground tunnels.

Mining Terminology

Mining in Co. Durham adopted several words of Scandinavian origin that had first been used in farming and were then adopted by lead miners before being transferred to the coal mining industry. **'In-bye'** was the direction underground away from the shaft or mine entrance whilst **'out-bye'** was the direction leading from the coal face to the shaft or entrance. **'Caviling'**, the process involving drawing of lotts by which areas of work were randomly selected for each man thus showing no favour in the allocation of the more productive areas, is thought to derive from the Scandinavian word for sticks used in lotteries. The term is still used by some people to refer to someone who has done better than expected, when they are said to have 'drawn a good cavil'.

Landing was the name given to the area where the loaded **tubs** were taken to be removed from the pit. In deep shaft mines it was the area around the base of the shaft. In drift mines it was the point in the drift where the cables from the stationery engine where attached in order to pull the **tubs** out of the mine.

Several other terms were borrowed from lead-mining but changed meaning slightly in the process. A **flat** was the name describing a lead seam where it changed direction from the vertical to the horizontal but in a coal mine the **flats** were the areas were the hewn coal was loaded into tubs. It then came to mean the area of working in a coal mine for which a Deputy was responsible. **Rolley-way** was the traditional name given to the passages along which the ponies pulled the tubs backwards and forwards between the **landings** and the **flats**. **Rolleys** were the flat wagons onto which the **corves** containing the hewn coal were loaded ready to be pulled to the **landings**. By the time the Mattimoes began work in the mines the **rolleys** had been replaced by **tubs** which were then coupled together to be pulled to the **landings**.

The **bankhead** was the area above ground where the coal was brought to be washed, screened and loaded onto the wagons for transportation. In Ramshaw it also contained the coke ovens.

Mining Jobs Underground

The first job a young boy would be given underground at the age of twelve, sometimes younger, would have been a **rapper**, a **trapper** or a **ventilation shaft minder**.

Rapper boys signalled the approach of a pony pulling a set of coal tubs in order that a pony and tubs approaching from the opposite direction could move into a siding. Signalling was by pulling on a communicating wire linked to a pivoted hammer which then struck a metal plate.

The mines were a network of tunnels and it was critical to ensure good ventilation of the workings both to enable the men to work below ground and to avoid the build up of

Fig. 44 Sandhole drift. Norwood and Railey Fell Collieries comprised a number of such small drift mines each connected to the bankhead by tramways.

dangerous gases. Air was directed through the tunnels as required by sealing of trap doors. Where these were positioned within active workings the **trapper** was employed to open the trap door to allow the passage of miners and the ponies pulling the coal tubs. This was a lonely, job for a young boy. He would have only brief contact with others as they passed. The majority of the time was spent in the pitch dark of the mine. In winter the boys left home in the dark, spent the day below ground and returned to the surface when it was already dark, only seeing daylight on the one day a week they did not work. The following account given by a **trapper** in 1842 describes their working conditions.

> "The clatter, the bustle and confusion, the darkness relieved only by glimmering flickering lamps, the men and boys flitting hither and thither, resembling grim shadows rather than human figures – all this seemed a fantastic dream, novel and bewildering. To direct the air currents of the mines, doors were placed at certain points, and it was my business to tend one of these, to open and shut it when the putters pass through on their way to the workings and on their return journey to the flat or station. The trappers hours were normally 12, really about 13, a day: his pay was tenpence a day, and he was expected to remain at his post the whole time in total darkness. There was a good deal of passage through my door, the putters with their tubs, empty and laden, men and boys backwards and forwards. This relieved the monotony, though exciting incidents were few. There were occasional stoppages in the work, sometimes for rather long periods. The dullness and loneliness were then oppressive."

Ventilation shafts were an essential part of the system of keeping air flowing through the workings. Air was drawn up the shaft by lighting a fire at its base. The fire was minded by the **ventilation shaft minder**. This was a job for boys perhaps as young as ten and was an even lonelier job for a young boy than being a trapper as he would rarely see other workers. A few years ago a ventilation shaft was exposed in the car park of the Trotters Arms in Ramshaw and at the bottom of it, alongside the remains of a fire was a straw pallet which the boy had used to provide some comfort in the dark, damp, lonely conditions he endured.

At the age of fourteen a boy would progress to become a **pony putter** or **driver**. Use of Shetland ponies, known as Galloway's, down the pits began in the 1840's and was widespread by the mid 1860's. Each pony pulled a set of tubs along the railway from the flats to the landings. In deep shaft pits the tubs were taken to the bottom of the shaft where they were lifted two at a time to the surface. In drift mines the tubs were attached to the cable of a stationery engine and dragged to the surface. The pony was then hitched to a set of empty tubs to be pulled back to the flat where the **putter** would be waiting with another set of full tubs. The boys would ride on the limmer to which the yoke is attached. There was always the risk of being crushed by tubs or scraping against the roof or sides of the tunnels which could cause serious injury.

The way for the **pony putter** and his pony was illuminated by a candle in a box hung on the side of a tub. If another horse and its tubs approached they would pass at designated sidings. In some mines engines and inclined planes were used to drag sets of tubs where the tunnel was too steep for the horses but there is no evidence of this mechanism having been used at Railey Fell.

George Welsh of Ramshaw gave the following description of his working day as a **pony putter** at Railey Fell Pit, Ramshaw where he started work on leaving school at fourteen in 1924. George told me that the job of a **pony putter** involved leaving home an hour before the start of the shift and walking up the bank to collect a pony from the stables behind Bowes Close. At its peak there were up to forty ponies stabled at Bowes Close to meet the demands of the multiple shifts. George led his pony to the Drift where he was caviled to work that day, and down to the landing. He had to be at the landing with the pony in time for the start of his shift. The pony was then harnessed to a set of empty tubs and taken to the flats where the hewers where working. The **hewers** started work an hour earlier so there were full tubs waiting

Figure 45 John Hannon (3rd from the left) with other pony putters at Railey Fell Colliery about 1916. The ponies were stabled above ground behind Bowes Close. The buildings still exist though are now converted to cottages.

Courtesy of Beamish the North of England Open Air Museum

and George would unharness the pony from the empty tubs and harness it to the full tubs to be taken back to the landing. The pony would pull up to ten loaded tubs. The **pony putters** did not ride the tubs as they had done in earlier times as this was not allowed instead they led them to the landing. Working conditions for men and horses were bad. They waded through muck and water halfway up to their knees. When they reached the landing the person in charge would attach the full tubs to a cable linked to a static engine at the surface. Two rings on the signal to the surface would mean take in the slack cable, three rings meant start hauling the tubs to the surface and one ring meant stop.

George and the other **pony putters** would not always use the same pony. They would be changed around after a week so that each pony had a share of both the hard and the easier drifts. George was familiar with handling the ponies before he left school as he and the other young school boys would collect the ponies at the end of a shift and ride them bareback down through Gordon Gill to the beck to wash the muck off their legs before riding them back to the stables. This was an unpaid activity but much enjoyed by the boys and must have presented quite a sight, and on some occasions alarm, to the families living in the Gill as their sons and the other boys galloped past their houses.

Four years later George went to work at Randolph Pit in Evenwood as a **pony putter**. This was a deep pit and the horses were stabled underground.

The ponies were well looked after, though instances of neglect and cruelty did occasionally occur for which the **putter** could be summoned. The local paper records details of cases where **putters** beat their horses or let them pull the tubs along the underground walkways unattended where they sometimes met with accidents seriously injuring the animal. **Putters** were reported by the Deputies for instances of ill treatment and received a fine if convicted. Fortunately such incidents were rare and none have been

Fig. 46 Pony putter riding the limmer. This photograph is taken from publicity material produced by Ashington Colliery showing that this practice was not frowned upon by all collieries.

found concerning the mines at Evenwood and Ramshaw where the ponies were far more likely to be spoilt by the boys with treats such as an apple from home, with or without their mother's knowledge.

The job of **pony putter** carried its own dangers. Inexperience and an awkward pony led to the following incident reported in the Auckland Chronicle of June 1899.

> "On Monday morning quite a consternation was caused when the sad news rapidly spread that a serious accident had happened to Jos. Cootes (17) son of Mr Robert Cootes platelayer of Leasingthorne. The deceased had only begun that morning as a pony putter, and had only got started with his work, and whilst coming out bye with his second tub, by some means or other he was severely crushed. The injuries (principally to the head) were of such a serious character that the deceased only lived about ten minutes. Great sympathy is felt in the above place for his parents in the great loss they have sustained. – Inquest held …
> The evidence of Adam Peverley, putter, who saw the deceased start with his tub, was that the pony was always kicking, and the boys who had it last quarter would make nothing of it. They had to let it go, and it used to toss the tub off when at the bottom. When witness got to the deceased he found him lying at the turn and the tub was "couped" up about 20yds further on. The Deputy had told witness to fetch a tub away in front of the pony, so as to prevent it running away. Complaints had been made last quarter about the animal, and the boys came out once and would not work with it. The jury in returning a verdict of "Accidentally killed" expressed the opinion that it was an unfortunate circumstance that the deceased should have been caviled a pony which was unquiet."

The Auckland Chronicle of July 1918 records the following fatal accident involving a pony putter.

> "The deceased was 'hanging' his pony to a tub of coal … when the pony walked away sharply and the deceased's head was badly crushed between the tub and a (pit) prop. He

Fig. 47 John Hannon (back row on right) having progressed to become a putter. Note the hobnailed boots and the lamps.

was rendered unconscious and died an hour later before he could be removed from the mine."

Tom Seagrave told me of a similar incident that happened to him in North Bitchburn Colliery, Howden-le-Wear. He was leading a pony pulling a set of full tubs when one of the tubs jumped the rails. Tom had to physically lift the tub back onto the rails but as he was doing this the pony started forward and Tom found his head trapped between the top of the tub and a pit prop. He was unable to move and there was no one near to help him. Fortunately, though trapped, he could reach out and bang on the metal pipe that ran the length of the tunnel. Eventually his fellow workers heard the noise and came to investigate and Tom was rescued and escaped with his life though carried a scar under his chin where the rim of the tub had cut into his flesh.

After a few years a **pony putter** or **driver** would usually be strong enough to become a **putter**. Once the coal had been brought down from the face it was loaded into tubs, each then weighing up to a quarter of a ton. It was the **putter's** job to push the loaded tubs from the coal face, along the tunnel floor, sometimes covered with metal plates to ease their passage, until he reached the flat where they were loaded onto the rolleys to be pulled away by the ponies. The work was extremely arduous and reserved for the strongest young men. If the seam was low the **putter** was in danger of scraping his back on the roof. These injuries would form scabs over the vertebra which were known as "buttons". The injuries would start to heal on the miners rest day only to be opened up again when they resumed work. Miners would say the proof you were a man were the marks on your back.

On reaching twenty one years of age a **putter** could progress to become a **hewer**. This was the job at the coalface for the strongest men and progressed to after they had served their "apprenticeship" as lads in other underground jobs. The men would make their way to the coalface often bent over due to the limited headroom, a stout stick helping them on the journey. Once at the coalface their manner of working depended on the depth of the coal seam. In Railey Fell it varied between 3' 8" (1.12m) to 5' 10" (1.78m).

The work of a **hewer** was hard and the domain of men in their prime. In 1842 a report described the manner of working which would have changed little in the following decades.

> "The ordinary posture is leg doubled beneath him and the other foot resting against, reclining his body to one side so as often nearly to touch the shoulder, he digs his pick with both hands into the lower part of the coal, or into a stratum of fireclay, or some other softer material beneath the coal. In this way he picks out an excavation often for a considerable distance under a mass of coal, beneath which he half lies to work. When he has, after two or three hours hard labour undermined as much as he judges it prudent to attempt; he inserts iron wedges by means of a heavy hammer between the coal and the roof above it, by which, and by the weight of the ground above, the mass of coal is detached and falls. The cramped posture, the closeness of the subterranean atmosphere loaded with coal dust and the smoke of his lamp, and at times the sulphurous exhalations, together with bodily exertions, cannot fail to be very exhausting."

Miners used gunpowder to help bring down the coal. This powder was their own personal stock which they purchased and kept in a wooden box at home though not without incident as the following shows.

> "In April 1853 at Toft Hill ... pitman Joseph Maughan .... Had 14 lbs of powder and thinking it was damp spread it out in front of the fire to dry out. After a while, when he thought it was dry, he took some and threw it into the fire to try it. It worked – it ignited and caught the loose grains and exploded the lot. The roof of the house was blown off and the two adjoining houses were damaged. Maughan lost much of his furniture but

Fig. 48   Hewer working with pointed pick to undermine the coal seam before bringing down the coal ready for removal. Note the crouched working position and the absence of safety helmet.

Fig. 49

Photograph of two miners from Houghton-le-Spring taken in 1893.

somehow managed to escape uninjured. Unfortunately an infant child standing beside him was badly injured and died the following day."

Miners were normally meticulous in the care of their blasting powder and incidents were rare however in September 1899 the Auckland Chronicle detailed the following.

"A serious explosion, happily though miraculously unattended with fatal results, occurred at Coundon near Bishop Auckland early on Saturday morning. It appears that a miner named Geo. Crosby … went home at one-o-clock in the morning and going into the pantry, presumably for something to eat, struck a match. In the pantry there was stored a small cask of gunpowder and "shot" made ready for use in the pit. Consequent upon the match … the powder became ignited, and a terrific explosion took place, the roof of the house being blown from overhead and the house wares and furniture considerably damaged. Remarkable enough Crosby escaped with his life though badly injured about the face, head

Fig. 50 A coal sorting belt. Here the coal from the mines was sorted or 'screened' to remove stone and other impurities. Judging by this photograph it was mainly a job for young boys.

Courtesy of Beamsih the North of England Open Air Museum

and hands, whilst his wife and three children, who were in bed upstairs at the time of the explosion, suffered no injury at all."

The practice of miners purchasing their own gunpowder persisted into the 1900's by which time the local Co-op store was a principal provider. In 1910 the Bishop Auckland Co-operative Society reported the following sales volumes.

"Bacon, 234 tons; sugar, 1,302 tons; lemon peel, 10 tons; tobacco, 28 tons; flour, 44,708 sacks; beef, 143,244 stones; **blasting powder, 167 tons**."

Hewers normally worked in teams of four, two on each shift. On the foreshift which was from 4am until 10am the **hewers** brought down the coal from the face. The **hewers** on the backshift which ran from 10am to 4pm would remove the coal. Miners would then swap shift weekly. The miners who you were teamed with on the other shift were known as your "marras". The earnings of marras were pooled and shared out equally encouraging them to work together to extract the maximum amount of coal from the workings. Those on the fore shift would often stay behind to help their marras get their shift off to a good start. Marras became good friends and could be relied upon to help each other both outside of pit as well as within it.

On times of high demand an afternoon shift would be worked running from 3pm to 11pm. This could be followed by a night shift to give 24 hour working.

The **Deputy Overman** was responsible for the management of the men underground and their safety.

He would inspect the workings before the men started work then direct them to the coalface on which they were to work. Allocation of a workplace, or 'cavil' was crucial as the miners would be paid according to the coal they produced and certain faces were more productive than others. Allocation of "cavils" was undertaken every three months by the drawing of lots known as cavilling and was organised by the **Deputy**.

The **Fore-Overman** was responsible for a number of **Deputies** who reported to him regarding the condition of the mine and as such was responsible for its overall safety and the effective deplyment of the men and boys working underground. He also kept accounts of the expenses and wages for his section of the underground workings, agreeing with the men the amount each had earned.

Above Ground Jobs

Miners were paid according to the amount of coal they produced. Miners attached their own tags to each tub they filled which was used to credit them with the coal produced when it was weighed at the surface. Weighing of the coal was therefore a crucial task which, by necessity, was undertaken in the absence of the miners. The weigher was appointed by the mine owner but, to avoid any concerns regarding the accuracy of the weighing process, a **checkweighman** was appointed by the miners. The job was established by statute in 1860 and in 1894 it was opened to any person freely elected by the work force. This process involved a number of ballots with the list of candidates being reduced each time. The **checkweighman** continued to be paid by the Mine Owner but could not be removed from office without a ballot of the workers or a court order. **Checkweighmen** were highly respected in the community and the job was only open to those who could command the respect of both owners and the miners for their integrity and knowledge of the mining process.

Screenmen were surface workers who screened the coal to remove stone and other impurities.

The coal from Railey Fell was of a high quality and suitable for turning into coke for use in the nearby ironworks at Witton Park and those at Teesside. Conical "beehive" coke burners were built at the mine and manned by **coke-burners**. The coal to be fed into the burners was first washed.

Enginemen tended the steam engines that ran night and day to pump the workings clear of water and were helped by a young boy working as a **fireman**.

In deep shaft pits the **onsetter** was responsible for putting the full tubs into the cage to be raised to the surface and unloading them when they returned empty.

Banksmen worked above ground and removed the full tubs from the cage or the stationery engine emptying them into the wagons or coal screens then returning the empty tubs underground.

Mention must be made of the **knocker-up**. This was a role often undertaken by a retired miner who went round the village in the early hours of the morning to ensure that those working on the fore shift were woken. Men would mark their front doors so that the **knocker-up** knew who to rouse.

Payment

Lads did not qualify for a full mans wage until they were twenty one years old. Wages were paid fortnightly and the second week of each fortnight was known as 'barth week' when money was often short and the family had to 'make do or go without'.

8 The Development of *'Little Ireland'*

Ramshaw is a small village on the edge of Evenwood, separated from its neighbour by the River Gaunless and surrounded by beautiful countryside comprised of gently rolling hills, fields and woods. Ramshaw grew rapidly during the 1850's and 1860's through development of coal mining. This was not deep mining requiring the sinking of shafts because here the Busty coal seam was just below the surface and exposed in places. Coal mining had been undertaken in the area since the 1300's when the Bishop of Durham owned the rights. Transportation of the coal won from the mines was for centuries by strings of pack horses which limited competitiveness and kept mining on a small scale. The development of the railways in the 1820's changed this. Efforts by the Earl of Strathmore who owned Norwood Colliery in Ramshaw, led to the opening of the Haggerleases branch line from the Stockton and Darlington railway in 1830 allowing cost effective transportation of coal from the local mines. Over time a system evolved whereby the railways brought iron ore through Ramshaw for the smelting works at Witton Park and took away coal and coke. The closure in later years of the iron works dramatically affected the economics of the whole area and particular the viability of the railway which eventually closed.

The mines at Ramshaw, first Norwood Colliery and then Railey Fell were collections of small drift mines dug into the sides of the hills to afford access to the seam. These drifts were scattered across the countryside making little impact on the rural landscape apart from the small spoil heaps and the smoke from the chimneys of the steam engine houses. The steam engines were essential to pump water from the workings which would otherwise have flooded.

The hamlet of Gordon Gill is on the edge of Ramshaw. Gill is an Old Norse word meaning small valley. The road from Ramshaw to Toft Hill rises up the hill, or bank as it is referred to in these parts. Halfway up to the crossroads at the top a farm on the left masks the track leading down to Gordon Gill. The houses nestle beside Gordon Beck on a junction of footpaths leading in one direction over the fields to Morley, in another across the hill to Lands and in another alongside the beck down to Ramshaw. For the inhabitants of the mining and agricultural communities of these small villages and hamlets footpaths were the essential routes by which they travelled to work, church, friends and social events at the local institute and public house.

In the tithe map of 1843 there are no buildings in Gordon Gill. There is a road leading to the Gill presumably to service Providence Pit which had recently opened. Bowes Farm is the only building noted on that area. Even in 1851 Gordon Gill was only occupied by one family, that of Robert Marley, a railway labourer.

To Ramshaw via Scotland

By 1861 things were very different. Twelve families were living in the Gill, some seventy four people. Of these fifteen people were born in Ireland and a further twenty five were their direct descendants. Not by chance were so many Irish families living together in the Gill. All but one had first moved to Scotland at the time of the Famine.

Michael Gaffney, Ann Mattimoe's brother, had left his native Ardcarne in Co. Roscommon around

The Development of 'Little Ireland'   91

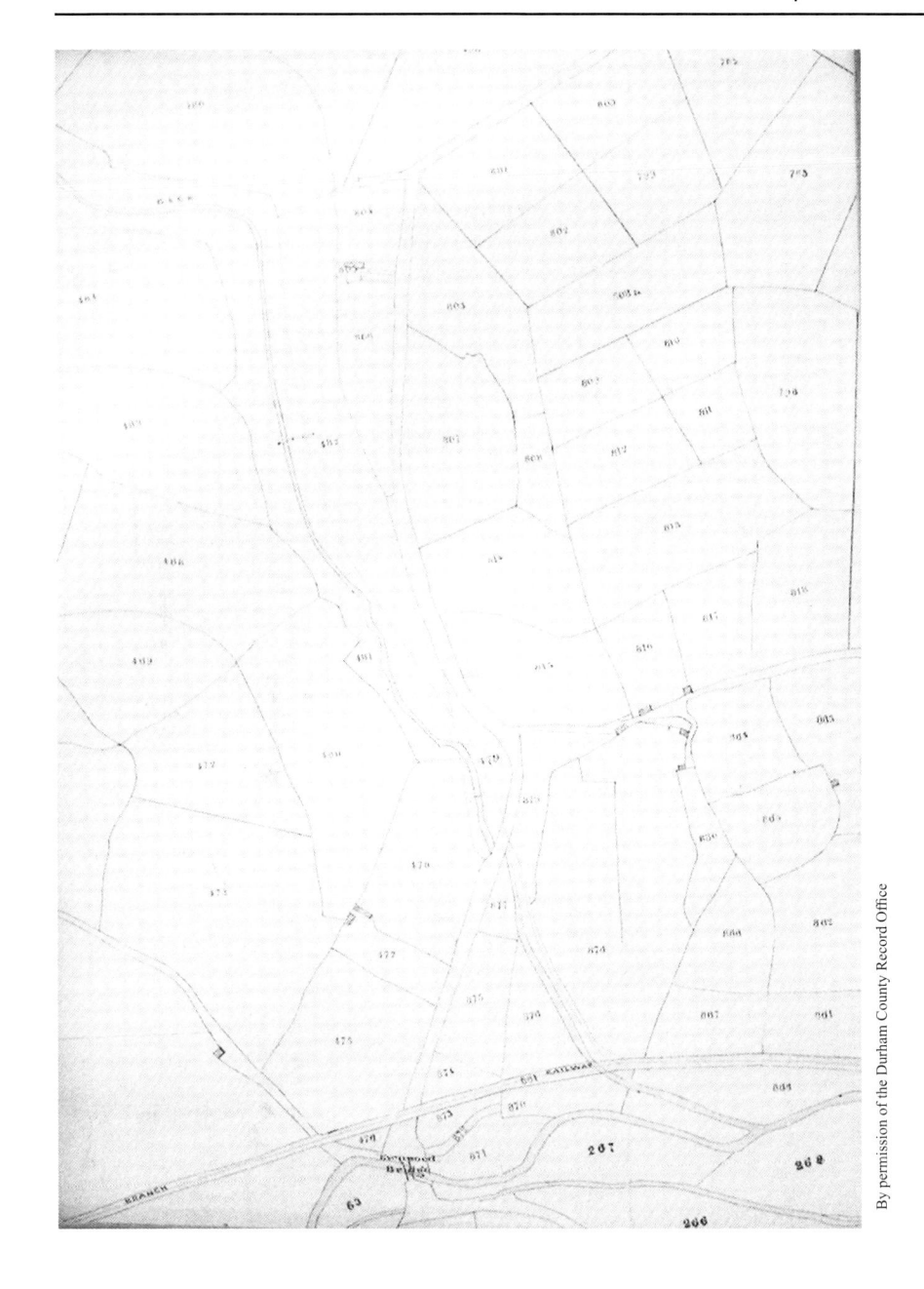

Fig. 51

The tithe map of 1842 shows that despite the Haggerleases branch line having been in use for over ten years the area surrounding Ramshaw had been unaffected. Small drift mines operated but had not been consolidated into one colliery nor was there any evidence of the sidings that accompanied later growth. The lack of housing supports the view that the railway was primarily supporting collieries further up the Gaunless Valley.

In the scattered community of Ramshaw farming was the principle activity.

There are no houses in Gordon Gill. Only Bowes Farm provides a landmark with which to compare later maps and identify changes.

By permission of the Durham County Record Office

1846/47 at the height of the Famine. He took with him his younger brother John who was then only fifteen. At about the same time the Tarbert family, the brothers John and Michael with their sister Ann, left nearby Kilronan, Co. Roscommon. Kilronan is near the Arigna Mountains where coal mining had been carried out since the 1500's and were at their peak in the early 19th century therefore the Tarberts may have been miners before leaving Ireland. Did the Gaffneys and Tarberts travel together? We do not know, but they all travelled to Coatbridge, Scotland, to the west of Glasgow where the families formed a close friendship and were to live as neighbours here and, subsequently, in the Gill for at least twenty five years. The links between the families were sealed when Michael Gaffney married Ann Tarbert in c.1847.

It is possible that they married in Co. Roscommon and then emigrated taking their brothers and sisters with them. Michael and Ann had five children whilst living in Scotland.

The other three men in the group were soon married to girls of Irish descent. John Tarbert married Ann, surname unknown, c.1848 and they had three daughters and one son whilst in Coatbridge. Michael Tarbert married Catherine Cassidy in 1848 and they had three sons and one daughter whilst in Coatbridge. John Gaffney married, Mary Stanton in c.1850 and they had two children whilst in Coatbridge.

The Scottish birth record for Michael Tarbert and Catherine's third son Patrick is very detailed. It not only gives the date of birth as the 25th February 1855 but also the time of day, 6.15am. Michael's place of birth is given as Kilronan, Co. Roscommon and Catherines as Co. Sligo further strengthening the links between those families who were to live in *'Little Ireland'*. The birth was registered by Michael Tarbert and a Peter Cassidy, presumably his Father-in-law or Brother-in-law. Both were miners and both could write. Their occupation and Irish descent were common factors amongst most of the fathers registering births around that time in Coatbridge. It seems certain therefore that all the Tarbert and Gaffney brothers were miners. Coatbridge had a thriving iron industry and nearby coal mines to support the process however two industries combined to create a poor living environment.

Coatbridge was a grim industrial town at that time surrounded by mines and ironworks. The Gaffney's and the Tarbert's may not have taken much persuading to move from there but why did they end up in Co. Durham? Perhaps a link with the mining interests of the Earl of Strathmore remains to be uncovered.

John Gaffney and his family were the first to move from Scotland to *'Little Ireland'* arriving sometime between 1853 and 1857, increasing their family by three in the following four years. John Tarbert and his family possibly moved from Coatbridge with the Gaffneys, initially living in nearby Cockfield where their youngest child was born. By 1861 the Tarberts were living in the Gill with a widower and three Irish bachelors as lodgers. The eldest four children of the Tarbert family are recorded in the census as 'scholars' including their oldest son who at ten years old had not been obliged to start work, though the legal minimum working age for children had been raised by statute in 1842. No occupation is given for the eldest two Gaffney boys though they were aged ten and seven. This could indicate an omission by the census enumerator or that they were needed at home.

Michael Tarbert's wife Catherine died in Coatbridge in 1859. It may have been this loss that triggered the move of Michael, his brother-in-law Michael Gaffney and their two families to leave Scotland as we find them living together in *'Little Ireland'* in 1860. Into this crowded household the Gaffneys's youngest daughter was born soon after they arrived in the Gill. Michael Gaffney's eldest three boys had already been put to work in the coal mine; John(13) and Michael(12) as drivers, hard and potentially dangerous work for young boys; Thomas(10) as a trapper, a lonely and boring job in the damp darkness of the pit tunnels. In contrast no occupation is given for Michael Tarbert's two sons aged nine and seven.

There was another Irish family, the Cox's, living in the Gill in 1861 who were to form a close relationship with the Gaffneys, Tarberts and Mattimoes. Patrick Cox had originated from Belfast and had to leave for reasons now lost to us. He had apparently tried to return but been forced to leave again. Patrick had married an English girl, Elizabeth Wanless, from Easington, Co. Durham. The Cox family lived in the villages between Evenwood and Gainford for at least nine years before moving to the Gill from Cockfield, together with their four children, in about 1860. The family continued to thrive and Elizabeth gave birth to three children in the Gill, a daughter, Sarah Jane and two sons. Sarah Jane, a gentle woman, was to become a good friend of the Mattimoes and would follow in the footsteps of her elder brother and sister by cementing links with the Gaffneys through marriage.

A recently arrived family was that of John Heal with his Irish wife Bridget Oushery, their four children and Bridget's brother, James. They had recently moved from Scotland to Gordon Gill. Perhaps John knew the Gaffneys and the Tarberts whilst in Scotland and been drawn to the Gill by their recommendation.

The last Irish family were a young couple, John and Mary Ann Philips. Little is known of them other than Mary Ann was born in the USA.

Distribution of 'occupations' given in 1861 were as follows.

Occupation	Number	Age range
Deputy Overman	1	20
Coal Miner (hewer)	11	29-47
Colliery Blacksmith	2	21-47
Coal Cleaner	1	19
Excavator	1	27
Masons Labourer	1	40
Colliery Engine Driver	1	52
Colliery Engine Fireman	1	12
Putter	2	15-17
Driver	4	10-13
Trapper	1	10
Farm Labourer	1	60
Housewives	11	22-48
Mother-in-Law	1	75
Daughters too old for school	4	14-22
Children at school	8	4-12
Children not at school	11	4-10
Infants and babies	12	2 weeks-3 years
Total	**74**	

Formal Schooling Begins in Ramshaw

The number of children attending school in 1861, whilst less than half those eligible is surprisingly high. The local school at Ramshaw was not opened until over five years later. Prior to this a school had operated in Evenwood since before 1857 though the suspicion must be that those recorded as scholars were being taught by a local woman at a Dame school or by their mothers.

Ramshaw school, which opened on 27 August 1866, was a Church of England National School built by, and under the patronage of, Henry Stobart & Company the owners of Railey Fell Colliery. The families in its catchment area were predominantly Methodists and Roman Catholics but there is little evidence of any difficulties the school encountered in accommodating the needs of the different religions. The funding link with the mine owners no doubt encouraged this ecumenical approach.

The first teacher of Ramshaw school, Francis Philipson, recorded in the opening entry of the school log that fifty children were admitted on that first day and, not surprisingly, found them 'very low in their attainment'. The parents were required to pay one pence per week for each child attending school. Children were organised into three classes and subjects taught were alphabet, geography, scripture, arithmetic, singing, reading, natural history, dictation and spelling. Francis records that he sold nineteen reading books and three slates to the children at half cost price.

Francis could not teach this range of subjects to three classes on his own so the 'monitor' system of teaching was employed. Older children of highest ability were selected and given tuition in order that they could teach what they had learnt to one of the classes. Whilst all children received homework that given to the monitors was tailored to lessons they would give to the other children. Monitors received a small payment for their assistance. Francis instilled discipline from the beginning and issued punishment for late arrival, disobedience and non completion of homework. Attendance at the school grew slowly and had reached sixty five by June 1868 though, interestingly, eighty four were present at a party given for the children.

Little Ireland

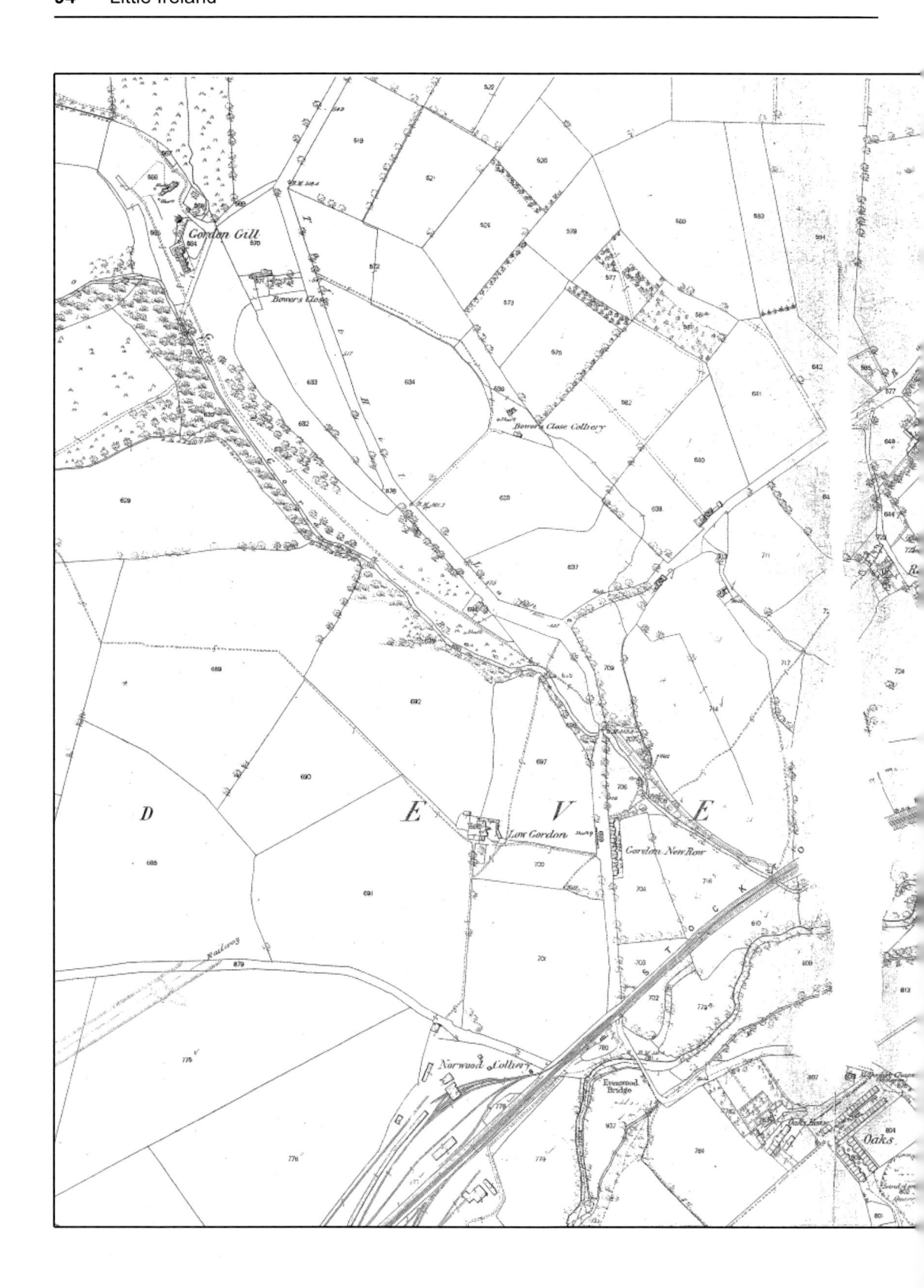

The Development of 'Little Ireland'

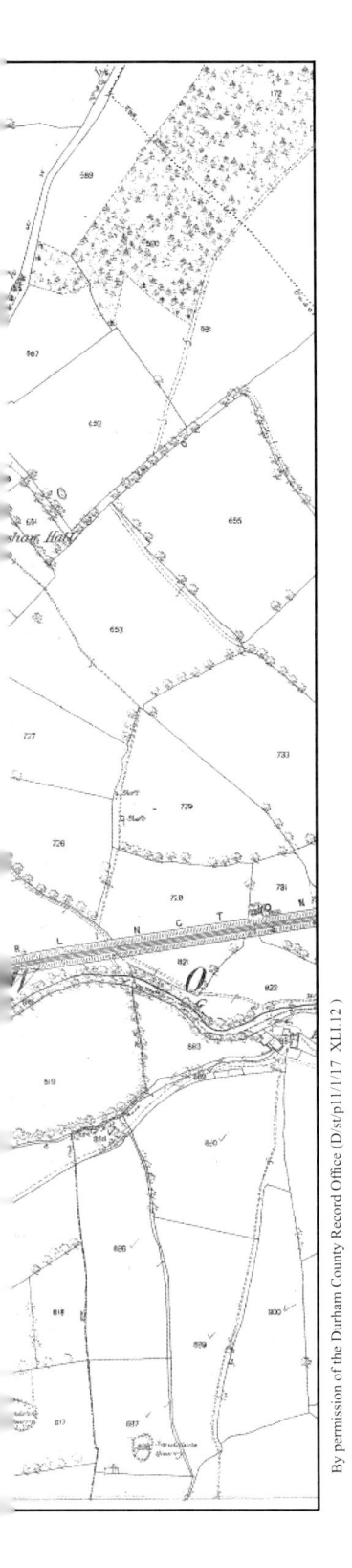

Fig. 52

This Ordnance Survey map, scale 1:2500, of 1853 shows the Haggerlease Line which had opened in 1830 providing a rail link between the pits of the Gaunless valley and the Stockton to Darlington Railway. The Haggerleases line provided the economic, large scale means of transporting the coal from the Gaunless valley and led to significant development of the mines in the area. Prior to this small drifts had been operating in the area surrounding Ramshaw and the map marks various shafts which were sunk to provide them with simple ventilation. Twenty years after the opening of the rail link the scale of the operation had changed dramatically. Norwood Colliery was well established with its sidings to receive and despatch coal trains. Compare this to the size of Bowes Close Colliery which would have been considered large before the arrival of the railway.

The railway boom was about to benefit Evenwood and Ramshaw still further. The initial construction works for the passenger line which would link Bishop Auckland and Barnard Castle can be seen just above Norwood Colliery.

This was a boom period for Ramshaw. The growth in mining led to the construction of the first terrace of cottages in Gordon Lane. Several terraces plus a Methodist Chapel had been built across the other side of the River Gaunless and were known as the Oaks. The Oaks were later to be condemned for the poor conditions they provided. A farmhouse and two short terraces of cottages had been built in Gordon Gill. The farmhouse and its adjacent single storey cottages still stand but the other terrace, destined to become the home of the Mattimoes and the Gaffneys has long ago been demolished.

Despite these developments the rest of the area is still largely a farming community. Small farms are dotted amongst the hills, Evenwood Mill still uses the power of the Gauless mill race to grind corn and the old hamlet of Ramshaw with its Hall nestles quietly in its rural location unaware of the full future development of Gordon Lane which would adopt its name.

Footpaths are clearly marked and there was as yet no sign of the small gauge rail lines which would link outlying drifts with the colliery bank head.

9 The Move to *'Little Ireland'*

In 1870, some three years after moving to Bishop Auckland, Thomas, Ann and their five sons took the opportunity to move to *'Little Ireland'*. Ann's brother John and his family had moved out of the Gill to nearby Evenwood so the Mattimoes moved into the house he had vacated next door to Ann's other brother Michael.

The gently rolling hills of this part of County Durham would have brought back fond memories to Thomas and Ann of the land, family and friends they had left behind in Ireland.

Settling In

The move to Gordon Gill must have been welcome after the cramped conditions of the town. Water came from a well or spring and, for some uses, the Beck itself. Slops would have been emptied into Gordon Beck to be taken down stream and deposited into the River Gaunless. In time the number of people occupying the Gill led to the establishment of ash privies the contents of which were emptied onto a common midden and cleared once a fortnight.

The living conditions strike us today as basic and insanitary but were not unusual for those times and it was far healthier to live in a small hamlet such as the Gill than in a crowded town. Gordon Gill provided the Mattimoes with a way of life more akin to that of Ireland. Lighting was provided by oil lamps. Heating was from the coal allowance they were entitled to as miners. There was a plot of land where they could grow and raise their own produce. They were amongst extended family and others who shared their memories, religion and traditions of the Old Country.

The Mattimoes moved to Gordon Gill in the Spring of 1870, the right time to plant a vegetable garden, acquire poultry and a piglet or two to fatten. By late Summer they were, for the first time since leaving Ireland, eating vegetables, fruit and eggs which they had produced for themselves. By the time the pigs had matured and been slaughtered their diet was probably better than at any time in their lives.

Whilst Gordon Gill kept its rural atmosphere surrounded by fields and tucked out of view of other habitation the links to mining activity were very evident. Mine ventilation shafts and disused coal shafts were close by the houses. The steam engine was in a building adjacent to the houses and ran night and day to keep the mine workings from flooding. Four hundred yards from the hamlet along the footpath leading to the bank head at Ramshaw were two drift mines linked by a tramway. Upon reaching the bank head there were areas for cleaning and storing coal, the coke ovens and workshops. Leading away from the bank head tramways crossed under the Barnard Castle/Bishop Auckland railway line to the Haggerlease line by the bank of the Gaunless.

Thomas found employment as a labourer at Norwood or Railey Fell Colliery. His eldest son Patrick, now fifteen, found work at the pit, probably as a pony putter. His second son, John, then twelve did not enrol at the local school but also found work in the mine. There were a number of activities for a young boy like John such as operating the trap doors that controlled ventilation, or rapping the warning of approaching coal trucks underground. Whatever the activity it would have been lonely work in the dark and damp of the mine. The three incomes and the opportunity to grow their own produce enabled the family to enjoy a life free from financial hardship for the first time since leaving Ireland.

Ramshaw in 1873

The Bishop Auckland to Barnard Castle branch line opened in 1856. The line passed near, but not through, Evenwood consequently the station to serve the village was built on land overlooking Ramshaw. Did Thomas and Ann Mattimoe travel by train to their new home? If they did then this article which appeared in the Newcastle Weekly Chronicle of June 1873 would have described the view which met them on their arrival.

"Looking northward (from the station), we have a village, a cultivated fell, and a fair sprinkling of trees, called generally Railey Fell and Toft Hill – a stretch of country on which may be seen groups of colliery cottages of an excellent type. Looking west, we catch far-off glimpses of Teesdale, and a striking view of red tiled Cockfield, from which the eye travels slowly in a stately direction, over a smoke-canopied valley and well wooded heights, broken only by colliery heaps and columns of smoke thereto pertaining, until the village of Oaks arrests the gaze, while above it, at the distance of a field or two, stands Evenwood, properly so called, and to the left or East the new clump of pitmen's houses called Tees-Hetton Row. Narrowing the range of vision, we get at our very feet Railey Fell Colliery, and three villages all in a row, one of which is called Ramshaw and another New Row, or New Moor Row, and the middle one doubtless has a name, although it is but a so-so 'pit row' squeezed in between the two. The whole used to be called Barony. But it will be more business like to step down from our elevation, and take a stroll up and down and all around. Before getting fairly into the inhabited region we have to cross a tramway and a brook. The former services the colliery of Railey Fell as a tributary to the old Haggarleases railway, and the latter does excellent service to the triple village on the other side. For the stream is intercepted and diverted through the valley as a drain-washer. On the East of the rivulet – on the bank side is a slowly dripping well, which contributes the sole water supply of the five hundred people living close by. It is an admirable school for training human nature to patience. Once fairly in the village, we observe that all the houses are good, those nearest the railway and the newest being far above the average of colliery dwellings. The middle row looks inferior to New Row, but they are very comfortable houses, and have the advantage of gardens, which the other two thirds of the row or street lack. There is a Primitive Methodist chapel, also a neat public –house. Then we cross the old railway, and rejoice to find it a much better railway ... it serves the two collieries of Norwood and Evenwood, the former of which has associated with it a number of coke ovens. Presently we come to the bridge across the Gaunless. Just now there is no Gaunless to speak of except a narrow mill-race which takes all the water the aged parent river has about her. In winter, however, the Gaunless can brawl with the best of them, and break bounds very often. By keeping [to] the roads instead of taking to the fields we get an easier ascent, and a better opportunity of visiting the village or hamlet called Oaks. This is a genuine pit village of the ordinary pattern, and accommodates indifferently well a large proportion of the six or seven hundred hands employed in the two collieries of Norwood and Evenwood. There is a Wesleyan Methodist chapel .... To the left or East, we observe an extensive cemetery, consisting of gates, a wall, some acres of turf, and a couple or so of gravestones."

Relationships between Owners and Miners fluctuated. The Union's were becoming a stronger voice. In 1870 thirty three miners at Norwood Colliery were members of the Durham Miners Association. By 1872 this had grown to one hundred.

The census records for Evenwood demonstrate, by the birth locations of miners children, that many of them moved from pit to pit across the Great Durham Coalfield to find employment when mines became worked out and new ones opened. Contrary to this however the Mattimoes and the Gaffneys were to remain in the Gill for the next forty years. Descendants of the Mattimoes through the Hannons were still living there in the 1930's and continue to live in Gordon Lane, Ramshaw close to the bridge over the Gaunless.

Gordon Gill in 1871

The 1871 census recorded a drop in the population to fifty seven. Of the ten families in the Gill at that time five were of Irish descent but there had been changes. John Gaffney's was not the only family to have moved from the Gill. The widower Michael Tarbert and his two sons had moved out as had John Heal's family and the young Philip's couple. In addition to the Mattimoes a young Irishman, Charles Hannan and his wife Bridget had moved into the Gill though do not appear to be related to the Hannon's who were to marry into the Mattimoe family at the beginning of the next century. Bridget was Scottish indicating a continued trend for Irishmen to arrive in the Gill via Scotland. Three of the other five families the Gair, Forster, and Place families had been living in the Gill since 1861.

The spread of 'occupations' was as follows in 1871.

Occupation	Number	Age Range
Deputy Overman	1	41
Coal Miner	14	12-60
Colliery Blacksmith	2	31-58
Colliery Labourer	1	32
Brakeman	1	25
Engineman	1	51
Mason	1	31
Servant	2	14-38
Housewives	9	20-55
Daughters too old for school	3	15-18
Children at school	17	3-15
Children not at school	3	5-12
Infants and babies	2	3 months-1 year
Total	57	

Sadness and Joy

The 1870's were to bring both tragedy and joy to the Mattimoe family. In September 1871 their son Thomas died at age of ten from "disease of the liver" which he had suffered from for the previous six months. Despite being only eleven years old his death certificate gives his occupation as colliery engine fireman, probably stoking the steam engine situated in the Gill. Five months earlier he had been recorded as a scholar in the census return. On St. Valentine's Day the following year their daughter Annie was born. Annie was to have a hard life. In June 1874 a son Frank was born who was destined to remain a bachelor and live with his sister and her family all his life. The last child Michael was born in December 1876 but sadly died in May the following year from bronchitis demonstrating that despite the family's improved circumstances living conditions were still harsh.

Upon moving to Gordon Gill the Mattimoe's worshipped at the Roman Catholic mission at Evenwood which had been established under the auspices of St. Osmund's at Gainford. This church was a distance of ten miles from Evenwood and the Priest would ride on horseback to officiate at Mass for the two hundred Roman Catholics, no doubt many of Irish descent, who lived in Evenwood and the surrounding villages. The Irish families of **'Little Ireland'** made up over 20% of the mission's congregation. Whilst the mission represented the bulk of the congregation of St. Osmund's this did not stop the priest from complaining about the difficulty of finding literate members who could undertake education of the children in the Catholic faith.

The Priest from Gainford also officiated at funerals for the Roman Catholics of Evenwood which took place at the cemetery on the hill which leads down to the bridge across the River Gaunless. These burials took place in the cemetery's unconsecrated ground.

Fig. 53 Patrick Mattimoe taken in the late 1870's or early 1880's. The outdoor scene complete with balustrade, column and artificial tussock being typical of that period as was the tight fitting suit with matching waistcoat.

There were still strict rules in force as to where marriage ceremonies could be conducted which did not extend to the Catholic mission in Evenwood so these were sometimes held in St. Wilfred's in Bishop Auckland as this was easier to travel to than Gainford. The Cox family, who had worshipped in the Church at Gainford when they lived in Killerby and Cockfield remained loyal to that Church consequently this was where their daughter, Elizabeth, married Edward the son of John Gaffney and their son Thomas married Mary Ann the daughter of Michael Gaffney.

Ramshaw School

The local school had now become established with attendance growing to eighty and a sewing mistress appointed. The majority of children of school age in the Gill attended the school. Notable exceptions appeared to be the children of Michael Gaffney who were not recorded in the census as scholars just as in the previous census. Again the enumerator may be at fault as the school log for 1870 records that an M. Gaffney, presumed to be Michael's daughter Mary, made three mistakes in a dictation test.

The funding basis of the school was illustrated when the log records

> *"could not admit one girl because she did not belong to Mr Stobart's workmen".*

Not all parents fully supported the regime of the school. The log records that

> *"some parents complained about girls doing homework and said if it persisted they would be obliged to send them to Evenwood school".*

Evenwood School had been constructed about the same time as that in Ramshaw and was also a Church of England school under patronage of the local pit owner. The parent's threat was probably a hollow one as the walk to Evenwood School would have been very arduous for the younger children.

The continued growth of the school led to the employment of 'pupil' teachers. These were in effect trainee teachers and paid 2s per week at that time. Average attendance had soared to one hundred and fifty five by 1876 who were taught by a master and four pupil teachers. Attendance was often severely affected by bad weather and illness. Children were poorly dressed and did not have the benefit of rainwear nor sufficient winter protection so spells of wet and snowy weather would keep children at home and even cause the school to close.

Epidemics of illness could strike at any time and did so frequently. Influenza, tonsillitis and scarlet fever were common during the winter. Whooping cough, mumps and measles were more frequent in the spring. The more serious scarlatina could prevail for months and lead to deafness in the children that contracted the illness. Diphtheria occurred in small numbers most years. Typhoid Fever was a rarer occurrence though would lead to closure of the school.

In November 1879 there was an outbreak of measles and 'fever' which did not abate until March the following year. Two children died of fever and parents kept children away from the school for fear they would contract the illness.

Strict discipline continued to be maintained at the school with the following entries in the log relating to incidents both within and outside its bounds

> *"George Raine punished for stupidity"*
> *"a number of children caned for coming late and playing during prayers".*
> *"caned fifteen boys for doing wilful damage at the pit".*

One hapless individual suffered when the teacher

> *"received a note from one of the parents that his child refused to come to school on Monday – caned the boy severely on Tuesday".*

Not all parents approved of such liberal use of corporal punishment and the log records details of complaints made by parents against members of staff for striking their children.

On a happier note the children received a day off school to celebrate the Railway Jubilee in October 1875. A football club and a cricket club were formed and attendance at the annual tea party continued to comfortably exceed that of the school itself. On other occasions the school seemed to bow to the inevitable and close allowing the children to take an enjoyable day away from their studies when the circus made its annual visit to Bishop Auckland.

The uncertainties of work in the mines had its own impact upon the school. In July 1878 the log notes

> *"a great many absent unable to pay school fees"*
> *"parents unable to afford to buy books".*

Kilmictranny Church, Co. Sligo, which has served the Mattimoes for over 250 years.

St. Teresa's, Carrigeenroe, Co. Sligo, where Thomas Mattimoe and his family worshipped, the children attending the adjacent school of which all trace has been lost.

Plate 1

Benbulben, Co. Sligo, viewed from Drumcliff cemetery, resting place of the poet W.B. Yeats.

Knockarea, Co. Sligo, viewed from Strandhill. This mountain is topped by Maeve's Cairn, the tomb of Queen Medb where she was reputedly buried in the traditional manner, standing facing her enemies.

The road leading from the Curlew Mountains down to Boyle. Sir Clifford Conyers forces climbed this road in August 1599 and were ambushed by the much smaller Irish forces of Conor McDermot and Brian O'Rourke. Knowledge of this treacherous pass through the mountains enabled the Irish to inflict an overwhelming defeat on the English.

Plate 2

Bricklieve Mountains, Co. Sligo viewed from Balinafad. These mountains have been important to the people of this area since the earliest imes. The mountains are topped by the important Carrowkeel, a megalithic cemetery comprising several passage tombs. The area surrounding these tombs provides beautiful views across the area occupied by the Mattimoes since records began.

Looking north from the gap in the Bricklieve Mountains toward the townland of Coolboy where records indicate the Mattimoe's were living in the mid 1600's and possibly earlier. From here those bearing that name spread primarily south to Boyle and the land surrounding Lough Arrow and Lough Key.

Plate 3

Parkes Castle on the banks of Lough Gill, just over the border into Co. Leitrim, built by Robert Parke on what may be the site of the moated castle of Brian O'Rourke who, like many in this part of Ireland, sheltered survivors from the Spanish Armada in the Autumn of 1588 saving them from being butchered by the English soldiers garrisoned in the area. Brian O'Rourke was arrained for high treason and for his humanity was executed at Tyburn in 1591.

Boyle, Co. Sligo. The grey buiding to the left of the cream building on the corner by the bridge is a public house named the Mattimoe run, at the time of writing by a Mattimoe whose brother ran a public house in nearby Ballymote.

Plate 4

Crannog's were lake dwellings built on small man-made islands linked to the shore by raised timber walkways. They date from 3000 BC through to early christian times. This photograph taken at Cavetown Lough, Co. Roscommon, shows evidence of the base island of a crannog now overgrown with trees.

During the years of religious persecution in Ireland Mass was often held in remote locations. The ruined friary of Mount Irwin near Gorteeen, Co. Sligo was one such location. The ruins now provide a peaceful backdrop to the cemetery located in the grounds of the friary.

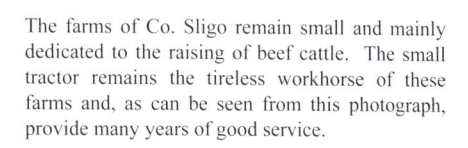

The farms of Co. Sligo remain small and mainly dedicated to the raising of beef cattle. The small tractor remains the tireless workhorse of these farms and, as can be seen from this photograph, provide many years of good service.

Peat beds remain an important resource to the farms and are cut and dried to provide fuel for fires and kitchen ranges both for the farmers and for those local families with open fires.

Old cottages in the countryside of Co. Sligo share mixed fortunes. Some are retained as well maintained comfortable living accommodation whilst others are used as farm outbuildings or animal byres before finally crumbling into ruins.

Plate 5

Thomas Mattimoe's cottage at Carrigeenroe, Co. Sligo. Despite its overgrown appearance the cottage was fairly sound and dry inside. The cottage consisted of three rooms with an extra room, possibly a scullery, built onto the back. The cottage is still owned by a Mattimoe.

Lough Key, Co. Sligo taken from the tower that now stands where Lord Lorton's Rockingham House once stood. The island where the MacDermot's had their castle can be seen in the centre of the photograph.

By permission of the National Galleries of Scotland

'An Irish Emigrant Arriving at Liverpool' by Robert Erskine, 1871.
This painting mirrors the situation Thomas Mattimoe and his family found themselves on arrival at Liverpool from Sligo in 1867.

Plate 7

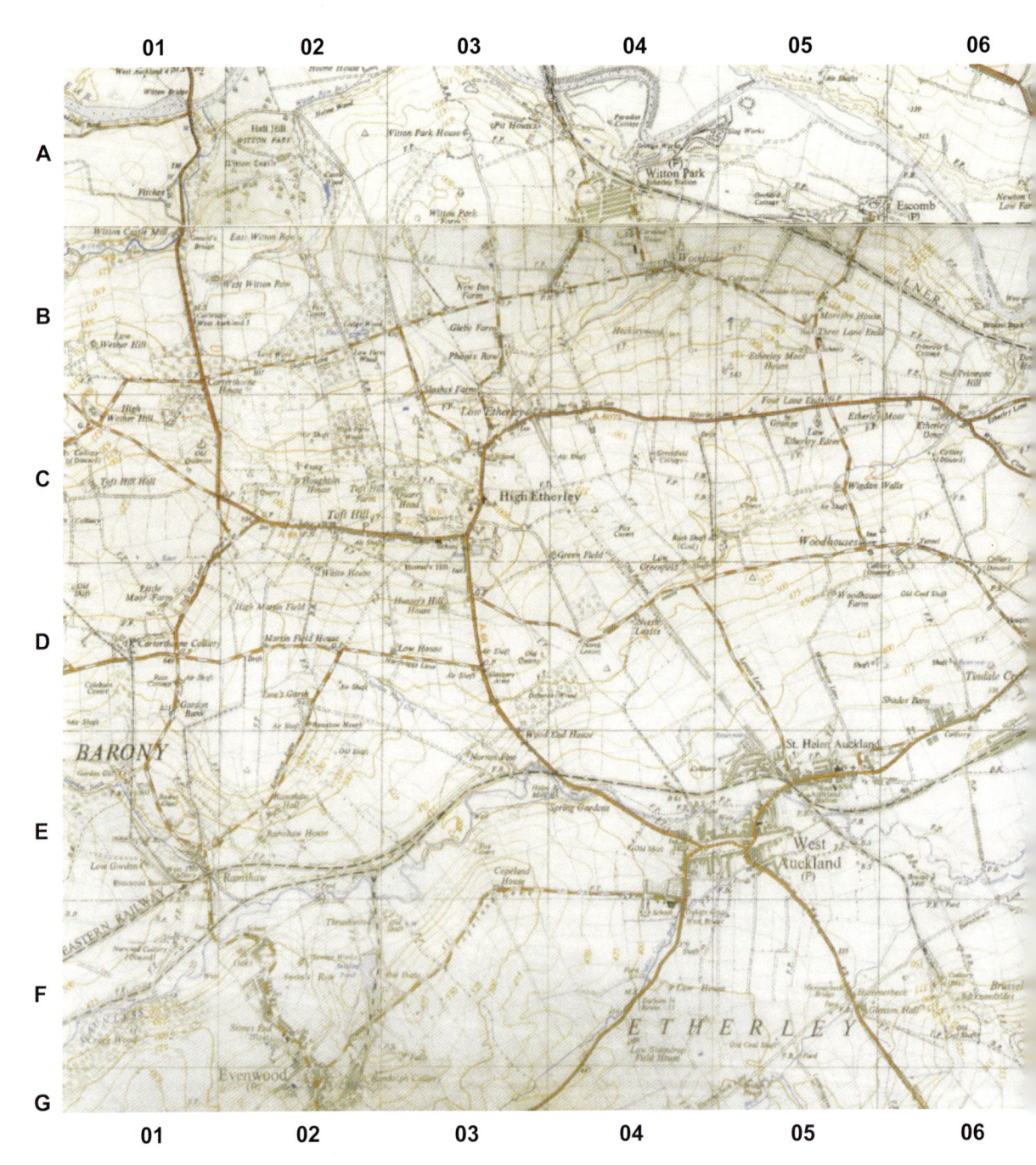

The section of the Provisional Edition Ordnance Survey map of 1945 covers the area where the Mattimoes lived from 1867 until the 1930's and where some of their descendants still live today. The road system has inevitably changed since this map was produced but as it still identifies the places where the members of the Mattimoe family lived and worked.

Thomas and Ann Mattimoe together with their three sons arrived in Bishop Auckland (B08) in 1867 then moved to *'Little Ireland'*, Gordon Gill (E01) in 1870. The men in the family worked at Norwood Colliery (F01) and West Tees Colliery (E01). As Thomas and Ann's sons and daughter married they began to move away from Gordon Gill. The eldest son Patrick moved to Bowes Close (E01). His daughter lived at Gordon Bank Top (D01). John and his family moved to Eldon Lane settling in Coronation the other side of the railway bridge (D09). Stephen also moved his family to Eldon Lane (D09/D10). They both worked at Eldon

Plate 8

Colliery (C10/C11). Stephen subsequently moved to Leeholme (B11) and worked at Leasingthorne Colliery (A12). Thomas's son Peter became checkweighman at Randolph Colliery (G02) and also became landlord of the Bridge Inn at Ramshaw (F01). Thomas's daughter Annie Hannon's family moved to Gordon Lane, Ramshaw (E01/F01) and her younger brother Frank lived with them all his life.

The family worshipped at St. Wifred's in Bishop Auckland, the mission established in Evenwood under the auspices of St. Osmund's, Gainford and subsequently at St. Chad's, Witton Park (A04). The 1km grid of the map gives an idea of the 9mile (15km) round trip to Mass which the Mattimoes and Hannons, and their visitors, made each Sunday.

Maps by permission of the British Library (Ordnance Survey Provisional Edition, Scale 1:25,000, sheets 45/12, 45/13, 45/22 and 45/23, 1949.)

Bridge Street, Bishop Auckland, Co. Durham, where Thomas and Ann Mattimoe moved to after a year in the difficult conditions of Corn Close. The road presents a steep walk up to the town but leads down to the River Wear and open country beyond.

The railway line ran behind the houses in Bridge Street and towered over them until crossing the River Wear on the Newton Cap viaduct. The railway has long since been closed and today the viaduct carries the main road which no longer winds down to the Newton Cap Bridge, the scene of many an accident in the past, and up the other side.

Newton Cap Bridge, at the bottom of Bridge Street now presents a peaceful scene as it crosses the fast running River Wear. This area must have been a popular play area for Thomas and Ann's sons, Patrick, John, Thomas and Peter.

Plate 10

Railey Fell looking across from Aunt Jane's house at Gordon Bank Top. Despite the strong link with coal mining in this area it retained its rural appeal throughout the busiest times and now has reverted to its agricultural past.

The location of *'Little Ireland'* in Gordon Gill. The houses occupied by the Mattimoes, Gaffneys, Tarberts and Hannons have long since been demolished together with the engine house where the steam driven pump ran day and night. Here too the land has reverted to its rural past.

Plate 11

By permission of Beamish, The North of England Open Air Museum

'Going Home', Ralph Hedley, 1889

This rather romanticised engraving of two miners returning home after their shift serves to show the work clothes the mining men of *'Little Ireland'* would have worn in the late 19th century. In their case however the wet conditions of the mines in Ramshaw, Co. Durham would have seen them returning in wet clothes which had to be dried before the shift the following day.

Plate 12

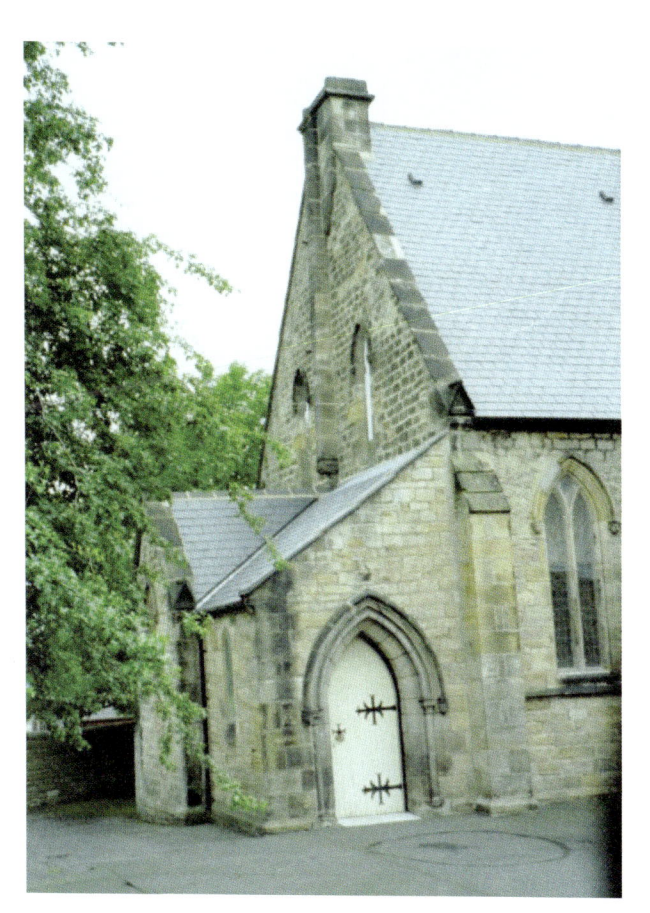

St. Wilfred's Roman Catholic Church, Bishop Auckland, where the Mattimoes worshipped, came to be married and brought their children to be christened in the sixty years following their arrival in the town in 1867.

St. Osmund's Roman Catholic Church Gainford, which supported a mission in Evenwood where the Catholics of Ramshaw and Evenwood could worship. Attendance at St. Osmund's itself was limited to weddings, christenings and, importantly the visit by the Bishop every seven or eight years for the First Holy Commmunion of those recently confirmed into the faith.

Plate 13

Gordon Lane, Ramshaw, as it is today. The Bishop Auckland/Barnard Castle rail branch line has long ago closed and the bridge which used to carry it across Gordon Lane has been demolished. The Haggerleases Branch line which served the mines of the Gaunless valley and crossed Gordon Lane just before Evenwood Bridge has also closed. A builders yard occupies the land previously occupied by West Tees (Railey Fell) Colliery but has retained the name. The tramways which brought the coal trucks from the drifts to the bankhead and then on to the Haggerleases line have also disappeared. The peace of this area was briefly lost when open cast mining took advantage of the coal seams close proximity to the surface in this area but calm has now returned and little remains visible of its proud mining past other than the risk of landslips the old workings present, particularly after heavy rain.

The house of Joe and Jane Peacock at Gordon Bank Top, Ramshaw. Aunt Jane's was the house on the far right. It was the only house in this small remote terrace which had a basement hence its choice as an air-raid shelter during the Second World War. Ironically it was next to Aunt Jane that John Hannon and his family lived when bombs fell from German bombers returning to their home base giving John the dubious honour of having been 'bombed' out of his home during both World War's, the first time having been by curtesy of a Zeppelin.

Plate 14

This card was sent to John Mattimoe by his eldest son Tom who was serving on the Western Front during the First World War. The card was made in France.

Frank Mattimoes grave in Trefcon Military Cemetery, near St. Quentin, France. Frank died less than two months before the end of the war in one of the last decisive battles. His surname has been spelt with an 'r'.

Trefcon Military Cemetery near St. Quentin, France. The cemetery is small containing 320 graves. It is in a quiet, peaceful location, surrounded by trees. On the October day the author visited the Autumn sun shone warmly and it was difficult to imagine the horror of battle which had been acted out eighty four years earlier.

Plate 15

Richard Terrace, Coronation, near Bishop Auckland, where Willy and Molly Gray nee Mattimoe lived with their young family. The fronts of the houses look over countryside and have the benefit of large front gardens.

Betty Lees nee Gray outside Coronation School which she and her brothers and sisters attended before the family moved to Bushey, Hertfordshire a few years after the tragic death of their father in a mining accident at nearby Eldon Lane Colliery where he was a Pit Deputy.

Plate 16

Fig. 54 In this faded school photograph of the children of Ramshaw school taken about 1890 James Moore is standing on the left in bowler hat. He had been master of the school for ten years. The man on the right is possibly Jonas Jackson, a pupil teacher, of whom we will hear more of later in this book. The girls appear to have their arms crossed under instruction from James giving them a somewhat 'I don't want to be here' image.

Though mining was the primary occupation farming would provide seasonal work and most families grew their own produce to supplement their incomes. Children were expected to help at peak times and the log makes mention of children potato gathering, hay making and -

"working in the gardens at home and the potato fields".

The school was regularly inspected by the local Church of England vicar, representatives of the patrons, Henry Stobart & Company, and the grant for the school depended on how well it was operating and how well the records were kept.

James Moore becomes Master

The school underwent a number of changes of Master in its early years. Some oversaw improvements whilst others struggled in the role. In September 1881 it embarked upon a long period of stability when James Moore was appointed Master. He was to remain in post for nearly forty two years until March 1923. He taught three generations of the families from the Gill. All remembered him as a strict disciplinarian but under his tutelage the children gained a sound basic education under the difficult teaching conditions of the school. He was steadfast in his duties and in his dealings with Patrons, Inspectors and parents.

10   A New Generation

By the time of the 1881 census the population of Gordon Gill had dropped to forty two. The Mattimoe, Gaffney (2) and Cox families provided four of the eight families in the Gill. The other families being Foster (2) and Place who had lived in the Gill for over twenty years and a new family, the Smiths. The distribution of 'occupations' of those living in the Gill in 1881 was as follows.

Occupation	Number	Age range
Coal Miner	13	13 to 67
Colliery Blacksmith	1	45
Rapper boy	1	15
Dressmaker	1	19
Widow	1	60
Housewives	7	21 to 66
Daughters too old for school	3	19 to 24
Children at school	10	4 to 14
Infants and babies	5	5 months to 3 years
Total	42	

Thomas had progressed to become a hewer as had his eldest sons Patrick and John. His son Peter, then fifteen, was working as a rapper boy. Stephen, Anne and Frank were attending the local school.

The 1880's saw the beginnings of the next generation of Mattimoes. The eldest son Patrick married Mary Ann Rutter in late December of 1882 and went to live in nearby Bowes Close. John married Mary Redfearn Parmley at St. Wilfred's Church, Bishop Auckland in November 1882. Mary, who was given her middle name after her paternal grandmother, was descended from a family of small farmers from Teesdale whose line can be traced back to the 1550's. Mary and her brother Joseph had left Teesdale in search of work. The Parmleys were not a Catholic family so, in line with the requirements of the Catholic Church at that time and for many decades to come, Mary converted to the Catholic faith committing to bring her children up in that faith.

Mary was four months pregnant when she married and gave birth in Gordon Gill to a son, Thomas, in April 1883. There were complications after the birth and Mary was to die from peritonitis one week later and Father Rodgers from St. Osmund's, Gainford officiated at her burial in Evenwood cemetery.

John felt he had no option but to hand his new born son over to his mother to look after. His mother was in poor health, suffering from tuberculosis, so the task of raising Thomas fell to John's sister, Annie, who had just turned eleven years old. Annie's life was already hard. She played a major role in running the home looking after her ailing mother together with her father and four elder brothers who all worked in the pit, plus a younger brother at school. Now she had a new born baby to look after and would have left school to cope with these demands, assuming that family commitments had not already forced this upon her.

The house had to run to a strict schedule through the day. Thomas and his son John were Hewers probably working on different shifts. The day began at about 3am when the person on the foreshift would have risen and Ann and her daughter Annie made a cup of tea or coffee for their man and prepared the 'bait' to sustain him until his return home. Once he left for work there was a brief respite for the women and perhaps opportunity for an hours sleep before the younger sons Peter and Stephen rose at about 5am in order to get to work by 6am. If one of the men of the house was working the backshift he would rise at about 8am and the process of preparing breakfast and 'bait' would be repeated. Finally it was time to get young Frank off to school before the women could attend to themselves and baby Thomas. There was then another short respite until the man from the foreshift returned at 11am. The tin bath would be set in front of the fire and filled with hot water. The man's top clothes were taken out and beaten against a wall to remove as much coal dust as possible. Dinner was provided following which, after a short rest and perhaps some work with the livestock and the garden the man would retire to bed. The remaining workers returned from their shift late afternoon and the bathing process began again, this time for three men, with three sets of working clothes to be beaten and dried. Dinner for the rest of the family was then served.

Around the schedule governed by the men's working day the chores of the house took place including cleaning, fetching water, making up the fire that would have burned all day everyday to provide hot water and heat the oven. There were chickens, geese and pigs to be fed, and the vegetable garden to be tended. Monday was reserved for wash day. This was a laborious task made more arduous by the need to clean the working clothes of four miners. On fine days the clean clothes would be hung outside to dry. All the women in *'Little Ireland'* did their washing on Monday and it is likely there was a communal area where the washing was hung providing a valuable opportunity for social contact between the women of the families.

The task of running the Mattimoe household would probably have been too much for an ailing Ann Mattimoe and her young daughter Annie so it is likely that one of the young women from another family in the Gill would have been employed to assist. It seems probable this would have been Sarah Jane Cox who was the right age and from a family where additional income would be welcome. Sarah Jane stood as godparent for more than one of the Mattimoe children of the next generation.

Fig. 55   Bowes Close, Ramshaw. Chimney of Railey Fell Colliery in the distance.

Fig 56

This photograph of Hannah Donlan taken in Galway during the late 1870's before she left for England. The painted bucolic backdrop and artificial tussock were typical of the 'outdoor' studio scene popular from the 1870's through to the end of the century. Hannah is well dressed in the fashion of the time with high necked bodice and an overskirt. Quality of dress is not a good guide to social standing and wealth as women were skilled home dress makers able to copy the latest fashions. Photographs of evicted families in Ireland often show mothers and older daughter dressed in smart dresses in stark contrast to the mens clothing and the circumstances the families found themselves in.

A Galway Girl

In November 1884 John married again, this time to an Irish girl, Hannah Donlan and moved into another house in the Gill. John's son Thomas did not move with him. Perhaps Hannah did not relish inheriting a young child though this was a far from uncommon situation in times where early death left widowers as well as widows with young families to raise. Therefore, whilst sister Annie's life had been made a little easier by the marriage and moving out of her brother, she remained primarily responsible for her nephew who was to prove a handful for the young girl. She was to say in later years that Thomas caused her more problems than all her own children put together. This is not difficult to understand as all the Mattimoe boys were high spirited. Hannah Donlan, who was known as Bridget, was born in Glenamaddy, Co. Galway and her father, Stephen, was a farmer. She had two brothers, Patrick and Martin, and two sisters.

Hannah's daughter, Molly, always referred to the family name as Donnellan. Edward MacLysaght viewed Donlan as synonymous with O'Donnellan, a sept of the Ui Maine, who had their origins in the south-east of Co. Galway thus linking it with Ballydonellan situated between Ballinasloe and Loughrea. Our Donlans came from Glenamaddy in the north of Co. Galway. In Gaelic the name is O Domhnallain thus claiming descent from Domhallan, lord of Clan Breasail.

Edward MacLysaght stated that in history the Donnellans

> "are chiefly known as ollavs or poets, many of whom are mentioned in the Annals of the Four Masters, the Annals of Connacht, etc."

The first record of Hannah in England is in the 1881 census, aged twenty three, working as a servant to a mining family and their boarders in Brandon, Co. Durham about ten miles from Ramshaw.

John and Hannah's first child, Stephen, was born in September 1885. John's brother Patrick and his wife Mary Anne had a son in December that year and also named him Stephen. The use of the same Christian names, not only from one generation to another, but also within the same generation, adds to the challenge of unravelling relationships within Irish families right up until the 20th century. Thomas, John, Stephen and Francis were most popular with the Mattimoes.

Fig. 57 (left)

John and Hannah Mattimoe with their first son Stephen probably taken at the end of 1885. John's suit appears rather old fashioned for the time and may have been 'borrowed' from the photographer. Hannah's dress is very elaborate and beautifully finished. It is clearly her own and in keeping with the high standard of dress exhibited by all members of the family. The 'outdoor' scene had finally gone out of fashion and the studio scene was now very plain with only the curtain in the background and the 'furry' accessory on the back of Hannah's chair providing added visual interest.

Fig. 58 (overleaf)

This family photograph was taken on the occasion of Annie Mattimoe's confirmation at St. Osmund's Roman Catholic Church, Gainford on 27 October 1887. Confirmations took place every six or seven years when the Bishop visited the church. Annie shared her conformation with Annie Cox and Rose Ann Gaffney from Gordon Gill. The back row from left to right are Annie Cox or Rose Ann Gaffney, Peter Mattimoe, Stephen Mattimoe, Annie Mattimoe, Patrick Mattimoe and James Francis (Frank) Mattimoe. The front row from left to right are unknown young boy possibly a Cox, John Mattimoe with his son Stephen on his lap, Hannah Mattimoe nee Donlan with Patrick's son Stephen on her lap, Thomas Mattimoe, Ann Mattimoe nee Gaffney, John Mattimoe's son Thomas by his first wife and Mary Ann Mattimoe nee Rutter. The women are dressed in the then highly fashionable elaborate blouses and dress bodices with sleeve frills at the shoulder.

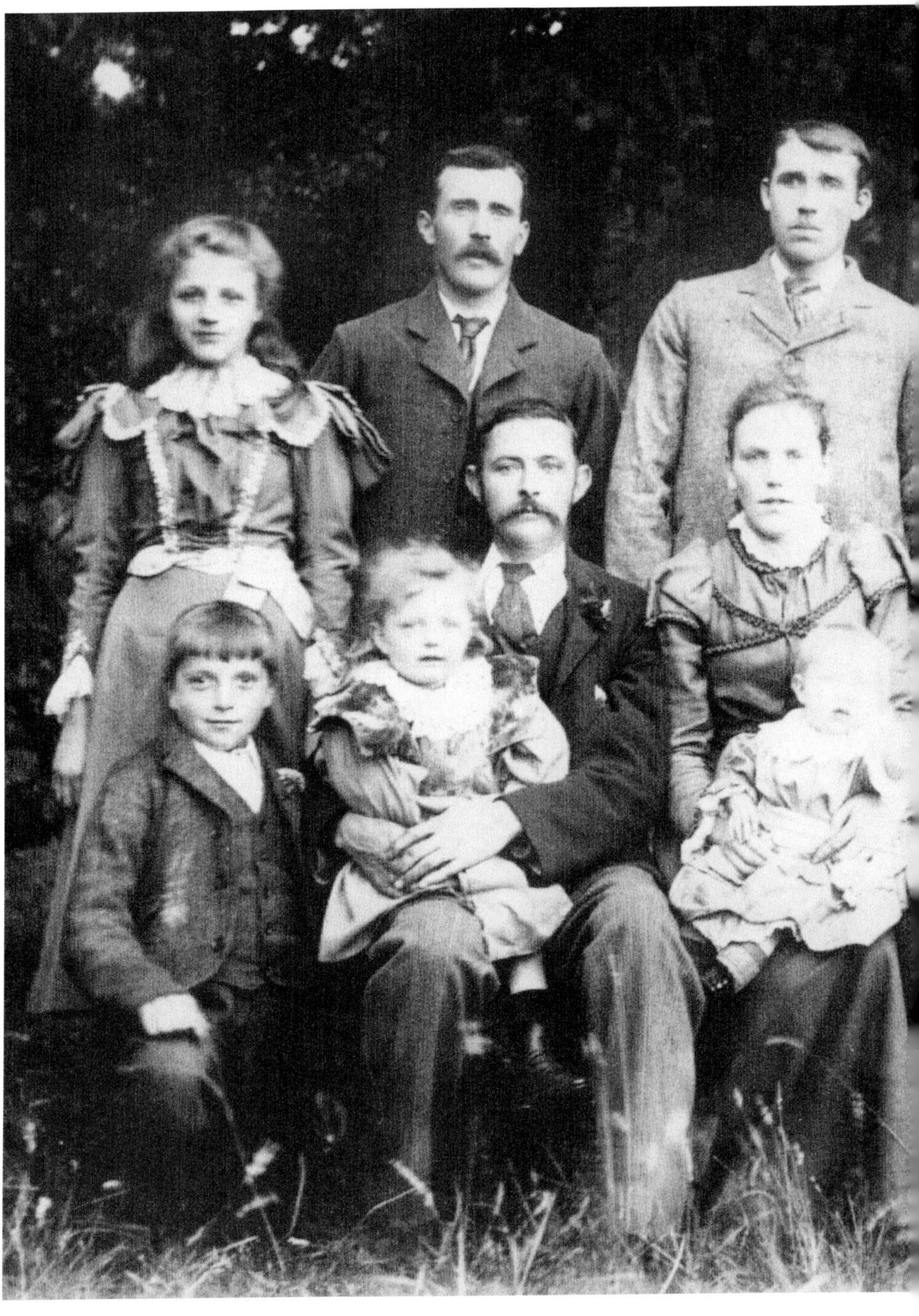

A New Generation 107

The Jubilee

Queen Victoria's jubilee was celebrated in June 1887 and whilst many towns unveiled memorials and drinking fountains to mark the event the pupils of Ramshaw School celebrated in the way they had become accustomed for such occasions as recorded by James Moore in the school log.

> *"Gave holiday on Tuesday for the Queens Jubilee, on which day we met at the school and marched to a field opposite the school where the children had tea, games, etc."*

Ann Mattimoe nee Gaffney Passes Away

Thomas's wife Ann, who had been ill for sometime, died in June 1888. The following extract from the words on her memory card express the debilitating nature of pulmonary tuberculosis from which she died.

> "I was so long with pain oppress'd,
> Which wore my strength away,
> It made me long for endless rest,
> That never can decay."

Pulmonary tuberculosis attacks the lungs and leads to coughing, breathlessness, chest pain, loss of appetite, weight loss, exhaustion and swollen joints. These symptoms worsen over a period weakening the sufferer. In the 19th century tuberculosis was the major killing disease. It was spread by inhaling droplets of an infectious person's coughs and sneezes but required prolonged contact with the infected person, which is why it often spread amongst family members and fellow workers.

A few months later in February 1889 the Gill lost another of its senior residents when Patrick Cox, who had lived there for nearly thirty years, died.

The decade was to end on a happier note with the birth of John and Hannah's second son John Leo in September 1888, the birth of Patrick and Mary Anne's daughter, Jane, in August 1889 and the marriage of John and Patrick's brother, Stephen, to Mary Ellen Hagan in October 1889. In addition the links between the Irish families continued to strengthen as the families grew. Gaffneys stood as godparents to Mattimoe and Cox children whist Cox family members stood as godparents of Gaffney children.

Changes took place regarding places of worship for the Catholics of Evenwood, Ramshaw and Gordon Gill. Money was raised locally to fund the building of a Roman Catholic Church in Evenwood. The building was constructed but the venture did not find the support of the Bishop. In the end the money appears to have disappeared and the builder of the new church let it out for housing before it was taken over by the Congregationalists as their chapel. The building still exists, but not as a place of worship, the Celtic cross on the roof showing the original intent of its construction.

A new Catholic Church, St. Chad's had been opened in 1881, not at Evenwood, but at Witton Park to serve, somewhat belatedly the growing community which had sprung up as a result of the ironworks opened by Blocklow and Vaughan in 1846. The mission at Evenwood appears to have remained open and the families of *'Little Ireland'* remained loyal to the Churches they had attended since their arrival. Patrick and Mary Ann Mattimoe had their daughter christened under the auspices of St. Osmund's, Gainford.

Fig. 59

Patrick and Mary Ann Mattimoe with son Stephen, in sailors outfit, and daughter Jane c.1890.

The 1890's

The last decade of the 19th century was to continue to prove eventful for the country as well as the families in the Gill and they, like the country, continued to thrive despite some setbacks.

In 1891 the population of Gordon Gill was virtually unchanged at forty four comprising nine families. Seven of these were of Irish descent. If the Gill had not acquired its 'Little Ireland' name before this date then it deserved it now. Thomas Mattimoe still occupied the same house, now with his two unmarried sons, his daughter and grandson. His sons John and Stephen lived in the Gill with their families. Michael Gaffney still lived next door to Thomas. Michael's nephew Edward "Teddy", son of John, had moved back to the Gill with his wife and four children. Elizabeth Cox, the widow of Patrick and her unmarried son and daughter remained in the Gill. Her eldest son, John, had married Annie Etherington and occupied the house next door with their four children. The two non-Irish families were that of Thomas Place, son of the original Place family, and a new local family, the Marshalls.

Little Ireland

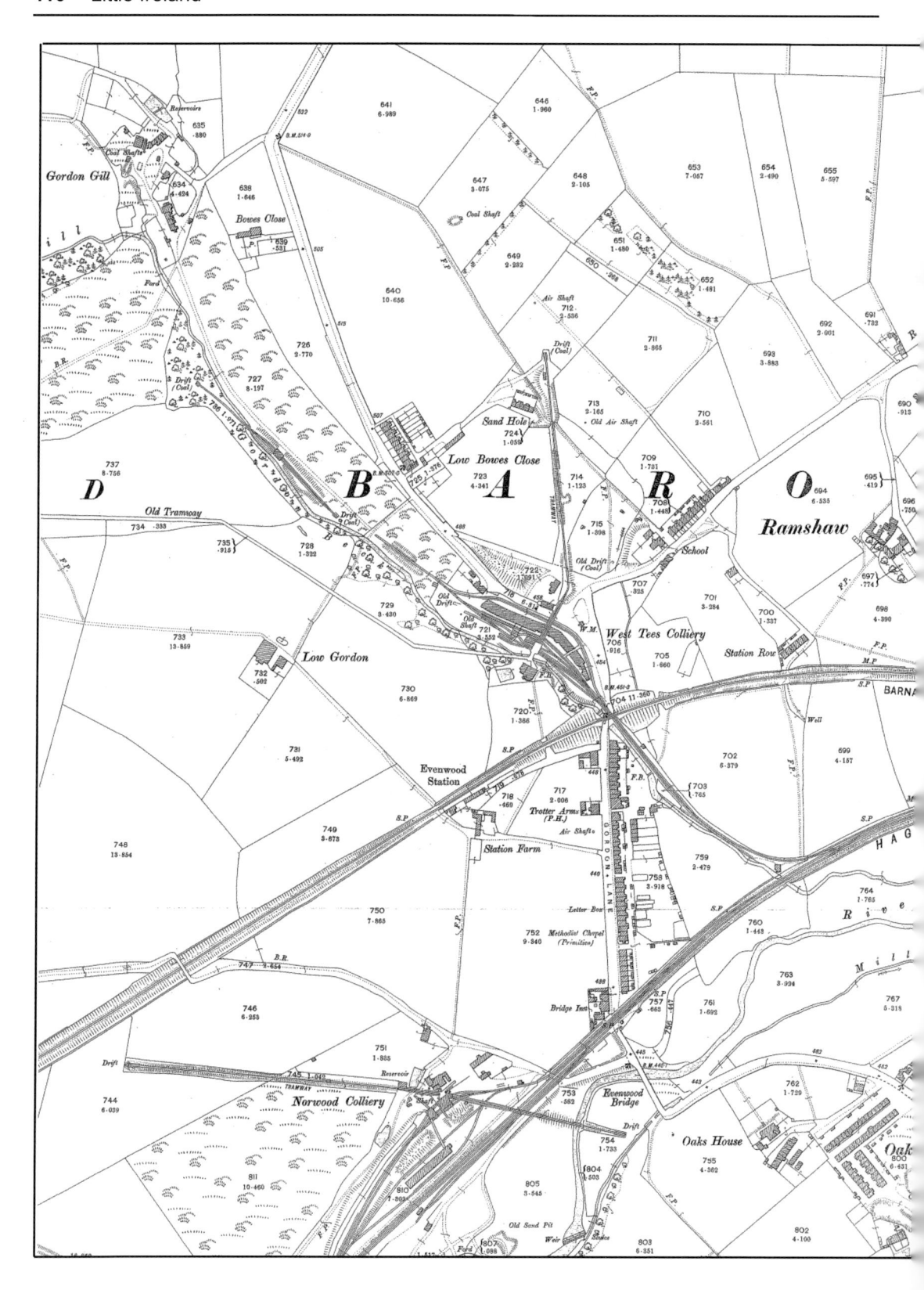

A New Generation

Fig. 60

This Ordnance Survey map, scale 1:2500, of 1897 illustrates the development which had taken place in the forty four years since the first edition map was produced. Using the description of the area which appeared in the Newcastle Weekly Chronicle of June 1873 it would appear that most of this development had occurred by that date.

The Barnard Castle & Bishop Auckland branch line was completed in 1856 and Evenwood railway station established near to Gordon Lane.

Railey Fell (West Tees) Colliery was the major mine though Norwood Colliery was still operating. A network of tramways link the isolated drift mines by Gordon Beck and at Sandhole, previously Bowes Close Colliery, to Railey Fell bank head. A disused tramway points to drifts that had been worked out. Further tramways now linked drifts to Norwood Colliery.

Three more terraces of cottages had been built in Gordon Lane together with a Methodist Chapel and two public houses, the Trotters Arms and the Bridge Inn.

In Gordon Gill no additional cottages had been constructed but a steam driven pump had been positioned over one of the old ventilation shafts and enclosed in its own building abutting the cottages occupied by the Mattimoes and Gaffneys. This was to pump water from the workings and two reservoirs had been built close to the cottages, probably to take the water from the workings. If this was the case the warm, if rather dirty water would have provided a 'swimming bath' for the children of Gordon Gill and nearby cottages. The water from the reservoirs discharged into a small stream which ran past the farmhouse in the Gill and into Gordon Beck. The stream still exists and has been incorporated into the garden of the farmhouse as a pleasing feature.

The cottages of Bowes Close had been constructed, one of which was occupied at this time by Patrick and Mary Ann Mattimoe with their young family

To the north of Railey Fell (West Tees) Colliery the school building is clearly marked together with a terrace of cottages constructed since the 1853 map.

On the Evenwood side of the river Gaunless, near the Oaks, the cemetery can be seen.

Despite these developments the area retained its rural atmosphere with 95% of the land still given over to agriculture. Evenwood Mill is still marked as a corn mill.

The distribution of 'occupations' of those living in the Gill in 1891 was as follows.

Occupation	Number	Age range
Coal Miner	14	15 to 58
Brakesman	1	42
Colliery Labourer	1	22
Agricultural Labourer	1	66
Housewives	7	22 to 60
Daughters too old for school	4	19 to 30
Children at school	9	4 to 12
Infants and babies	5	2 months to 3 years
Total	**42**	

During the 1890's Stephen and Mary Ellen had six children, Thomas who died aged five, Frank, Annie who lived only one week, Teresa who lived only one month, Mary Eveline and Joe.

In the early 1890's Thomas Mattimoe, then in his sixties, developed chronic bronchitis no doubt brought on by the damp working conditions and the coal dust of the pit.

The Cox family forged a further link with the Gaffney's when the eldest daughter of the late Patrick Cox, Sarah Jane, married Michael Gaffney's son Thomas in 1892. Sarah Jane purchased a family bible and made the first entries regarding Thomas and herself. She maintained the entries as the family grew and her descendants have kept up this valuable task and it is pleasing to report that the bible is still in the family's possession and rightly treasured.

John and Hannah completed their family with the births of Frank and Molly. Hannah was a lovely woman much loved by her children but she had the 'Irish temper' and her son Frank would tell how she kept a stick by the fire and would chase the boys with it if they were naughty. They would hold the backdoor shut so that she could not reach them, giggling helplessly whilst their mother shouted at them from the other side of the door. Like all the Mattimoe boys they liked to have fun and were quite a handful.

To accommodate his growing family John combined two of the houses in the Gill into one. He grew vegetables for the family, selling what the family did not need, and raising ducks, chickens and pigs. Killing of the pigs would probably have been undertaken by a local butcher.

In years to come John's nephew Frank became a butcher in Evenwood. His wife Kathleen told me how every family kept a pig if it was able. Frank and his helper on these occasions, the aptly named Jack Hogg, would travel to the house whose pig was to be slaughtered. The pigs throat was cut and the blood saved. The carcass was then taken back to the butcher's shop to be cut up. Roasting joints, and chops were set aside along with cuts to be cured for bacon. Off cuts were made into sausages and the blood was boiled together with added fat, milk and other ingredients to make black pudding.

Changing Fortunes in Mining

During this settled time there were periods of uncertainty brought about by the changing fortunes of the mines and the Owners relationship with their workforce. Falling coal prices led the mineowners to seek to impose a 7½% reduction in miner's wages in early March 1892. Miners throughout the Durham coalfield balloted on strike action. The mine owners took pre-emptive action as recorded in the Auckland Chronicle in the middle of March.

> "Intelligence reaches in from the Auckland district that in one case the Owners are boarding up about the pit heaps, with a view to prevent possible trespass for coal in the event of a strike."

By the end of March 70,000 miners were on strike. Mass meetings of miners were held throughout the

Fig. 61

John and Hannah Mattimoe with their children Molly, Leo, Stephen and, seated at the front, Frank taken c.1894. Note the sailor suits still popular for the younger boys and the elaborately painted backdrop.

coalfield including one at nearby West Auckland.

During April the miners and their families were already suffering hardship trying to manage on the meagre strike pay available. The local Co-op began to advance credit to mining families and money was received from other trade unions and Co-op's. The headmaster of the school, James Moore, records in the log that the children could not afford school books because of the miners strike.

The strike created some friction in the local community. The Auckland Chronicle recording details of a court case that month when James Metcalfe was charged with threatening Mary Ann Marney who accused him of being a blackleg.

Worse was to come. At the end of April the mine owners revised their offer to a 10% wage reduction, to be reviewed at the end of July, giving as their reason the anticipated cost of getting the mines operational after the strike.

The strike dragged on into June with the mine owners proving intransigent. In early June a revised offer of a 13½% reduction in wages appears to have sapped the will of the miners and a deal to limit the reduction to 10% was struck and the miners returned to work.

In 1894 it was reported that the Norwood Colliery in Ramshaw was working the Brockwell seam, 5ft 6in thick at a depth of fourteen fathoms and the Busty, 4ft thick worked by two drifts north and south. The annual output was 120,000 tons and it employed over 200 men growing to one hundred and eighty seven underground workers and forty surface workers by 1896. The Railey Fell Colliery was not working at this time though the coke ovens were handling coal from the nearby Lands Colliery. It seems likely that the men of Gordon Gill were working at Norwood Colliery, possibly at drifts not far from the Gill itself.

The dangers of colliery life were sadly demonstrated that year when twenty two year old George White of Gordon Lane was killed by a fall of stone at Norwood Colliery. His grave and headstone can still be seen in Evenwood cemetery. Some eighty years later Mrs Tate of Gordon Lane, who had been thirteen at the time remembered the funeral cortege passing her as she filled a bucket with water from the spring opposite the terraces in Gordon Lane.

Randolph Colliery, a deep shaft mine sunk in 1892, was destined to become the major employer through to the middle of the 20th century. In 1895 a set of 'Coppee' coke ovens were built at the colliery by a Belgian Company using their own bricklayers.

Ramshaw School – Discipline, Fun and Education

Throughout the 1890's the families of the Gill provided eight to ten pupils for the local school. The children walked up the track to Gordon Lane then took the footpath across the fields, passing under the bridge carrying the tramway from Sand Hole drift before walking down the hill to the school, a journey long enough to provide tempting reasons for dalliance. Perhaps Mattimoe or Gaffney boys were amongst those who in October 1890 were -

"punished ... for being absent on Thursday afternoon brambling"

The boys from the Gill liked to have fun and in doing so could incur the wrath of their mothers, fathers and teacher though the incident reported by James Moore January 1891 was more serious

"Punished John J Gaffney on Thursday morning for putting his hand in another boys bag in the porch, as there had been complaints of dinners taken, and his father came here about it in the afternoon"

Not all the punishment was justified. In September 1891 an indignant James Moore records

"sent Gaffney children home because their father came to school drunk on Monday afternoon, & wished to fight Jonas Jackson, and used very abusive language".

Teddy Gaffney may well have had just cause to be upset with Jonas Jackson as the pupil teacher had previously been cautioned about striking the children following complaints from parents. Teddy Gaffney's condition, mood and behaviour would have caused uproar at the school where the complement of some one hundred and thirty children continued to be taught alongside each other in one room. The children, no doubt seeing the funny side of the altercation, would have been laughing at the shenanigans whilst a worried Jonas Jackson sought the protection of an obdurate James Moore. The Gaffney children would have had mixed feelings as their Father ranted at the Master demanding satisfaction for the hurt done to them. Only they would have known the extent, if any, to which they contributed towards the incident by their earlier actions. Teddy, once sober, dwelt on the matter and no doubt concluded that, regardless of the degree to which right had been on his side, the manner in which he handled the situation had made matters worse. A realisation no doubt reinforced by his wife, Elizabeth, who had to endure the

Fig. 62 Ramshaw school photograph 1893. John and Hannah's three sons are in the back row, Frank on the far left tall Stephen seventh from the left, showing an indication of a future □
Anne's children are both in the picture Stephen is in the back row second from the left and Jane is in the middle row seventh from the right Stephen and Mary Ellen's son Frank is on the far right of the front row. James Moore on the far left.

children under her feet at home for a week. Consequently a week later James Moore was able to record that

> *"Ed Gaffney brought his children to school on Monday, and asked to have them readmitted, which was done after he had apologised for his conduct last Monday".*

The affect on Jonas Jackson appeared short lived as James Moore had to caution him again six months later for striking a child. Jonas eventually concluded that teaching was not for him and resigned. He later set up a successful shoemaking shop in Evenwood and went on to become a Parish Councillor. Teddy Gaffney himself was to fall foul of the authorities some years later when in June 1899 the Auckland Chronicle recorded.

> "An elderly man named Edward Gaffney, was summoned to appear at Auckland on Monday at the instance of Mrs Emma Place of Evenwood for using obscene language to her on Saturday week – Complainant … stated that when her husband was alive , defendant was constantly molesting them, and in March she found it necessary to summon him and have him bound over to be of good behaviour. On Saturday week he went over to her place and threatened her in several ways. She had tried to get peace, but had not been able to get peace at any price – Defendant, who pleaded guilty, was fined 40s including costs or one months imprisonment."

Emma was the second wife of Thomas Place, some twenty years his junior, and the couple with their family were recorded as neighbours of Teddy Gaffney's family in the 1891 census. Perhaps the root cause of the antipathy that twice landed Teddy in court lay in a dispute between neighbours.

It is difficult not to construe from these incidents that, even allowing for a degree of provocation, Teddy Gaffney was a belligerent character but this would not be the whole story. To balance this trait he was also known for his sense of fun and cheeky sense of humour. It is fair to say that he liked a drink and he composed the following poem for his headstone.

> *"Who lies here, who do you think?*
> *Poor old Teddy for he liked drink.*
> *Drink to me as you pass by,*
> *For poor old Teddy was always dry."*

Like many of his generation 'poor old Teddy' never got a headstone so his invitation to those passing has gone unheeded.

The School Report

The school improved under the management of James Moore but incurred criticism albeit for conditions largely beyond the control of the master. The inspection report for the year ending March 1894 reads as follows.

> *"The rooms are very much crowded (the average attendance being within three of the accommodation), the floor space is covered with desks, and the infants are taught in the same room as older children. In these circumstances teaching is very trying to the Teachers, the concentrated and sustained attention of the children*

is difficult to secure, and satisfactory progress almost impossible to obtain. The needlework of the girls has improved, and generally speaking fair results have been produced in the Elementary Subjects but oral Arithmetic and the written Arithmetic of the fourth and sixth Standards fall below this level, and the children's knowledge of English and Geography is so meagre and wanting in intelligence in the upper division that it is only with hesitation that a Grant is recommended. The work of the Infants is poor in character. They cannot be efficiently trained under existing conditions and their instruction interferes with that of the older scholars. ... I am able to state that unless a classroom is provided for the exclusive use of the infants ... the next grant will be paid upon the attendance of the elder children alone. The ventilation of the offices (earth closet toilets) must be improved and the division between the boys and girls yard completed."

The threat to withdraw the grant for the younger children was carried out after the next inspection and three years later the school was still reported as being *"overrun and overcrowded".* The noise in the school as classes were taught simultaneously in the same large room can only be imagined though the discipline was far more rigid than children at today's schools would expect.

Attendance at the school continued to be affected by illness with frequent mention in the log of influenza, scarlet fever, scarlatina, measles, mumps, whooping cough, inflammation of the eyes and even diphtheria and typhoid fever, the last mentioned leading to closure of the school for a period.

Happier reasons for dropping attendances included the show in Bishop Auckland, the arrival of the circus to that nearby town and the inevitable helping in gardens and with the potato harvest.

Children of Roman Catholic families, who appeared to account for some 20-30% of the pupils, had their own reasons for absence on occasions as James Moore records in the log for December 1895

"the Roman Catholic children have all been absent nearly all the week attending special services at Witton Park preparatory for confirmation."

Children of other denominations sometimes had opportunity to miss school for less serious reasons. In July 1895 James Moore reported that

"Most children Wesleyan and Primitive Methodists were on a day trip to Redcar."

However all children enjoyed two days holiday when in July 1893 the Prince of Wales, the future Edward VII, married the Duchess of York.

The Man from Knocknaskeagh

In the late 1890's a man arrived in the Gill who was to become an important member of the Mattimoe family. His name was Thomas Hannon. He and his younger brother Frank had recently left Knocknaskeagh near Ballymote in Co. Sligo, not far from where the Mattimoes originated. Thomas and Frank had left under a cloud. The story told by the family is that they had stolen a cow and sold it to get enough money to pay their fare to England. Their eldest brother Michael, known as 'Peeler Hannon' for the time he spent in the Garda, caught up with them both in Liverpool and tried to persuade them to return. They refused

118 Little Ireland

and Michael returned home to Ireland. Some years later when their mother lay dying Michael again tried to persuade his brother, Thomas, to return but again he refused and never returned to the country of his birth. It is said that Thomas felt if he ever returned to Ireland he would be unable to leave it again.

Edward MacLysaght stated that Hannon is the anglicised version of the Gaelic names *O hAnnain* family of Co. Limerick and the *O hAinchin* family of southeast Galway where it is a corruption of Hanneen. He placed the roots of this family firmly in the west of Ireland in Co.'s Clare, Limerick, Galway and Roscommon, the last three being strongholds of the name today. Thomas's ancestors had farmed at Knocknaskeagh for generations. Bartholomew Hannon, probably Thomas's Grandfather, was recorded as farming at Knocknaskeagh in the Tithe Applotment Valuation of 1833. The original house is still occupied by a descendant of Michael Hannon and is of the traditional single storey layout. Michael acquired nearby Knocknaska House which is still farmed by his descendants.

Given that the Hannon's had always farmed the land since moving to Knocknaskeagh why did the brothers Thomas and Frank feel it necessary to steal a cow? The answer probably lies in a family disagreement. The two sons could see that they would not inherit the farm and were anxious, as most young men, to make their own way in life without delay so probably in the absence of reaching agreement with the rest of the family on their needs 'stole' one of their own families beasts as their part of their inheritance to provide the money with which they could start a new life. The loss of a single beast would have been significant to the family because then, as today, the farms are small with on average forty animals and often a lot less.

Michael Hannon is buried in Mounterwen Cemetery which is in the grounds of Knockmore Abbey, ¾ mile from Knocknaskeagh. This small friary has long been abandoned, and only a few rough stone walls of the buildings remain to give an indication of their size and layout. The story is told that those against the Catholic Church murdered the monks by putting them into barrels, sticking spikes through the sides then rolling the barrels down the hill which rises above the Abbey. The site is remote and is one of the locations locally where Mass was held during the years of religious oppression. Today the remains of the Abbey provide a most beautiful and peaceful setting for the cemetery.

Whilst Thomas Hannon became a miner he did not enjoy the good fortune of the unrelated Patrick Hannan (1842-1925) of Co. Clare who discovered the Kalgoorlie goldfield in Western Australia containing "the richest square mile of gold in the world".

On moving to England Thomas Hannon took up lodgings with Thomas Mattimoe and his family in *'Little Ireland'*, whilst Frank moved to nearby Stanley. Did Thomas know the Mattimoe family before arriving in the Gill? Knocknaskeagh is not far from Boyle and the families in the area kept contact with each other. Whilst no link has been found between the Mattimoes and the Hannons prior to the two sons emigrating it is a strong possibility the Hannons would have known Mattimoes living not far away who would be aware of the good living Thomas Mattimoe had established with his family in Gordon Gill.

Whilst Thomas Hannon never returned to Knocknaskeagh his descendants did not share his reluctance and have maintained contact with the family in Knocknaska House through visits to Ireland and by welcoming their Irish relatives when they visited Ramshaw. Such contact has continued up to the current day.

Fig. 63 (right)

Annie Mattimoe in the mid 1890's dressed in a tight corsetted, decorated top with 'leg-of-mutton' sleeves. The top came to a point at the front over a plain skirt. Her hair is worn high on the head. Her beauty and strength of character shine out from this photograph.

11 The Twentieth Century Opens

In 1901 the population of Gordon Gill had grown slightly to fifty. Of the eight families only three were of Irish descent and all were Mattimoes. The other family surnames were Place, Stewart, Handley, Heslop and Robinson.

The distribution of 'occupations' of those living in the Gill in 1901 were as follows.

Occupation	Number	Age range
Checkweighman	1	35
Deputy Overman	2	40 to 50
Coal Miner (hewer)	6	19 to 34
Colliery Engineman	1	52
Colliery Joiner	1	50
Pony Putter	1	17
Colliery Screen Boy	1	15
Colliery Bank Boy	1	16
Widow	1	26
Housewives	5	20 to 45
Housemaid	1	15
Servant	1	35
Young Sons Not Working	2	15 to 17
Daughters too old for school	2	15 to 16
Children at school	15	4 to 13
Infants and babies	6	1 month to 3 years
Total	**50**	

Thomas Mattimoe Dies

The 1900's were to start traumatically for the Mattimoe family. Thomas, the patriarch of the family, who had brought his family from Ireland and worked to give them a settled life in good surroundings, died in February 1900. The chronic bronchitis he had suffered from for eight years led to a heart attack from which he died ten days later. The sadness his children felt at the loss of their father is encapsulated in the wording of his memory card.

"Dear Father and Mother you now have left us,
And your loss we deeply feel;
But 'tis God that hath bereft us,
He will all our sorrows heal.
But again we hope to meet you,
When our day of life is fled;
Then in heaven we hope to meet you,
Where no farewell tears are shed."

Annie Mattimoe having nursed first her mother through serious illness and then her father was deeply affected by the death of Thomas. She grew ever closer to Thomas Hannon and in November 1900 gave birth to his child, a daughter to be named Annie. Annie retained the support of her family and Thomas after the illegitimate birth. Thomas and Annie married in early 1901 at St. Chad's Roman Catholic Chapel and continued to live in the family home in the Gill with Annie's two brothers and nephew. Sadly Thomas and Annie's daughter died at the age of five months in May 1901 but the couple were destined to raise a large family.

Fig 64 Tom Hannon with his wife Annie who is holding their first son, John. Standing behind them are Tom's younger brother Frank and his future wife Sarah Robinson. The photograph was taken in 1902. The impressive *Trompe-l'oeil* scenery is very effective in this photograph.

Fig. 65 This faded photograph shows Peter Mattimoe standing in the doorway of the Bridge Inn, Ramshaw. He is holding his daughter Jane in his arms. The man to his right is probably holding Peters second daughter Annie. On this basis the picture was probably taken in 1907. It is tempting to believe that the men either side of Peter are his brothers John and Stephen, the old man his father in law, William Kelly, and the young boys his nephews from Gordon Gill.

A Well Respected Family

By the start of the 20th century the Mattimoes were well respected both locally and by their employers and work colleagues. John had progressed to the position of Deputy Overman whilst his younger brother Peter had recently been voted into the important and influential position of checkweighman a position he was to hold for thirty years. Peter was elected to the recently established Parish Council in 1901 after an unsuccessful attempt in 1897. He was to be re-elected at every election up to the First World War and took an active role in village life until his death. Peter married Elizabeth 'Lizzie' Kelly from Cockfield in April 1904. Lizzie was born in nearby Morley but her father was born in Rathfarnham, Dublin.

Whilst marrying late in life Peter and his wife Lizzie wasted no time in raising a large family. Their first daughter Jane, born in 1905 was followed in the years leading up to the First World War by Annie in 1906, twins Elizabeth and Mary in 1907 who sadly died in infancy, Esther in 1909 then three sons, Peter in 1910, Patrick in 1912 and Thomas in 1914.

In the early 1900's Peter, retaining his job as checkweighman, also became landlord of the Bridge Inn, Ramshaw, which lies next to the bridge carrying the road over the Gaunless and up to Evenwood. Amongst all his other duties and commitments he found time to become a member of the Evenwood Silver Band which itself actively supported the activities and endeavours of Ramshaw and Evenwood.

Happy Times in Ramshaw and Evenwood

The 1900's were a time of optimism and prosperity in Ramshaw and Evenwood with opportunity taken to celebrate national as well as local celebrations. The engagement of a local correspondent for Evenwood and Ramshaw resulted in frequent references to local activities as well as specific references to the families of *'Little Ireland'*.

For example The Auckland Chronicle records the following in May 1900.

> "The village of Evenwood presented a gay appearance on Monday afternoon on the local celebration of the Relief of Mafeking. A huge procession of the children attending Evenwood and Ramshaw schools was formed near the Railway Station and headed by the village band, the banner of the Randolph Colliery Miners Lodge and a troop of mounted scouts wound its way through the village. The crowd of onlookers will not soon forget the animated sight of 700 waving flags carried by the young Britishers. Sports of various kinds took place in the Randolph Colliery Gala Field."

Outings had, until this time, been limited to day trips to Barnard Castle and the pretty local villages such as Stanhope and Piercebridge but the introduction of buses opened up opportunities further afield and coastal resorts such as Redcar became popular. Before this many local people never saw the sea. In the early 1970's, when she was in her nineties Suzie Tate told of her mother who never saw the sea but always imagined it moving like a field of waving corn.

In August 1900 the Randolph Coke Works were visited by the Duchess of York who was to become Queen Mary. Five years later a second royal visitor to the works was Prince Henry of Battenburg. These visits illustrated the importance and success of the new works.

Peter Mattimoe was playing an active part in supporting charitable occasions both for organisations and individuals. In August 1900 it was reported that

> "A treat was given to the aged men of the Miners Permanent Relief Fund at Norwood Colliery a week past Saturday by their workmen and friends. The Party took brakes to Piercebridge where some time was spent refreshing the "inner man" and looking round the village then on to Gainford. Dinner was provided at the Trotters Arms. Peter Mattimoe responded to the Chairman's speech on behalf of the Committee."

Fig. 66

This photgraph is probably Annie Hannon's eldest surviving daughter, Mary, taken about 1910. The thicker sole on the shoe of her left foot reflecting the slight handicap with which she was born. The adult style clothes and artificial country setting were typical of photographers studios in the early years of the 20th century.

Whilst in December 1903

"Charity is never more evident than at Christmastide and therefore we note with pleasure that the helping hand is to be held out to Mr Thos. Gaffney of this place who on account of ill health has been unable to follow his employment for a considerable time past. A benefit concert owing its promotion to the active efforts of the Chairman of the Parish Council (Peter Mattimoe) has been arranged for Monday night in Christmas week and as the Rev. H J H Faulkner lends his presence to the gathering and the artistes engaged are all well known it is hoped that gratifying success will be realised."

Thomas Gaffney was the husband of Sarah Jane Cox and Peter's cousin. Peter would have known Thomas all his life but this does not detract from Peter's efforts in support for his cousin. Thomas was probably suffering from a chest illness such as bronchitis or possibly tuberculosis to which he succumbed in September 1905.

Peter Mattimoe and his wife were good hosts at the Bridge Inn with reports of events there commenting upon the "sumptuous spreads" that were provided. The Bridge Inn was then very much a working men's public house. Suzie Tate who worked there for Peter and Lizzie told that it had wooden tables with black legs and the table tops had to be scoured with sand to keep them clean. These were the days before Licensing Laws and the Bridge Inn would open in the morning to cook kippers for the miners returning from the fore-shift and they would throw the fish heads onto the floor. Suzie remembers cooking the meat for Peter and Lizzie's wedding party in April 1904 at the Bridge Inn following which a dance was held in the evening.

Dancing was a popular pastime and Patrick Mattimoe like his brothers was a good dancer. Suzie Tate remembered her mother, also a good dancer, dancing a threesome with Patrick on one side and another man on the other side. Other members of the Mattimoe family made their contribution to local evening events through song.

The people of importance to the local community received recognition. In January 1904 the Auckland Chronicle recorded the following.

"Mr G H Coates Stationmaster at Evenwood for 36 years was recipient of a testimonial from the inhabitants of the surrounding area at Ramshaw School. A purse of gold a silver mounted walking cane and a beautifully designed ring for Mrs Coates. £21 was collected. A programme of vocal music was rendered in good style by Messrs T and F Mattimoe and others...."

Fig. 67

A handwritten note on the reverse of this section of a postcard identifies the women as Jane Rutter and her mother. If this is correct they would have been related to Patrick Mattimoe's wife, Mary Ann. The postcard is of Evenwood Station and the stationmaster could well be Mr Coates. The postcard was hand tinted and the local station appears to have been a popular choice for such cards.

Fig. 68 Evenwood Prize Silver Band. Peter Mattimoe, in the light coloured waisrcoat on the right of the back row.

The village band regularly provided entertainment for the residents as in June 1904.

> "On Sunday afternoon the Silver Band again played on the village green but on this occasion a collection was made for Mr Thomas Gaffney a miner who has not been able to work for about two years owing to ill health. The weather was fine crowds of people gathered to listen to the music … .The sum raised was about £3-12s."

Whilst in August 1904 the paper reported.

> "Monday – Bank Holiday all the collieries in the District were idle. Grand gala held in Randolph Colliery Field. At 1.30pm a cycle parade headed by the Silver Band started from Ramshaw and proceeded up to the gala field where prizes were given for the best decorated machine. The Silver Band played during the afternoon. In the evening there was dancing for which a string band was provided."

In October 1904 the Silver Band played at the opening of the Cooperative shop Evenwood.

The quality of the village band can be judged by this entry from the Auckland chronicle of January 1911.

> "An excellent supper was provided at Mr Peter Mattimoe's Bridge Inn on Saturday evening when a good number of members and friends of the Evenwood prize band (winners of the Kirtley Cup, 1909 – Northumberland and Durham Association and the Boothroyd Cup Auckland Charity Carnival) sat down. Mr Mattimoe presented to Mr Raine, bandmaster, on behalf of the committee and members an enlarged photograph of the band, given by Mr J R Hymes, Bishop Auckland, the picture to hang in the band room. Mr Raine heartily thanked Mr Hymes for his gift on behalf of the bandsmen and said it was one which would ever be a reminder of the successes the band has achieved (Applause). It was a pleasure

126 Little Ireland

to him to know that the band was appreciated by workers and employers alike. The following contributed to the harmony of the evening:- Messrs Mattimoe, Jackson, Smith, Watson and Hymes. Mr Raine presided at the pianoforte. The band rendered a number of pleasing selections."

All these activities were taking place against a backdrop of a booming local mining industry as witnessed by the following reports of September and December of 1906.

> "It seems that the Old Raily Fell Colliery owned by Messrs Stobbart and Co is about to take a new lease of life. A drift has been put through from the Five Quarter to the Brockwell seam where it is estimated there are about 14 acres of whole coal besides a large area that has been partially worked out but left a few years ago owing to the lack of pumping machinery to cope with the water hence was "drowned out". This seam is between six and seven feet thick and is of the very best quality for household and working purposes."

> "Owing to the great demand for coke the management of Raily Fell Colliery has commenced an extra night shift. This will enable them to draw coal 17 hours instead of only 10 each day."

There was evidence that the families in the Gill were continuing to use the land surrounding the Gill as a smallholding in the following report in December 1906 describing an incident that would have lessened the Christmas cheer of the Hannon family that year.

> "Mr Thomas Hannon miner of Gordon Gill Ramshaw met with an unpleasant surprise on Saturday morning. On going to look after some geese that he kept in an outbuilding – and which were fed fat to be disposed of at Christmas – he found the building had been broken into and the geese, ten in number, missing. They were subsequently found lying in an adjoining field, not many yards from where they had been, four with their necks broken. It is hoped that the perpetrator of the act will be found...... Mr William Kay of Ramshaw Heugh had fourteen head of poultry stolen only three weeks ago."

The Mattimoe families continued to thrive, though not without the occasional sad event. After the loss of their first daughter Thomas and Annie Hannon had four sons and three daughters

Fig. 69

"At the Bridge Inn on Saturday night Dr. Sheedy presented certificates to those who had passed the St Johns Ambulance examination including Mr T T Mattimoe and PC Mattimoe. A sumptuous supper was provided by Host and Hostess Mr and Mrs Mattimoe."   (Auckland & County Chronicle, Thursday March 25 1909)

Several Mattimoes were present at this evening presentation. In the middle row from the left are Peter Mattimoe, Stephen Mattimoe, John Mattimoe's sons Thomas and Stephen the recipients of the certificates, John Mattimoe himself and John's tall brother-in-law Martin Donnelly. On the far right of the back row is John's younger brother Frank. The young girl in the front is Peter's daughter, Annie. Dr. Sheedy is seated in the middle of the front row. He was of Irish descent and a good doctor to the mining families but had the 'Irish temper'. One time he was summoned for assault and stated, unrepentantly, to the Magistrates that he had assaulted the victim because 'he deserved a good thrashing'.

John's son Stephen had left mining by this date to become a policeman but had returned for the ceremony wearing the bowler hat off duty policemen were expected to wear at that time. Martin Donnelly was also a policeman and similarly attired.

before the end of the decade, John, Mary, Sally, Elizabeth, Tom, Joe and Mattie. Stephen and Mary Ellen Mattimoe completed their family with the births of Cornelius, Timmy and Tommy.

Annie Mattimoe's husband Thomas Hannon was a strong supporter of the Irish cause. His eldest son, John, remembered as a young boy his father sending him out to put up Fenian posters in the local area. We will never know how strong his Fenian views were and how actively he was involved but it seems likely that he restricted himself to promoting the cause through rhetoric and posters. We do know that two of his brothers back in Ireland were members of the IRA. One brother later joined the Garda after independence and entered this fact on his application form. The other brother was so active that he had to leave Ireland and spend some time in America. On his return he spent some time in Co. Durham but allegedly after some incidents of rick burning his niece wrote to the family in Ireland asking them to call him home.

In April 1906 Stephen, the son of the eldest brother Patrick married Sarah Ferguson. They began the next generation with Theresa and Harold. In October 1907 John's eldest son Thomas, who had

Fig. 70

Molly Mattimoe was aged about ten when this photograph was taken. The artificial outdoor scene of the previous photograph of Molly has been swapped for a contrived and busy indoor scene. The pedestal with the potted plant obscures the fireplace and crowded mantle on the painted backdrop. These elements plus the large chair and fluffy rug all compete for the viewers attention. Molly's dress adds to these distractions. Despite this the photographer has beautifully captured the image of a serious young girl whose eyes look out from the image directly into those of the viewer.

been brought up by his Aunt Annie married Caroline Samms descended from an Essex family who had, with other families from that county, moved to Butterknowle in search of work. The area they moved to in Butterknowle became known as Essex Row.

A report in the paper of November 1908 featured Thomas and demonstrated the dangers of pit life.

> "On Thursday night at Railey Fell Pit Thomas Mattimoe Ramshaw, a hewer in the night shift met with an accident the cause being a large fall of cannel coal which caused severe bruising on the face and other parts of the body."

John's second eldest son Stephen also followed his father to work at the mine but soon decided this work was not for him and left to become a policeman with the Durham Constabulary a course of action his younger brother Frank was to take five years later.

The Move from *'Little Ireland'*

Fig 71 Thomas Mattimoe, John Mattimoe's son by his first wife.

Just as the first decade of the 20th century had started traumatically for the Mattimoes, the second was also to bring difficulty and sadness. In February 1910 the work at Railey Fell pit started to reduce and was recorded in the Auckland Chronicle as follows.

> "The Hutton seam at Railey Fell Colliery (Gordon bank Top) is about to be closed the coal being worked out. Last week the whole of the men and boys, 49 in number, received notice to terminate their engagement."

The pit struggled on and in February the following year a brief respite was announced.

> "The life of Railey Fell Colliery has to be prolonged a little longer, the whole of the workmen being re-engaged, but to terminate their employment at a day's notice. It is alleged that cannot continue beyond a week or two."

The uncertain future of the mine must have been a constant worry to the families of the Gill through into the following year but then in June 1911 personal tragedy struck. Patrick Mattimoe the eldest brother died. The loss was felt widely throughout the village as described in the following article in the Auckland Chronicle.

Fig.72 Patrick Mattimoe

Fig. 73 Patrick's wife, Mary Ann Rutter

"It is with regret that we record the death of Mr Patrick Mattimoe, Gordon Bank, which took place on Thursday after a few days illness. Deceased, who was 53 years of age was of a hearty, genial disposition, and was held in high esteem. The funeral took place on Saturday, when a large company of relatives and friends attended. Father Myler, Witton park, officiated at the graveside. Among the immediate relatives present were Mrs Mattimoe (widow), Mr Stephen and Miss Mattimoe (son and daughter), Mr John Mattimoe, Mr Peter Mattimoe, Mr Stephen Mattimoe (brothers), with their wives and families, Mrs Welch (sister), Mr H Rutter (father-in-law), Miss Rutter (sister-in-law), Mr T Rutter, Mr E Rutter, and Mr J Rutter (brothers-in-law). Among the general public were Messrs T and C Brown, B and W Arkless, Mr and Mrs R Bell, Mr and Mrs L Henderson, Mr S Roe, Mr R Straughan, Mr J Moore, Mr D Carrick, Mr I Raine, Mr J Gent, Mr G S Robinson, Mr J and R Anderson, Mr and Mrs Sewell, Mr and Mrs W Marshall, Mrs Brunskill, Mr J Coatesworth, Mr E and R Place, Mr T Crosby, Mr and Mrs A Moffat, Mr J Wilkinson, Mr I Bailey, Mr and Mrs J Walker, Mr M Whitehead, Mr M Armstrong, Mr J Tarn, Mr W Sutton, Mr W Kaye, Mr and Mrs J O'Neil, Mr and Mrs H Fawcett, Mr J Bradwell, Mr Stainthorpe, Mr Barron, Lands bank, and others. Mr R Howe was undertaker."

In evidence of the importance of the local paper report the following appeared in the next edition.

"In last weeks issue, among the list of those who attended the funeral of the late Mr P Mattimoe, we regret the omission of the names of Mr and Mrs Hannon, Gordon Gill. Mrs Hannon was a sister of the deceased."

The sadness of Patrick's death was compounded for the Mattimoes when his granddaughter, Theresa, died a few days later from diphtheria.

"Sympathy goes out to Mr and Mrs Stephen Mattimoe, Gordon Gill, owing to the loss they have sustained by the sudden death of their eldest child, Theresa, aged five years, which

Fig. 74 Ramshaw School photograph taken c.1905 shortly before the school moved to the new building on the other side of the River Gaunless. Molly Mattimoe is sitting on the far right of the middle row. The girls are well dressed with polished boots. The boys sport the high white collars on their shirts which, though fashionable, must have been the bane of their mothers who had to wash, starch and iron them. The suspicion must be that the children had been sent to school in their 'Sunday Best' clothes for the benefit of the school photograph but it still indicates that the families were not poor. Molly's dress appears to be that worn in the photograph in **Fig. 70** so it is probable that children were expected to make their 'Sunday Best' last at least two years.

> took place on Saturday morning. Deceased was granddaughter to the late Mr P Mattimoe, whose remains were interred only a week before her death, and with whom she had, for the most part, resided, and both were much attached to each other. The remains were interred on Monday."

On top of these tragedies came the announcement that Railey Fell pit was to finally close. John and Stephen Mattimoe felt they had no alternative but to move their families to an area where they could find pit work. The local paper caught the sombre mood of the decision.

> "The stoppage of Railey Fell Pit is causing some of our most respected families to leave the locality, the latest of these being the brothers John and Stephen Mattimoe and their families who removed to Eldon on Monday. It is considerably over 40 years since their father came to Gordon Gill, and now the fourth generation is represented there. When people have known no other home from childhood to well over middle life the severance is keenly felt. The best wishes of their many friends go with them for their success in their new sphere."

132 Little Ireland

John's eldest son Thomas left Ramshaw at about this time and moved his family to Leeholme. Only the Hannon family remained in the Gill as descendants from Thomas and Ann Mattimoe. Since moving to the Gill in 1870 Thomas and Ann's family had grown from seven in number to an extended family of thirty nine by September 1911. This included twenty nine grandchildren and one great grandchild of Thomas and Ann. They had faced sadness at the loss of children but the family had thrived vindicating the decision by Thomas and Anne almost fifty years earlier to leave their beloved Ireland. The families had enjoyed a close relationship with each other, supported by their close friends and had gained the respect of the community in which they lived and worked.

The Hannon family were to leave the Gill soon after John and Stephen's families moved to Eldon but they remained in Ramshaw moving to Gordon Lane, where they were to remain, moving only once, into the adjacent house. Some of their descendants still live in Gordon Lane.

In Evenwood the Auckland Chronicle recorded the death of a member of the Gaffney family in January 1914.

> "The death took place on Wednesday of Mrs Gaffney wife of Edward (Teddy) Gaffney, Stonesend. The remains were interred on Sunday, with the rites of the Roman Catholic Church"

Eldon Lane

John Mattimoe started work at Eldon Lane Colliery where he was to spend the rest of his working life as a Deputy Overman.

Eldon Lane Colliery had one unusual feature, an outdoor heated swimming pool. The idea had come to the colliery manager when he saw teenagers playing in the stream into which had been discharged hot water pumped from the pit. The proposal was that a swimming pool be constructed using filtered hot water from the pit. The colliery owners provided the construction materials and the miners carried out the building work. They were deducted one penny a week to fund the swimming pool which was opened in 1911. The pool had a diving board, wooden changing cubicles, two coal-fired heated changing rooms, one for men and one for women. A water polo team was formed which became very popular and successful and swimming galas were held therefore two wooden grandstands were constructed for spectators. An Institute was constructed next to the swimming pool. It had a gymnasium where Eldon

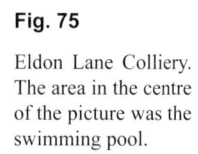

Fig. 75

Eldon Lane Colliery. The area in the centre of the picture was the swimming pool.

The Twentieth Century Opens

Fig. 76 This photograph of John Mattimoe's family and his brother in law Martin Donellan was taken in 1912 shortly before Martin emigrated to the USA in August of that year. From left to right those in the picture are Hannah Mattimoe, Stephen Mattimoe, John Mattimoe, Frank Mattimoe (sitting), Leo Mattimoe, Martin Donnelly and Molly Mattimoe. The Mattimoe men were tall but Martin's 6' 7 1/2" (2.02 m) towered over them. Consequently the photographer, in achieving a balanced photograph, has seated Martin on a low stool. The result is successful but Martin's long legs bent at an awkward angle give the game away.

Band also practised, a reading room, table tennis room, billiards room and, upstairs, a concert room where dances where held. The Institute and the pool were commandeered by the Army during the Second World War and never reopened. No trace is left of the Institute but a commemorative stone marks the site of the swimming pool.

The Donnellan's Emigrate to the USA

At the end of the 19th century and the early years of the 20th century Hannah Mattimoes brothers and sisters emigrated to the USA. The only one for whom a firm date has been identified is Martin Donnelly. He left England in August 1912 aboard the Lusitania bound for New York from Liverpool.

The Lusitania was later to be sunk by a German U-boat on May 8 1915 whilst off the coast of Ireland and 1,198 of those aboard perished. The British Government denied that the liner was carrying munitions but an unexplained second explosion resulted in the vessel sinking in a horribly short eighteen minutes. It is widely cited that the loss of the Lusitania precipitated America's entry into the First World War though history does not support this. It was not until March 1917 when U-boats sank three US merchant ships bringing supplies to Britain that America, albeit somewhat reluctantly, declared war against Germany. The speed of response by the American forces supports this view with US naval boats not joining the Grand Fleet until December 1917 and land forces not fighting in France until June 1918.

In the passenger manifest Martin gave his age as thirty, though he was probably nearer forty, and his last country of permanent residence as Ireland. The age given was no doubt intended to ease his entry into the country whilst the reference to Ireland reflected the country where he felt his roots belonged. On arrival at Ellis Island in New York he stated he was from Bishop Auckland. The manifest shows that all his personal possessions were held in two pieces of luggage. When he emigrated Martin gave his occupation as police constable and on arrival in America joined the New York City Police where he achieved fame by being the tallest person in the Force at that time.

Why did Martin emigrate? He was very close to Hannah and her family and enjoyed many good times with them. He was single and remained so all his life. Was it a case of 'lost love'? He did not join his sisters and brother in USA but made his own life in New York therefore was it the lure of making a new life in a country of opportunity? We will never know but he did keep in contact with Hannah and John after his arrival.

Hannah's brother, Patrick and her two sisters emigrated before Martin, perhaps as early as the 1880's judging from the dress Hannah's

Fig. 77 Hannah's sister, probably Mrs Foley who settled in Denver, Colorado. The photograph was taken in Pittsburgh, Pennsylvania. The standing collar of the tight-fitting bodice, buttoned to the throat is a style from the 1880's whilst the skirt, full at the back with overskirt dates it to the first half of that decade.

sister is wearing in a photograph taken in the USA.

One sister settled in Denver, Colorado and the other moved to San Francisco, California. Hannah could not write at the time of her marriage to John Mattimoe in 1884 but the sisters did correspond. It seems likely that Molly wrote the letters on her mother's behalf.

Willy Gray

Molly married John William 'Willy' Gray in October 1913 at St. Wilfred's, Bishop Auckland and they moved to Mary Terrace, Coronation.

Willy Gray was born 14th April 1884 in Hartlepool, Co. Durham. His great grandfather was James Gray, born in the late 1790's in Aughanagh, Co. Sligo, thus the surname is likely to be the anglicised version of the Gaelic *Mac Giolla Riabhaigh* (son of grey youth). Aughanagh is the parish where Molly's Grandfather, Thomas Mattimoe, had been born in 1833 though there is no evidence the families were close.

James Gray married Anne Ferrall at Boyle in February 1819. Their son Peter, born in 1823 in Aughanagh, Co.

Fig. 78 Molly and Willy Gray taken around the time of their marriage in October 1913.

Sligo, came to England around 1850 and became a coalminer. In April 1853 he married Margaret Conway in St. Michaels Catholic Church, Houghton le Spring, Co. Durham. Margaret had been born about 1832 in Co. Longford, and her father was also a James. Margaret and her father had lodgings in Houghton le Spring at the time of the 1851 census. Her mother is not with them though there was a Margaret Conway lodging not far away who was married and about the right age.

Margaret and Peter's eldest child a boy, not surprisingly named James, was born in Houghton le Spring 2nd June 1855. Whilst no trace has been found of the family in the 1861 and 1871 censuses from the children's birthplaces given in the 1881 census they had moved around Co. Durham, living in Hunwick in 1861 (Thomas), Crook in 1865 (Cornelius), Spennymoor in 1867 (Margaret), West Auckland in 1870 (Mary), and Bishop Auckland from 1874 (Elizabeth). When the census was taken in 1881 they had a lodger, Frederick Blake, aged 18. Frederick's start in life had been harsh as he was born in Hereford Goal.

James married Elizabeth Ann Haigh in St. Wilfred's Church Bishop Auckland in October 1881. Witnesses to the marriage were James' brother Cornelius "Con" and Julia Collins whom he subsequently married.

Fig 79

This photograph taken in the early 1910's shows Elizabeth Gray nee Haigh then in her fifties, her daughter Jennifer who was in her thirties and her mother Mary haigh nee Purtill who was in her seventies. Elizabeth is dressed in early Edwardian style whilst her mothers dress and hat hark from the late 1880's.

James died of a cerebral abscess six and a half years later when he was only thirty three and was buried in Bishop Auckland cemetery where his grave stone can still be seen incorporating his parents Peter and Margaret who died in 1898 and 1910.

Elizabeth was left to bring up her children, Margaret Jennifer born in Southchurch 1882, John William born 12th April 1884 in Hartlepool, Alice born in Southchurch 1885 and Mary born in Southchurch 1887.

Alice married Jack Hunter a hairdresser. She was his second wife and married late in life. Jack Hunter had a son before he married Alice called John Hunter who had several hairdressing shops in Darlington and all over the North.

Mary sadly died young.

Elizabeth Ann Haigh was born about 1863 in Yorkshire in Bedale or Burneston, between Richmond and Ripon. Her father John Haigh was born about 1835 in Klekheaton near Huddersfield and is the only English ancestor on this side of the family.

John Haigh had married an Irish girl, Mary Purtill, on 11th September 1860 in the Register Office, Ripon. They were living in North Stainley, a village to the north of Ripon. He was a farm labourer and she was a domestic servant. Mary had been born in Ireland about 1839 and her father was John Purtill, a farmer. The Griffith's Valuation identifies two John Purtill's both farming in Co. Clare.

John and Mary had six children in addition to Elizabeth Ann namely John William born about 1864,

Louisa born about 1866, Mary born 26th August 1868, George born 1872, Alice Inman born 9th August 1875, Maria born 1878.

Mary Haigh nee Purtill died on 17th June 1913 at Bank Top, Shincliffe of cirrhosis of the liver and senile decay. She was seventy four years old. Her son George who worked at Eldon Colliery was present at her death. John Haigh died 1st March 1918 also at Bank Top, Shincliffe of bronchitis. He was eighty three years old. His daughter Louisa Stockdale was present at his death.

Births, Death and Marriage in 1914

John Mattimoe's wife Hannah died in February 1914 at Mary Terrace, Coronation and was buried in Bishop Auckland cemetery.

John Mattimoe's son, Frank, had left mining and joined the Durham Constabulary. He married Nellie Welsh in April 1914. A month after his marriage Frank was posted to Chester-le-Street where he was to remain throughout his career. Nellie gave birth to a son, Francis 'Frank' in July 1914.

In an eventful month for the Mattimoe family and the country Molly and Willy's son James, 'Jack', was born on 3 August two days before Britain declared war on Germany.

Fig. 80
The reverse of this photograph correctly identifies Willy Gray standing on the right then indicates that the man sitting is Jim Hannon. It seems most likely that this is Thomas Hannon who married Annie Mattimoe. The man standing on the left is Annie's brother Frank. It has not been possible to positively identify the young woman but it seems most likely that she is one of Willy Gray's sisters. The photograph appears to have been taken around 1910 shortly before Willy and Molly married.

12   The Great War

The Home Front

The First World War began on the 5th August 1914. The outbreak of war did not touch the Mattimoe and Hannon families as directly as families in other parts of the country due to underground jobs in coal-mining being reserved occupations. Despite this the family were unable to avoid tragedy.

Local men responded to Kitchener's appeal for volunteers "for three years or the duration" and the Auckland Chronicle recorded the following on the 10th September with regard to Bishop Auckland.

> "The 'call to arms' has been responded to during the week-end by a good number of recruits. The railway station presented quite an animated appearance on Tuesday morning when about 20 left with the 9am train for Bishop Auckland. Most of the recruits are married men."

The full horror of what was to come was not realised by anyone consequently those who joined up were cheered on by patriotic crowds.

Belgium bore the initial brunt of the war as German forces swept through that country to bypass the fortifications on the Franco/German border. Despite a brave defence the Belgian forces were no match for the larger German Army and its superior heavy guns. Rumours of atrocities, some substantiated, against the civil population by the German Army resulted in Belgians fleeing their homes and becoming refugees.

Tens of thousands Belgian refugees came to Britain, some ending up in Evenwood. For this reason and perhaps also because Belgian workers had built the coke ovens at Randolph Colliery a few years earlier the population of Evenwood and Ramshaw rallied to their aid. In October 1914 a social was held in the school for the benefit of the Belgian refugees and the following month the Auckland Chronicle reported that

> "Belgian Flag Day was celebrated at Evenwood on Saturday, when flags and bunting were exhibited from a large number of dwellings. The band paraded through the village, and a number of ladies were busy selling bows representing both the British and Belgian colours. A dance was held in the evening, when a large company was present. The proceeds of the day, which were in aid of the Belgian Relief Fund, amounted to over £20."

In December the war seemed even nearer when the sound of the German naval bombardment of Hartlepool, Scarborough and Whitby could be heard in Evenwood.

The patriotic zeal was undiminished in the early part of 1915 when the local paper noted 'hearty send offs' for recruits and was able to proudly announce that thirty thousand Durham miners had enlisted by that time. This was the time of the 'Old Pals' Brigades when brothers, friends and workmates joined the same regiment. The paper carried a picture of five brothers who had joined the Northumberland Fusiliers together. There was even a report of a Durham amateur football team who, after their match, all enlisted together. This was not a response on their part to a string of bad results as they were top of their league at the time with a healthy goal difference. Less prosaically a write-up on the proceedings of Bishop

Auckland's Magistrate's Court noted a case of alleged poaching at which the two defendants failed to appear as they had both enlisted. The case was dismissed.

Pictures of soldiers from local families were a regular feature, together with accounts of bravery and successes from the front, mixed in with horror stories such as the deaths of French women and children from German Artillery. As the year progressed the captions beneath the pictures were increasingly accompanied by the words 'wounded' and 'killed'. From mid year the individual write-ups on casualties gave way to lists reflecting the mounting losses. To emphasise the scale of the casualties details of a parliamentary answer were printed in the paper stating that those killed and injured up to that point exceeded half a million.

Alongside the details of the war which occupied a significant number of columns in the paper the reports of local life continued together with the regular articles such as 'Chats with the Doctor' and 'Cottage gardens'. There was concern on the Home Front about the increasing cost of food.

Developments of the Mattimoe and Hannon Families

John Mattimoe married again in April 1915 to Sarah Wilson "a German lady". His daughter Molly was a witness at this wedding in St Wilfred's Church. All does not seem to have been well as John later wrote her out of his will in February 1919. During the war years John also gained a number of grandchildren. Molly and Willy had Mary in 1916 and Laurie in 1917, whilst Frank and Nellie had Winifred three weeks before the end of the war..

At the outbreak of the war John's sister Annie Hannon was living in one of the terraced cottages in Gordon Lane with her husband Tom and ten children. Sadly her son Mattie died on 3rd August 1915 aged six years old. Showing the resilience necessary to cope with her hard life six weeks later on 20th September she sends the postcard shown below to her sister-in-law Sarah at West Stanley and writes in a positive vain. The spelling of certain words indicates Annie retained a strong element of her family's Irish accent.

Fig. 81   Gordon Lane, Ramshaw. Annie Mattimoe and her large family lived in the second house from the right.

A Roll of Honour from ... Catholic Congregat...

Pte. Dick Toole (6th D.L.I.)

Pte. A. Toole (D.L.I.)

Pte. J. Toole (14th D.L.I.) killed.

Cpl. J. Quinn (6th D.L.I.), wounded.

Driver W... in ...

Pte. W. Sinclair (6th Durhams), wounded.

Driver Thos. Harker (R.E.).

Bugler M. Burns (D.L.I.) wounded.

Pte. T. Mattimore (N.F.) in France.

Fig. 82

These photographs are part of an amazing set of sixty two serving soldiers and sailors drawn from the congregation of St Joseph's Roman Catholic Church, Coundon, which appeared in the Auckland and County Chronicle on 27th January 1916.

St Joseph's served the Catholic communities of Coundon and the adjacent village of Leeholme and numbered many miners families in its congregation including Mattimoes.

The caption accompanying these photographs was as follows.

"Over 100 men of the above small parish have enlisted in His Majesty's forces, and a few have already been fighting for some months. A few of the photographs are given here"

Many of those whose photograph was printed shared common surnames indicating close family links. Their surnames also hint at Irish origins from where they drew their faith.

Three Tooles all in the Durham Light Infantry, one of whom had been killed; three Quinns, one of whom had been wounded; seven Conlons of whom four were in the Durham Light Infantry and two of these had been wounded; three O'Neills; two Kelley' both in the Northumberland Fusilliers; two Gallaghers; two Callaghans; two Dolans. Other Irish names included Murphy, Cleary, Sharkey, Mulligan, Kelly and, of course, Mattimoe.

Of the sixty two listed eight were reported wounded and one killed and the war was only 18 months old with the worst of the fighting and casualties still to come.

"Dear Sarah

I write to see if ye are all well when you have not written. Joseph his a lot better now he can walk about by himself. Tom his working on bank and he is keeping fairly well. Write and let me know if ye are all well and how is your Mother. This is the street we live in.

Your Loving Annie"

Losses at the Front

The first local casualty of the war was reported in September 1915. In this month John's first son Tom joined the Northumberland Fusiliers. Tom was married with three children, Mary, Jack and Teresa. His wife, Carrie, was seven months pregnant with their daughter Winnie. The family were living in Coundon near Bishop Auckland. Tom was one of over one hundred young men from the congregation of St Joseph's Roman Catholic Church in Coundon who had enlisted by the end of 1915. In January 1916 the Auckland Chronicle printed photos of sixty four of them including Tom who was by that time serving in France.

Several soldiers in the photo have the same name indicating they were related and they also were in the same regiment. The tragedy this practice could lead to has been documented many times but it was brought home to those living in the Bishop Auckland area when the local paper reported the deaths of two sons belonging to Mrs Oxhill. The soldiers were together in the same dugout in France when a shell exploded killing them both instantly. Their brothers-in-law were serving in the same part of the battlefield and one had visited the two brothers shortly before the tragic incident. They had asked him to stay but he had insisted on returning to his position and consequently survived the attack. Mrs Oxhill had previously lost a son during fighting in the Dardenelles.

Tom was later transferred to the Labour Corps. This may have just been for his physical strength but miners were often employed to tunnel under "no mans land" to the German trenches where bombs were set to explode beneath the enemy trenches. This was a dangerous activity for those involved due to the disturbed nature of the ground in no-mans land and even more dangerous if the German soldiers came to suspect what was taking place beneath them.

Tom was then transferred to the Sussex Regiment where he served until the end of the War. He was injured in the war and bore deep scars on his back. He was awarded the Victory, British and 1915 Star medals. His military record was lost along with the majority of other such records during the Blitz of the Second World War. What has survived is a card he sent back to his father from France bearing the simple message "To my Dear Father with Love & Best Wishes From your affectionate Son Tom". Tom apparently managed at least one spell of leave as his wife gave birth to a son, Thomas, in 1918.

Stephen Mattimoe, his wife Mary Ellen and family had settled in Eldon Lane after leaving Gordon Gill. The eldest son, Frank, was independent and high-spirited and was to enlist in the army. We will hear his story in the next chapter.

John Mattimoe's youngest son Frank had followed in his brother Stephen's footsteps and joined the Durham Constabulary. In February 1916 he was a constable attached to Chester-le-Street police station and is mentioned in the court write-up of the local paper appearing for the prosecution against a hapless cyclist who was on his way to work at 4.30 am and whose bicycle did not have a rear lamp. Frank stated, perhaps in an attempt to mitigate the seriousness of the offence but I am sure as no surprise to those gathered in the court, that when the offence was committed "there were very few people about". The magistrates appear to have been unmoved by the additional information and fined the offender four shillings.

Peter Mattimoe continued to play a full role in the community. In March 1916 he was re-elected to the Burial Board and in April was elected vice-chairman of the Parish Council. In May he was appointed steward of Evenwood Working Men's Club.

Zeppelin Raid over Evenwood and Eldon Lane

The war was brought closer to home by air raids carried out by Zeppelins, Germany's fleet of dirigible airships. During the war there were only fifty three such air raids, twenty two of them in 1916 but the

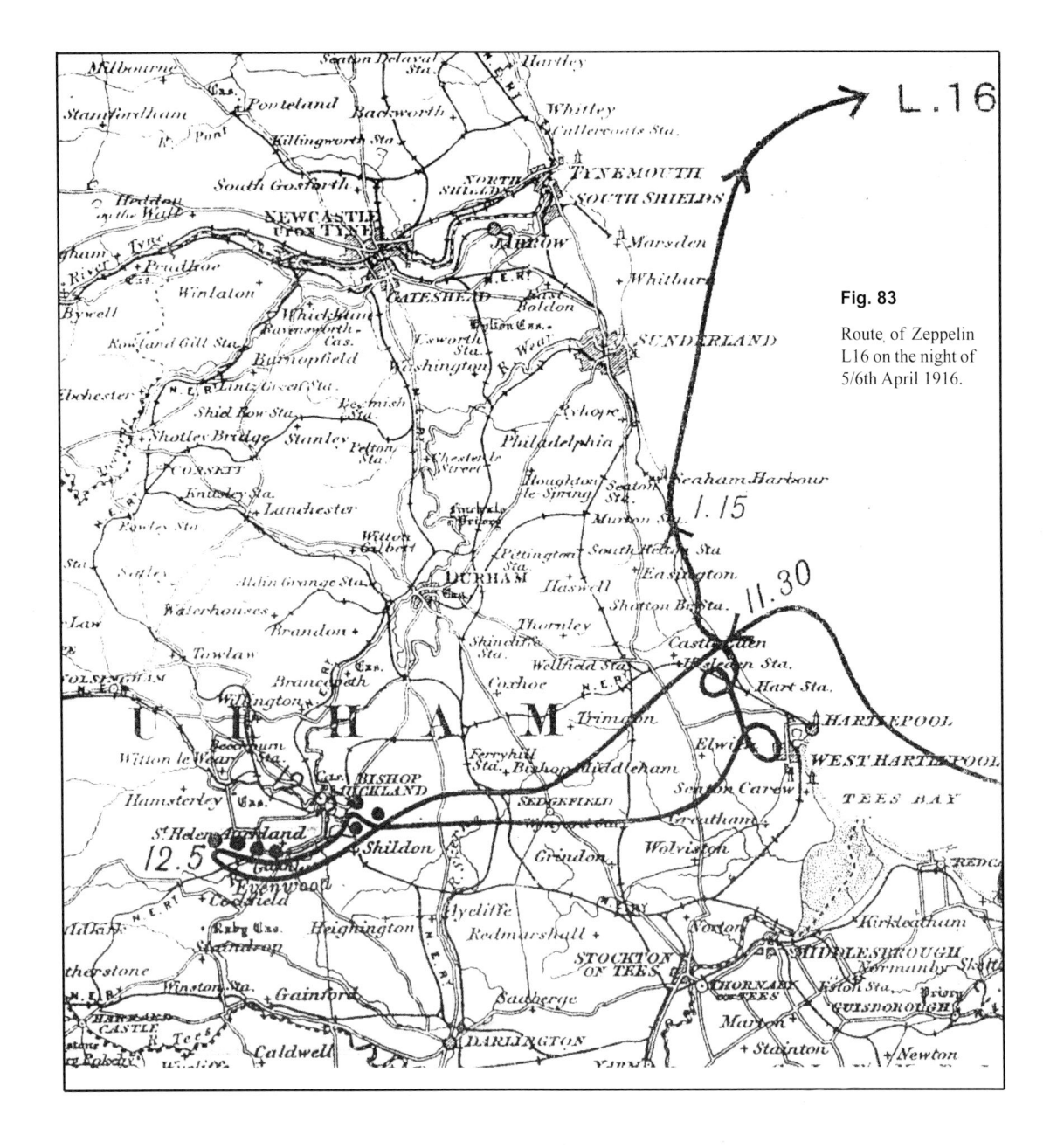

Fig. 83

Route of Zeppelin L16 on the night of 5/6th April 1916.

Fig. 84 Zeppelin L12 was the same type as Zeppelin L16 which attacked Ramshaw and Eldon Lane on the night of 5/6th April 1916. Its immense size can be judged from the machine-gunner sitting on the top of the airship above the front gondola. Zeppeilins were filled with hydrogen gas and burst into flame when their enormous hulls were pierced during ground or air attack. They were slow moving with a distinctive sound to their engines giving warning of their arrival but the models introduced in 1916 flew high and out of reach of British air defences. Improved air defences including deployment of fighter aircraft brought raids to a halt by the end of 1916.

threat of such attacks caused significant fear amongst the civilian population of cities and industrial areas. In March that year a raid on Hull had caused forty four civilian casualties including twelve dead. There was concern locally about the possibility of such an attack and lighting restrictions were introduced.

Local concern proved justified. On the night of 5/6th April Zeppelin L16 crossed the North Sea coast north of Hartlepool shortly before midnight and headed inland. Navigation by the crew was by eyesight and maps. A difficult task made more difficult by the need to fly the airship at high altitude to avoid anti-aircraft batteries. Was Evenwood their intended target that night or had they mis-identified it for their true objective Leeds? The people of the village were convinced that the coke ovens were the intended target as Germans had been involved in their construction prior to 1914, some of them lodging with families in Gordon Lane. Whatever the intended target the crew seem to have been attracted by the light from the burning spoil heaps of Randolph Colliery and dropped twenty three bombs on Evenwood destroying fifteen cottages and damaging a further seventy including that occupied by the Hannon family in Gordon Lane.

Some bombs fell on Ramshaw damaging a number of houses including that occupied by Thomas and Annie Hannon's family. The school was also damaged, losing forty eight panes of glass. The school was closed for over two weeks for repairs though replacement glass was not to be had. When it reopened on the 21st April James Moore recorded the following in the school log.

> *"The attendance was very poor when the school reopened after the Air Raid, only 50% of the children were present on Monday morning but it improved later. ... The school was very cold – notwithstanding the heating apparatus – owing to the broken windows which have not yet been repaired."*

The L16 then made to return to Germany passing over Eldon Lane where John and Stephen Mattimoe were then living with their families. More bombs were dropped damaging the school at Eldon Lane, the Co-op, Quaker Meeting House and other buildings at nearby Close House and shaking buildings and their occupants at Eldon. The L16 was seen passing over the coast at Seaham Harbour at 1.15pm. The only casualty of the raid was a young boy killed at Close house, the son of a soldier serving in France who himself was to return home but die of his injuries.

The crew of the L16 subsequently transferred to another airship which was shot down over Essex in September 1916 with the loss of its crew.

Germany flew one hundred and fifteen Zeppelins, of which seventy seven were destroyed. George Welsh told me of the time when as a young boy he was called out of the family house in Evenwood by his father to witness the shooting down of a Zeppelin over Hartlepool. He watched it slowly fall to the ground in a huge ball of flame.

Fear of further raids in early May and again in September led the local population to spend uncomfortable nights in the fields and, for those living in Gordon Lane, the 'snecker' drift mine.

School attendance suffered following these alarms as recorded in the school log.

> *"Attendance ... much reduced on Tuesday owing to the rumours of another Air Raid about midnight on Monday which caused many families to sit up all night"*

The air raid would have caused some concern in the Willy and Molly Gray's household in Coronation, just the other side of the railway bridge from Eldon Lane where their second child, Mary, had been born just three weeks earlier.

The War Drags On

The War entered a new year and the local paper continued to print pictures of local men who were serving in the Army and Navy though increasingly with the annotation 'killed' or 'wounded'. As the year progressed individual write ups on soldiers who had been injured were replaced by lists of local men killed, wounded or missing in action. At home there were reports of Women Land Workers being 'put to the test' and mention of soldiers home on leave. On 17th December 1917 the entry for Ramshaw described the return of one soldier to Gordon Lane.

> "The many friends of Pte. 'Jack' Burney are pleased to see him at home again after being wounded for the third time. He has been recuperating in hospital in Southampton. Pte, Burney has been through the Dardenelles campaign, and many encounters in France."

No doubt the return, just before Christmas was a joyous occasion, though sometimes soldiers who had seen a great deal of action and confronted the horrors of war found it difficult to settle at home and impossible to talk of their experiences. This difficulty must have been made more poignant by the news, reported in the same article, that Cpl. L T Cox, the son of Mrs Cox, who lived at nearby Oaks, who had been missing in action since 5th November 1916 had just been confirmed killed on that date.

By 1918 photographs of local soldiers which had appeared weekly in the early years of the war had been replaced with long lists of casualties. Alongside this sombre news the local paper continued to report the other events in the village in the manner in which it had done in the years before the war. In January the quiet of the village was upset by the following.

> "An exciting incident occurred on Friday afternoon. A horse attached to a flat was standing at the Station steps and evidently took fright and galloped furiously down the Station Road its head smashing into the plate glass window of Mrs Jarret's shop opposite the Station gates. Fortunately no one was passing down Gordon Lane at the time. A little before the accident Mrs Jarret was cleaning the outside of the windows."

Fig. 85 John Mattimoe's sons, Stephen and Frank were in the reserved occupation of policemen. Stephen did leave the police force and join the Army in April 1918 but, as this photograph shows both he (fifth from the back of this group) and his younger brother Frank (far right) participated in training sessions for the Army before that date. Their police background shows not only in their formal stance but also in the way they wore their military caps which mirrored the way they had to wear their policeman's helmets and caps.

Then in March an entertainment took place which would now be rightly frowned upon.

> "The Evenwood Nigger Troupe gave a concert in the Railey Fell Institute and rendered a lengthy programme of nigger songs, choruses and monologues."

In May an entertainment was arranged which was one of the very few that succumbed to the weather.

> "The village bandsmen turned out on Saturday evening dressed in their new band suits which gave them a smart and military appearance. To raise money to defray the cost of the suits they intended to give a concert on the Railey Fell Institute grounds but after playing a couple of pieces thunder showers intervened and the programme had to be abandoned."

John Mattimoe's second son, Stephen, left the police in April 1918 and joined the Army. He was to return safely and rejoin the Durham Constabulary in February 1919.

Spanish Flu, which would prove to be deadlier than the fighting on the Western Front, struck at home. In July the Auckland Chronicle reported that the illness had reached Evenwood and at one pit where forty six boys were employed only seven were present on one shift. One hundred and fifty cases were reported at nearby Coundon. The epidemic closed Ramshaw School. By November the paper reported seventeen deaths from influenza in one week at Cockfield.

Amongst this sadness the life of the village continued its normal path and the local paper was able to report that one of the winners at the Ramshaw Vegetable and Livestock Show held at the Railey Fell Institute in October was a Mrs Mattimoe who won first prize in the brown bread category. This was most likely Patrick's widow, Mary Ann but could have been her daughter-in-law, Sarah.

The reports of life in Ramshaw are a stark contrast to the hardships being suffered by civilians in the cities of Germany in 1918. The riots on the German home front together with a German Army now much weakened after four years War and a final push by the British, French and Belgian forces aided by the fit but inexperienced Americans was to bring the War to an end after four years. This last push by the Allied forces was to involve Stephen and Mary Ellen's son Frank.

13   Frank's Story

Frank Mattimoe was the second son of Stephen and Mary Ellen Mattimoe but his older brother died at the age of five so Frank donned the mantle of eldest son. He was born and brought up in Gordon Gill attending the local school and being taught by the no-nonsense James Moore. He grew up with a group of boys including his cousins and the sons of neighbours. They lived in the country with fields, woods and a stream nearby and, an added benefit for boys, amongst the current and past buildings and workings of the coal mines. The boys had no difficulty making their own entertainment but like boys everywhere the lure of the forbidden would have proved a strong draw leading to investigation of disused shafts and drifts as well as the big steam engine housed in the Gill to pump water from the mine workings. Frank and his cousins would have incurred the wrath of their parents from time to time but as most were of Irish descent the anger would have subsided as quickly as it rose to be replaced with smiles and laughter. Frank inherited this spirit that would make him popular amongst his friends but also get him into serious trouble.

Frank's family moved from the Gill to Eldon Lane in October 1911. Frank was determined not to follow his Father by finding work in the pits. Instead he initially found work as a barman but his life was to take a significant turn when Lucy Daykin of Eldon became pregnant with his son in early 1913. Frank seemed not to want to marry Lucy as she resorted to obtaining an affiliation order in January 1913 ordering him to pay maintenance of 3s per week until her son reached his thirteenth birthday. It does not seem a particularly amicable arrangement as Lucy is awarded costs of £3-9s-6d. It seems likely that Frank had moved to Middlesborough by this time or soon afterwards and worked for a short while in the steel industry.

The First World War had broken out on 5th August 1914 and after the initial confidence of "It'll be all over by Christmas" had been shaken by the losses and setbacks of the British Expeditionary Force in France recruitment began in earnest. Thus it was that in November 1915 Frank enlisted in the Army. He made a good impression and in February 1916 was made Lance Corporal. Four months later he found himself in trouble for the first, but not the last, time when he received a severe reprimand for neglect of duty whilst on active service at Gosforth.

It was at the time of enlistment, or soon after, that Frank met Hannah Smith from Middlesbrough who was to become his wife. The relationship in those troubled, unsettled times did not follow the traditional pattern. Hannah became pregnant and gave birth to their daughter Esther in September 1916. That September was an eventful month. Not only did he become a father for the second time but he was posted to the 81st Training Reserve Regiment stationed at Usworth and promoted to full Corporal.

Frank did not follow his mother's example in sound management of his finances. In June 1917 the Army made an Order for Stoppages of Pay against him in regard to what appear to have been arrears in maintenance payments to Lucy for his son. The amount of the stoppage was four pence equating to 2s 4d per week, eight pence less than the order Lucy had obtained from the Magistrates in Bishop Auckland. Earlier the same month Frank, who had been worried that he had not heard from Hannah thinking he may have upset her, writes thanking her for her letter and the money he had received from her which he hoped to pay back in the next two weeks. Hannah could not write so her letters must have been written for her by a relative or friend. In his letter Frank finalises the arrangements for their wedding. An Army friend

Fig. 86

Frank Mattimoe on duty with the 81st Training Reserve Regiment whilst based at Usworth. The trainees were living in tents. Frank was well thought of by the Regiment and was promoted to Lance Corporal but a hot-headed moment was to set in train a sequence of events with fatal consequences for young Frank.

was to be his Best Man and also provided initial accommodation for the couple in Middlesbrough.

Middlesbrough was in the middle of an influenza epidemic and out of bounds to service personnel; therefore Frank requested a pass for nearby Stockton. Frank and Hannah married in St. Patrick's Roman Catholic Church, Middlesbrough 14th July 1917.

Later that month Frank writes to Hannah to tell her he has arranged a pass, ostensibly to Stockton, to meet her and their baby daughter. In the letter he thanks Hannah for a further letter and money.

Frank received a further letter from Hannah which he replied to in late July. There had been some difficulty for Hannah with members of the Tully family who were related to Frank's Mother and lived in Middlesbrough. Frank tells her not to worry and in a blunt manner that he would sort things out on his return. He is still clearly short of money though this did not appear to stop him having a good time with his mates in true Mattimoe style. In a touching passage he tells Hannah not to worry about him as his battalion seemed set to stay in England for the foreseeable future. Events were soon to unfold which would undo his reassurance.

Frank Gets Into Trouble

On 5th August he is arraigned in front of his Lieutenant Colonel charged with striking a private soldier, found guilty and deprived of his rank. The offence seems relatively minor though the punishment inevitable for a corporal in a training regiment. The incident however was to have tragic consequences for Frank and Hannah.

The Training Battalion treated the offence seriously and transferred Frank out, consequently on 18th October 1917 he found himself embarking at Dover for the Western Front in France.

At this time the Western Front had long been established as a line of trenches running from the Belgian coast to the border of Switzerland. The local Bishop Auckland paper had for the previous year printed long lists of men from the area who had been killed, wounded or were missing in action. The Battle of Passchendaele, where over a quarter of a million soldiers of the opposing armies had been killed, had just taken place. It is not difficult to imagine the trepidation which Frank and the other soldiers would have felt when boarding the ship to France, nor the worry felt by his wife in Middlesbrough and his family back in Bishop Auckland.

On arrival at Boulogne Frank travelled ten miles south to Etaples near Le Touquet. Two days later he was transferred to the 2nd Battalion, Yorks and Lancs Regiment which was undergoing instructional training in the area. The Battalion strength at this time was thirty six Officers and seven hundred and ninety one Other Ranks.

The Battle of Cambrai

On 15th November the Battalion entrained for Peronne arriving in the evening from where the troops marched the 2 miles (3 kms) to their billets. Peronne was one of the towns that the Germans had destroyed the previous February in their withdrawal to the specially constructed line of defences known as the Hindenburg Line. The Battalion were to take part in an attack on the Hindenburg Line to become known as the Battle of Cambrai.

The Battalion took up position for the battle on the night of 19/20th November. Two platoons were sent into 'no man's land' to establish an outpost to prevent German patrols reaching the Battalion's lines.

The sun rose on a fine and misty morning. At 6.20am the British artillery, using a new electrical method for registering their guns providing greater accuracy, unleashed a hurricane bombardment from one thousand guns onto the German trenches. Almost simultaneously over three hundred tanks set off followed by waves of infantry from eight divisions. Frank's Battalion attacked in conjunction with troops on right and left. A Runners Post and Visual Signalling were quickly established to keep in touch with Battalion HQ.

The German garrison at Cambrai was surprised by the ferocity of the bombardment and the massed attack by tanks and infantry. This was the first time in the War that tanks had been used in such numbers and, although slow moving (3mph) and in danger of ditching when trying to cross the sunken roads that criss-crossed Flanders, they made a significant contribution to the battle. The tanks attacked in threes, the first engaging the enemy whilst the other two crossed the barbed wire defences and German trenches.

After two hours fighting the Battalion had advanced to the Hindenburg line and captured all its objectives and were consolidating their positions. Casualties were defined in the Battalion's War Diary as slight, namely three killed, and nineteen wounded. The Battalion captured six machine guns, three trench mortar machines and one heavy minenwerfer and crew. The minenwerfer was a heavy trench mortar whose shells made virtually no noise and were nicknamed 'Minnies' by the British troops. One hundred and seventy prisoners were also taken by the Battalion. Overall some ten thousand German troops surrendered on that first day of the battle, more than on any day in the war up to that point.

On 22nd Frank's Battalion were establishing a main line of resistance along the captured ground whilst numerous German planes flew very low trying to locate their position.

There was heavy enemy shelling the following morning, both where the Battalion had dug in and along the front line trenches. The Battalion incurred three casualties. They came under heavy shelling the next day suffering further casualties with two killed and seven wounded. The following two days were quiet with little shelling, though again numerous planes appeared over the Battalion's line. Then on 26th the Battalion was relieved and withdrew to the support line.

Despite success on both flanks where British forces advanced up to four miles with few casualties the centre of the German line still held. Following their initial setback the Germans assembled twenty divisions and counter-attacked. On 30th Frank's Battalion came under considerable shelling in the early part of the morning. At 10.00am news was received that the Germans had broken through the British line and the Battalion had to withdraw to form a defensive flank on the right. Arriving in a valley after tracking a considerable distance in open country orders were suddenly received for the Battalion to make an attack on a village with the aid of tanks. The order was cancelled but replaced with orders to take Quentin Ridge but this attack could not proceed owing to the dark and the difficulty tanks had in crossing the Sunken Road. The Battalion moved up across the Sunken Road and dug in. A further attack to capture the Ridge was ordered for 10am the following morning but owing to the considerable number of machine guns the advance was stopped.

Exchanges took place between the opposing sides on 1st December following which the Battalion was ordered to make an attack with the aid of tanks which failed owing to darkness setting in. They were again ordered to make an attack on Quentin Ridge at 1am but due to the suddenness of the order the attack had to be made without artillery support other than a few guns. The Battalion started to move forward but had not got far before the Germans became aware of them and brought up many more machine guns. In spite of this the Companies still went on until the fire of the enemy machine guns finally made them give up and they returned back to their former position. The Battalion suffered heavily in this encounter with two Officers killed and four wounded whilst about sixty five Other Ranks were killed, wounded or missing. One of those injured was Frank Mattimoe who received a gunshot wound to his forearm. He received initial treatment at a Field Dressing Station and was evacuated to the hospital in Etaples.

By the end of the battle British forces had managed to hold on to some of the ground gained on 20th November but had lost ground elsewhere thus the Battle of Cambrai ended in stalemate.

In twelve days of battle Frank's Battalion had suffered casualties of one hundred and five Officers and Other Ranks killed, wounded or missing, nearly one in eight of its complement. It had been Frank's first taste of battle. He had been on the Western Front for just one month. He had witnessed the first mass deployment of tanks and the use of planes. He encountered military success and setback, the hardship and danger of trench life when not at the battlefront plus the chaos that can follow a counter-attack. He had lost comrades and suffered injury himself.

Frank rejoined his Company on 16th January. They were now undergoing training in a back area away from the Front where they remained until 4th February with only a brief, uneventful time in the front line trenches where they relieved the Leicestershire Regiment.

In early February the Battalion provided labour for working parties, probably strengthening the defences of their new position. On the first day Frank committed a misdemeanour, details of which are not noted on his military record but the punishment of seven days Field Punishment Number One (FPN1) is recorded. FPN1 was harsh and humiliating. It could involve being handcuffed to a wagon wheel for up to two hours each day. In between there would extra duties, normally of the more unpleasant kind, and extra drill. FPN1 could be given for minor offences such as arriving late for parade.

German Offensive Spring 1918

In early 1918 the British Army was short of manpower. It reorganised, disbanding one hundred and forty five Battalions in order to strengthen the remainder. In early February Frank's Battalion was reinforced by eleven Officers and two hundred and twenty one Other Ranks from the disbanded 10th Battalion bringing its complement up to approximately 1,000.

In Spring of 1918 the Bolshevik Revolution removed the Russian threat on Germany's Eastern Front. This together with Germany's fear of the growing deployment of American Forces led their Army to make a decisive move on the Western Front. They moved their elite Divisions from the Eastern to the Western Front and on 21st March opened an attack on the area between Arras and Rheims with an awesome artillery barrage.

Frank's Battalion was one of those that bore the brunt of this attack. The War Diary records that at 5am on 21st March the German barrage, including high explosive and gas shells, commenced and was put down extremely heavy on Lagnicourt trench and the Sunken Road immediately in rear of the Battalion HQ. Only a slight barrage was put on the front line and reserve line until 7.30am when an intense barrage was put on the front line for one hour. It then lifted to the reserve line for fifteen minutes then returned to the front line where it remained with only a brief respite. The barrage lifted from Battalion HQ and Lagnicourt trench at 9am but by this time it had killed or wounded practically the whole of one Company. Only fifteen Other Ranks survived and managed to get back to the reserve line. The barrage did not however cut the wire of either the front line or reserve line.

The enemy attacked the Brigade on the Battalion's right and captured the front line. They spread out towards the Battalion's front line and, though the remnants of the Battalion fought hard for some time, they were forced back to the reserve line. They were gradually surrounded during the night, the enemy having got into the outskirts of Lagnicourt village, by this time no more than ruins which provided cover for the German troops as they worked down the streets behind the houses. Another Company was ordered to reinforce the reserve Company but having suffered a large number of casualties from the barrage could not provide much help. The Battalion's third Company were being flanked on both sides and also from the right rear and were eventually driven out of the line and withdrew. The fourth Company, who had moved into their battle position in Lagnicourt trench engaged the enemy advancing on them and fought it out to a finish. The only survivors were a few men who had been left behind in the dugouts. The Battalion HQ was nearly cut off and forced to withdraw to Vaulx Wood but the Battalion were driven out of there and fought as they went inflicting heavy casualties on the enemy. They eventually withdrew to Vaulx Morchies strengthening that garrison and stayed there the night.

Fig. 87   Frank Mattimoe's tour of duty on the Western Front from 18th October 1917 until he was killed in action at the Battle of St. Quentin on 18th September 1918.

Frank's Story

Dunkirk

Calais

········· Frank's tour of duty
— — — — Western Front
✻ Fighting involving Frank

Poperinghe ✻ **Ypres** *11 Apr 1918*
Dickesbusch ✻ **Lankhoff Farm**
13 Aug 1918 ✻ *5 Jun 1918*
Kemmel
28 Jun 1918

Arras
21 Mar 1918
Lagnicourt ✻
Vaulx Morcheis
Cambrai
19/20 Nov 1917
Bapaume

15 Nov 1917
Peronne
Amiens ✻ **Fresnoy-le-Petit**
1 Sep 1918 *18 Sep 1918* **St Quentin**

On the battlefield as a whole over seven thousand British soldiers died on this first day of the German offensive and twenty one thousand were taken prisoner.

On the morning of the 22nd the remaining one hundred and fifty with the remainder of another Regiment had orders to make a counter attack on Vaulx Wood but owing to the deadly fire of enemy machine guns it was impossible. The German army attacked along the Vaulx Morchies line and the Battalion fought until nearly surrounded when they withdrew to the next sunken road. After holding for a further hour against advancing Germans forces orders were received to withdraw to the Army line. The battalion was relieved at midnight but their respite was brief. At 9.15 am they received orders to dig in a position on the ridge Longeast Wood to Achiet-Le-Grand Baphume Railway as the enemy had broken through at Mory.

On 24th the Battalion entrained from Doullane for Rousebrouge. Whilst at the station a hostile plane flew over and dropped six bombs but no casualties were inflicted upon the Battalion.

Losses suffered by the Battalion during the offensive were twenty four Officers and three hundred and ninety one Other Ranks killed wounded and missing, 40% of its complement.

On 1st April the Battalion relieved another Battalion East of Ypres and then relieved the Buffs on the front line on 5th/6th. This area which had suffered heavy shelling was a sea of mud only accessible across duckboard paths. The trench map identifies this area as 'Hellfire Junction' a name no doubt earned during the ferocious fighting in this area.

By early April the German forces had advanced twenty miles since the start of the offensive but their push had stalled. Despite this the front line and support trenches remained under artillery attack suffering twelve casualties on 11th/12th from high explosive shells. The Battalion dug a new line which, due to further withdrawals, became the front line trench. There was a heavy barrage on 28th but the War Diary records "only a few casualties". In early May, the Battalion were in a support trench and came under

Photograph courtesy of the Imperial War Museum, London (Q8432)

Fig. 88 Soldiers of the Yorks and Lancs Regiment repairing damage to their trenches. The muddy, cold conditions are self-evident as is the limited protection provided by the trenches.

heavy shelling losing one Officer killed and ten Other Ranks wounded.

In early June brilliant sunshine and moonlit nights had the affect of curtailing enemy activity. Relief was short-lived for Frank and the rest of his Company because on 5th June they, together with Reid Company, some two Officers and sixty eight men, carried out a raid on Lankhoff Farm, zero hour being 11.15pm. Lankhoff Farm was a fortified position across the canal from the British positions. Some artillery cover was provided but the Farm was strongly held and the party came under heavy fire forcing them to withdraw. Eleven Other Ranks were wounded and one Officer and two Other Ranks posted missing.

The Battalion was reinforced by two Officers and fifty Other Ranks and on 12th June weather continued warm and sunny whilst they carried out musketry training and then returned to the front line on working parties relieved only by the Brigade Sports. On 21st the German artillery fired shrapnel over the line causing two casualties. By 28th June the Battalion were in trenches at Kemmel. The German Army was very active at night time with machine guns, rifle grenades, aerial darts, and trunenwerfer wounding one Officer and nine Other Ranks. The good weather continued into July when the Battalion relieved the Forces at Marin Farm Southeast of Poperinghe. There was shelling but they did not suffer any casualties. The Battalion was deployed burying cables and on Lewis Gun practice until 20th July, when it moved up to the front line North of Dickesbusch. The British artillery shelled the German lines at night.

Familiar names given to positions in this area such as Gordon House and Auckland Farm would have brought little comfort to Frank. Similarly, soldiers from north London would have viewed wryly the area known as Willesden Junction.

The Final Allied Push Begins

The War was about to enter its final decisive phase on the Western Front. Two factors were critical at this time. Firstly the Allies superiority in tanks. Whilst the German Army had approximately two hundred, most of which were captured British and French tanks, the British had five hundred and the French also had several hundred tanks. The other key factor was the American Army which by August had four million men mobilised or in training. An American Expeditionary Force of one million men had already reached France. These were, not surprisingly, noticeably stronger and well fed when compared to their equivalents in the British, French and particularly German armies who had endured and survived four years of gruelling, horrific war the like of which had never been experienced before. The Americans strengthened the French Army substantially and successfully saw action alongside them in the Second Battle of the Marne. Other American units bolstered the strength of British Army Divisions. On 27th July one such unit joined Frank's Battalion for instructional purposes. The shelling from German artillery that night would have left the Americans in no doubt as to the difficult and dangerous task they faced alongside the British.

In early August the Battalion was in Brigade reserve. Their role was to counter attack any part of the Dickesbusch line penetrated by the enemy. The 105th American Army were undergoing trench training with the Battalion. The back areas continued to be shelled by the German artillery.

On 13th August the Battalion were in the front line at Dickesbusch with the American 107th facing Germans described as "fairly good" who were active with artillery and machine gun fire. . Orders were that the line was to be held at all costs. On 16th the good weather broke temporarily and the afternoon was very wet making for uncomfortable conditions in the trenches. That evening an artillery barrage dropped near the first line killing eight and wounding twenty five men.

On 21st August Frank received a gunshot wound to the chest and was admitted to the 177 Ambulance station. It does not appear to have been a serious injury as he rejoined his Company on the 24th.

On 1st September the Battalion entrained to Heilly and then onto Amiens from where on 8th August a tank led attack had succeeded in pushing the German Army back to the Hindenburg Line.

Amongst all the preparations for the next battle the Brigade Horse Show was held on the afternoon 10th September. The war had started with mass movements of mounted cavalry but trench warfare had made mounted cavalry attacks impractical. The horse remained important to the Army as the "engine" to pull its supply transport, ambulances and artillery pieces though even here motorised transport was becoming increasingly important as the war progressed. Despite ample evidence the horse would never again play the key role it had in the wars of the previous century it seems the Army still valued horsemanship skills enough to parade them, virtually on the eve of the battle where tanks would undertake the driving role previously belonging to the cavalry. The horse show was a morale boosting exercise. Events included show-jumping, racing, tent pegging and wrestling on horse-back. Prizes were awarded for the best turned out horse and waggon teams. Horses were dressed up and some soldiers donned fancy dress in the characters of the day such as Charlie Chaplin.

It was about this time that Frank was to make one last fateful decision. He was due to go on leave which would have spared his participation in the coming battle to take St. Quentin. Instead of accepting leave he agreed to another man going in his place. This man also wanted to see his wife and daughter and it is quite possible that he had waited longer than Frank for a spell of leave but as a result of his generous act Frank was never to see his own wife and daughter again.

Photograph courtesy of the Imperial War Museum, London (Q5521)

Fig. 89 Horseback wrestling was one of the less serious events of the Brigade Horse Show though keenly contested as can be seen from this photograph. It provided an opportunity for the lower ranks to participate and for the onlookers to give partisan support to entrants from their battalion or company whilst probably engaging in some illicit wagering on the results. The horses, some of whom, were dressed up for this or other events, were the draught horses which provided the power to move the army's heavy equipment and artillery. They were in use as such throughout the war suffering heavy losses, injuries and terrible hardships in the process.

The Battle for St. Quentin

In the early hours of 11th September the Battalion marched to Fouilloy then three days later embussed to Tertry where the men were quartered in bivouacs. The battle objective was to capture St. Quentin which, following attacks by the British and Australians during the previous few weeks, and despite counter attacks by the Germans, was only three and a half miles beyond the front line. The good weather started to break. The date set for the attack was the 18th. Assembly of Frank's Battalion, part of 6th Division, began on 17th. The War Diary records the following.

> "About 3pm the battalion moved to assembly positions just west of St. Quentin Wood, and took cover in the wood until midnight. Weather:- fine but threatening.
> About midnight ... the battalion moved forward to assembly positions S.E. of Badger Copse ... Battalion HQ was situated in the quarry in St. Quentin Wood. Whilst in these assembly positions rain fell heavily and the companies were shelled considerably with high explosive and gas.
> At 5.20 am under a splendid creeping barrage the battalion moved forward to the attack on enemy positions. The entire objectives allotted to the battalion and named the Green Line, being the line of Douai Trench, Champagne Trench and Fresnoy Trench ... were captured ... at 6.30am. At 10am a determined enemy counter attack was delivered ... from the direction of Fresnoy Cemetery and Wood. This counter attack succeeded in driving our left Company (to which Frank belonged) back into Champagne Trench. Mainly on account of

Photograph courtesy of the Imperial War Museum, London (Q9365)

Fig. 90 In this photograph taken during the battle for St. Quentin British troops can be seen at rest during a lull in the fighting. A group of German prisoners sit and stand resignedly amongst their captors who themselves show little interest in them. In the distance three of the tanks display the mounted equipment used to help them cross the German trenches.

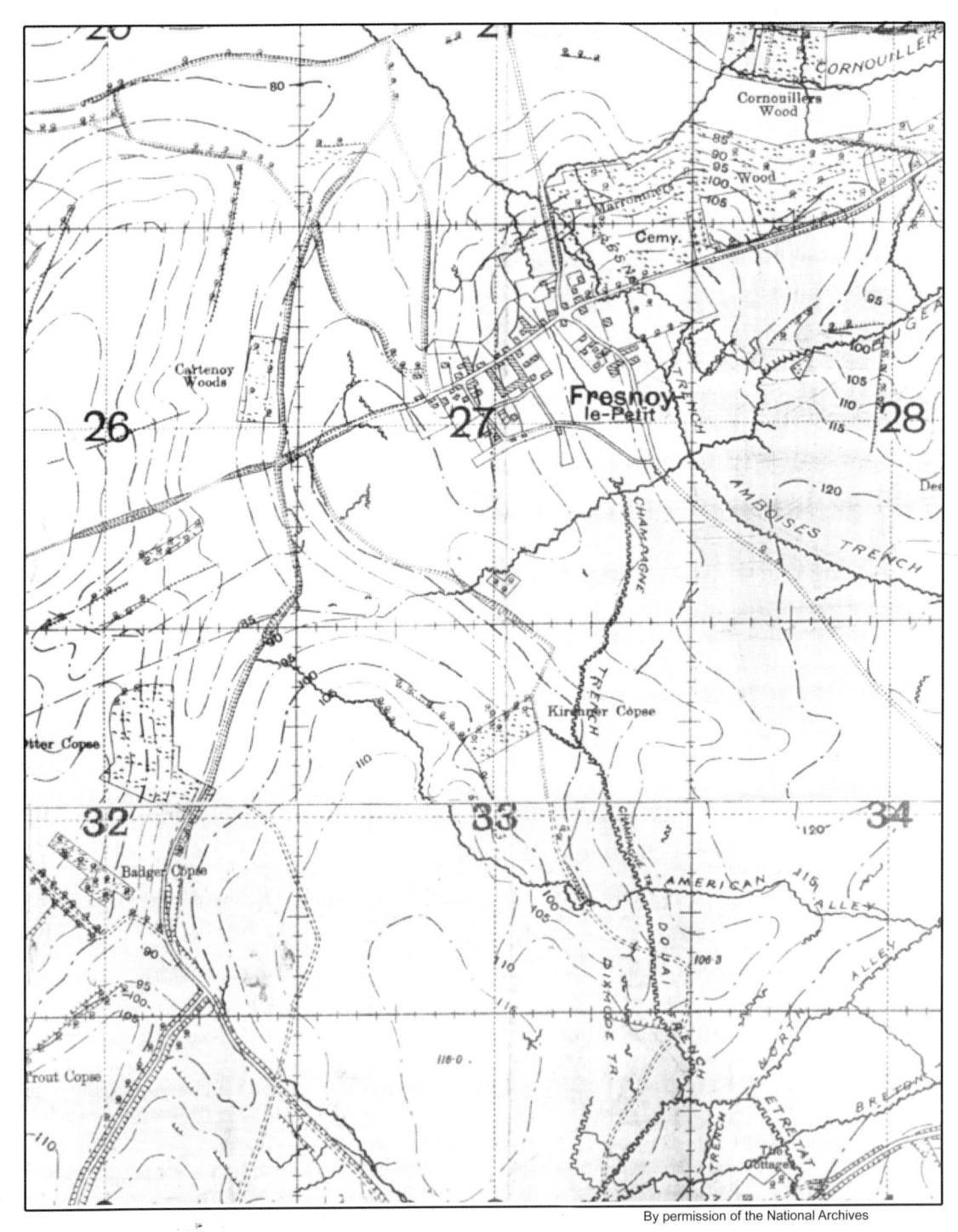

Fig. 91 Trench map of the area south of Fresnoy le Petit where Frank Mattimoe's Company attacked the Douai, Champagne and Fresnoy trenches from Badger Copse, three quarters of a mile to the east. The slightly rising ground would have provided some cover during the initial stages of the advance but they would soon have come under direct fire from the German trenches. Despite this they captured the trenches and held them until a fierce counter attack from the German stronghold in Fresnoy Wood and cemetery forced them back to the Champagne trench.

casualties suffered during the advance, the left Company was too weak to counter attack. From the junction of Champagne Trench and Bugeaud Alley, the Green Line southwards was held and consolidated.

As a result of these operations about 50 prisoners were captured and many enemy left dead. The casualties suffered during the advance, by the battalion were :-

| Officers | killed | 3 | Wounded | 2 | Missing | 1 |
| Other Ranks | killed | 27 | Wounded | 140 | Missing | 43" |

Sadly Frank Mattimoe, who's Company, had faced the stiffest resistance from Fresnoy Cemetery and Wood, was one of the Other Ranks killed. He had been in France eleven months, fought in three major battles, been injured twice and then made the ultimate sacrifice.

The 6th Division's attack on the 18th together with that of the 1st Division gained 3,000 yards on that first day. The heavy rain had created slippery conditions which severely disadvantaged tanks. The strong German response from Fresnoy Cemetery is accounted for by the fact that it contained a Redoubt, a strongly fortified position, which was the location of a German Brigade Head Quarters. A further Redoubt known as the Quadrilateral was just beyond the Douai Trench east of Holnon Wood and many British lives were lost in overcoming both this and the Fresnoy Redoubt.

The battle for St. Quentin continued with much hard fighting until the town was entered by French troops on 1st October. The surrounding area was not fully liberated until 25th October but the battle, part of a major offensive along the Western Front, was decisive in bringing the War to an end. By the beginning of October the German Army was ready to sue for peace and on 11th November the Armistice was signed.

Buried in France

Frank Mattimoe was buried in Trefcon British Military Cemetery situated just outside Caulaincourt on the left of the road to Trefcon, 14 kms west of St. Quentin. On a warm, sunny October day in 2002 eighty four years after the battle I visited the cemetery. Frank's grave is in the front row flanked by those of his comrades from the Yorks and Lancs Regiment and soldiers of the Durham Light Infantry who also fell in the action to retake the two villages. Frank's name has been spelt Mattimore as it has on the war memorial in Middlesbrough.

The cemetery is not large. It contains approximately three hundred graves and is in a very peaceful location surrounded by trees. One of the stone pillars at the entrance to the cemetery has a cubby hole which contains a register listing the details of all those buried, including next of kin. There is also a visitors book which showed that the cemetery, though small and not signposted from the main road, was visited several times a month, sometimes by those paying their respects to one soldier in particular as I was but also by others moved by the sight of the graves of those who died and should not be forgotten.

Frank's wife Hannah received notification of her husband's death in a letter dated 7th October. Hannah subsequently visited Frank's family and in their shared sadness was insistent they keep contact with Frank's daughter Esther. Hannah kept her word. Cornelius and his brother Tommy would travel to Middlesbrough, a difficult journey in those days, and bring Esther back to Leeholme for holidays from the age of four until she was fifteen years old and able to make the journey on her own. Esther became particularly close to her cousin Mary, daughter of Cornelius. When I met Mary in 2003 she spoke fondly of Esther and said that they were more like sisters than cousins and had stayed close until Esther's death earlier that year. Hannah married again but that did not alter her commitment to Frank's family.

14 Jubilation and Depression

The signing of the Armistice led to great rejoicing throughout the country with Evenwood and Ramshaw being no exception as the local paper recorded.

"Local buzzers were blown as a signal that hostilities had ceased. The glad event was celebrated by young and old. The village band played national and patriotic tunes on the village green and some dance music to which many 'tripped the light fantastic toe'. Children at Ramshaw School were given a half day holiday. A feature of Monday night's celebration was a parade of the village children waving their flags."

Many local families were still mourning the loss of husbands, fathers and sons. Stephen Mattimoe and his wife Mary Ellen were mourning the death of their son Frank news of which had been received a month earlier. Frank's wife Hannah received her husband's medals three days after the Armistice was declared.

Other families were celebrating the return of loved ones. John Mattimoe's eldest sons Tom and Stephen returned home safely in early 1919.

The local paper reflected this bitter sweet time carrying stories of returning soldiers together with details of others whose fate had been changed from 'missing in action' to 'killed'. The influenza epidemic was still raging leaving deaths in its wake including the wife of Cornelius Gaffney, son of Teddy whose altercation with the school teacher James Moore twenty seven years earlier had enlivened proceedings at Ramshaw School.

Despite the number of local families who had lost loved ones in the war and the Spanish flu epidemic the residents of Ramshaw and Evenwood were still able to welcome the peace. The inhabitants of nearby Bishop Auckland had been criticised in the local paper for their apathy and lack of support for a dinner laid on in honour of returning soldiers. The village of Ramshaw, however, showed no such apathy and at a party to celebrate peace the village band led a parade of children to the venue where ex soldiers, sailors, children and adults over sixty years of age were able to enjoy a free feast and all present were able to enjoy the sports including 'foot running', tug-of-war and quoits.

Then in June 1921 the Evenwood Village Band led a parade of ex soldiers sailors, Girl Guides and Boy Scouts through the village to the cemetery where a memorial obelisk to those who had given their lives in the Great War was unveiled. The band played stirring music and concluded by sounding the Last Post.

Black and Tans

Those of Irish descent maintained a strong affiliation with Ireland. Many were the children or grandchildren of Irishmen who had emigrated from the Old Country. In the years following the First World War there was a strong feeling amongst the Irish that the British Government had reneged on its promise, made during the conflict that Ireland would be granted Home Rule in return for Irishmen joining the British Forces. The Irishmen had kept their side of the bargain and acquitted themselves with gallantry but the Government refused to grant Home Rule. This perceived injustice strengthened the Irish communities bond with each other. For most this saw expression in the singing of 'Rebel' songs when they gathered together.

One other development during this period further strengthened sympathy for the Irish not only from those of Irish descent in Great Britain but also the public at large. This was the establishment of the Black and Tans. In the early 1900's action by the IRA, including attacks on police stations and barracks, made it difficult for the British Government to recruit policemen into the Royal Irish Constabulary. Their response was to advertise on mainland Britain for men who were willing to "face a rough and dangerous task" by serving alongside the RIC. The pay was ten shillings a day and many ex-soldiers were recruited. These men were soldiers not policemen and an ill-disciplined poorly trained force resulted. They proved to be a brutal, ill-disciplined and lawless force which terrorised and committed atrocities against the civilian population of Ireland. This was not by accident as shown by the following alleged extract of a speech to his constables by a recently appointed Division Commander of the RIC in June 1920 by which time fifty five constables had been killed, sixteen barracks destroyed and hundreds abandoned.

> "....If a police barracks is burned or if the barracks already occupied is not suitable, then the best house in the locality is to be commandeered, the occupants thrown into the gutter. Let them die there - the more the merrier. Police and military will patrol the country at least five nights a week. They are not to confine themselves to the main roads, but make across the country, lie in ambush and, when civilians are seen approaching, shout "Hands up!" Should the order be not immediately obeyed, shoot and shoot with effect. If the persons approaching carry their hands in their pockets, or are in any way suspicious-looking, shoot them down. You may make mistakes occasionally and innocent persons may be shot, but that cannot be helped, and you are bound to get the right parties some time. The more you shoot, the better I will like you, and I assure you no policeman will get into trouble for shooting any man ..."

One person I spoke to, eighty years later retained the vivid memories and perceptions of those times and told me:

> "England promised the Irish home rule if they joined up to fight during the First World War. As soon as England got on top they went back on the promise. So the Irish rebelled and because the English soldiers would not fight them they got all the scum of Britain, they emptied the prisons, and formed the Black and Tans."

These views were shared by the rest of the Irish community and their descendants. My mother remembered her mother, Molly, talking about the Black and Tans with anger and disgust.

Jackie's Moran's father was serving with the British Army in Ireland at the time of the troubles and whilst on duty on the bridge in Dublin a crowd approached. He fired warning shots over their heads but they kept coming and he was tipped over the bridge into the Liffey with a full pack on. If he had not been a champion swimmer he would have drowned.

The local Irish communities knew who had been recruited locally into the 'Tans'. A relative of Jackie's wife married a man down South and when they met him he told them he once had this good Government job in Ireland. Jackie asked him "Were you a 'Tan'?" He never answered so Jackie knew.

News of the activities and reputation of the Black and Tans spread beyond the shores of Great Britain and affected the Armies Irish Regiments. The Connaught Rangers were a well respected force who had served Britain with valour and distinction in many campaigns including the Napoleonic Wars and then the Peninsula Wars under Wellington who had said of them "I don't know what effect they'll have on the enemy, but by Gad they terrify me". They had served bravely during World War I in various theatres including the Dardenelles and France. In a link with the Mattimoe's home land the Connaught Rangers had their headquarters in Kings House in Boyle. My paternal Grandmother's half brother, Brian

Little Ireland

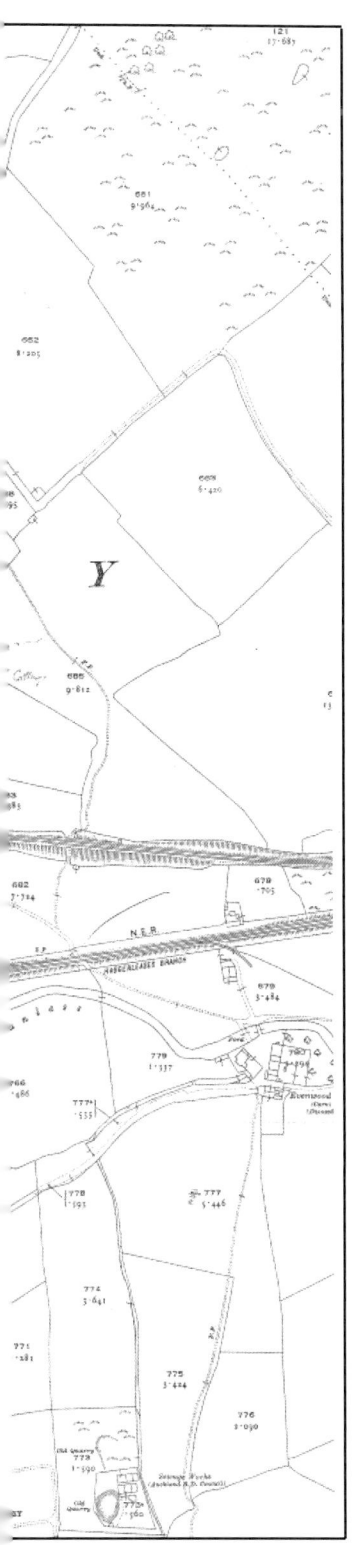

Fig. 92

By 1921 the revised Ordnance Survey map, scale 1:2500, covering Ramshaw shows some significant changes since the previous edition in 1897. Norwood Colliery had closed and its buildings, tramways and rail links to the Haggerleases line removed. Only the excavations in the ground give away their earlier location.

Railey Fell appeared to have expanded. The drift mines along Gordon Beck had been abandoned but a major new drift had been opened to the west of Gordon Beck. This drift was served by a direct rail link to the Barnard Castle/Bishop Auckland line which was now carrying goods as well as passenger traffic. A second rail link ran along Gordon Beck then branched off to drifts at Gordon Bank Top to the north where it, and a tramway were served by a steam driven haulage engine. A bridge crossed the tramway near Gordon Gill. The houses in the Gill no longer had to endure the sound of the steam engine and pump running day and night as this had been removed and the building housing it demolished following a downturn in the coal industry some years earlier. However they now had the noise and danger, particularly to their children of the unmanned trucks running up and down the rail link. Sand Hole drift had been abandoned but the tramway serving it had been extended to service new drifts to the north.

The changes in mining had at best maintained the level of employment in the area and hard times were soon to follow therefore there had been no house building since 1897. Today the pattern of housing in the area differs little from that shown on this map.

Old Ramshaw School was now the Institute and the new school can be found north of the Oaks on the road winding up from Evenwood Bridge toward Evenwood itself.

Whilst the countryside still retained its rural and agricultural outlook Evenwood Corn Mill had closed and was now disused.

Mulholland, had fought with them in World War I in France and then, as a sergeant, fought with them in Afghanistan where he was killed in action in the hills just across the border in what is now Pakistan and is buried in the grounds of a roadhouse.

When the Black and Tans were in Ireland the Connaught Rangers were in India. On hearing the stories of the treatment being handed out to their fellow Irishmen the Connaught Rangers mutinied. This was not a violent mutiny, the troops just refused to go on duty and made it clear they would hand over peacably to a relieving regiment. A number of soldiers were court martialled and one was executed by a firing squad. On establishment of the Irish Free State the Regiment was disbanded and a number of soldiers who had been court martialled, including four from Boyle in Co. Roscommon, were released. When the four returned home they were greeted by a large enthusiastic crowd of well-wishers on arrival at Boyle station.

Happiness and Sadness in the Mattimoe and Hannon Families

The mixture of happiness and sadness felt by the general population in these post-war years was reflected in the family lives of the Mattimoe's. John Mattimoe lost a grandchild in February 1919 when Winifred the daughter of Frank ad Nellie died. The sadness of this loss was to a degree assuaged by the birth of Frank and Nellie's daughter Veronica, always known as Ronnie, in September 1920. Before his death in July 1922 John gained two further grandchildren, Nora in November 1919 and Monica in December 1921, the children of his daughter Molly and her husband Willy. The two Mattimoe families were to complete their families in the inter-war years with the births of Mary, Stephen, and Ann to Frank and Nellie, and Peggy and Betty to Molly and Willy. John's son Leo and his wife Ginny had three children Annie, Jean and John.

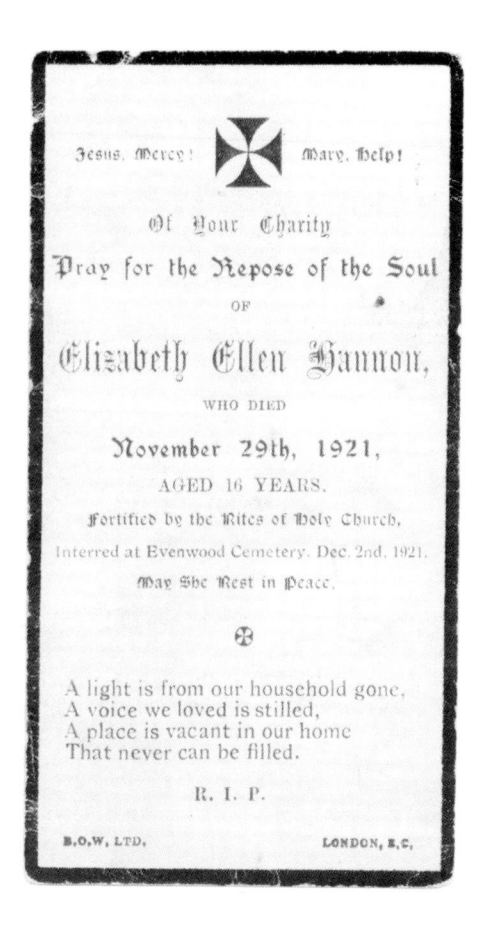

After the death of their son Mattie Annie and Thomas Hannon were to suffer the loss of two daughters. The Auckland & County Chronicle recorded the death of Elizabeth Ellen in December 1921.

> "Mr and Mrs Hannon, Gordon Lane, Evenwood, have sustained another bereavement by the death of their daughter, Elizabeth Ellen, aged 16 years and eight months. The funeral took place on Friday, the Catholic priest from Witton Park officiating. Mr and Mrs Hannon have a large family, and much sympathy is felt for them."

Annie and Thomas then lost their daughter, Mary, in July 1922. Mary had entered service but caught pnuemonia by sleeping in a damp bed and died at home.

Fig. 93 Memory card for Elizabeth Ellen Hannon

Fig. 94

This faded photograph has been included because it is the only image the family have of Mary, the young woman standing with Kitty, her youngest sister. It is probably her elder brother John who is taking the photograph whilst two of her other brothers, Joe and Tom looked on from the doorway of the house. It seems likely that the photograph was taken outside the house of Frank Hannon, Mary's uncle, in Stanley, Co. Durham.

Mary went in to service at a house in barnard Castle but caught pneumonia from sleeping in a damp bed and died at the age of nineteen only a few months after this photograph was taken.

1922 Miner's Strike

The ending of the war which had rightly been so joyously welcomed now produced a sting in its tail. Britain's export trade reduced dramatically as its traditional trading partners dealt with the war's aftermath. This affected the staple industries such as coal by reducing both export demand and demand at home from the industries they served. There were early signs of industrial unrest when local life was affected by a railwaymen's strike. Coal mining, like the other staple industries, was also suffering from under investment during the war years. Consequently, after an initial period of prosperity, an economic depression set in during 1920 impacting the coal industry and its workers. The Auckland Chronicle noted that by March 1921 local mines were idle on Saturdays and Railey Fell had laid off thirty men.

In April 1921 the Mineowners reacted to the poor market conditions by offering lower wages combined with a 'lockout'. The miners went on strike against the imposed reduction. In 1915 they had forged a 'triple alliance' with the railway and transport workers, where each agreed to support a partner calling a strike. The Miners partners in the alliance initially committed to join the strike but in the event a disagreement within the alliance lead almost immediately to its collapse on a day which became known as 'Black Friday' because of its impact upon the union and labour movement. The miners were left to continue the strike on their own.

There was strong support for the strike amongst miners. In May there was a mass meeting of miners on Evenwood Village Green at which the Silver Band played. Hardship was quick to show itself in the mining communities.

Miners were quick to find coal from other sources such as disused drifts for their own needs. In one instance this quickly achieved the scale of an industrial process which drew an equally quick response from the Owners as the Auckland Chronicle recorded in May.

> "The old Carterthorne Pit, disused since about 1898, has been yielding coal of profiteers, but the boon was too good to last, and Messrs Pease & Partners have posted a notice on the gate leading to the drift that no person will in future be allowed to take coal away without first securing a permit, and that not more than three cwts will be allowed to each person.
>
> This old drift is situated near Toft Hill and Hamsterley. It was known to the old miners in the Witton Park district who worked it years ago, and a few days after coal dissents commenced some of these miners tackled the old drifts and began to hew in earnest. They were followed by hundreds and soon it became known in most of the districts west of Bishop Auckland that coal in plenty was to be had for the working.
>
> The old drift became again a busy hive as carts, hand-carts and motor lorries passed into the field, and some hundreds of tons changed hands at about 7s 6d (37.5p) to fetch and made as much as 70s (£3 50p) on delivery. Householders in Witton Park and district are said to have stored it in every conceivable place they could find, even using bedrooms.
>
> It is rather a laborious process bringing the coal to bank, for the only way is to hand it up by bucket. However it is easy to get and men, working in batches of half a dozen and staking out the best 'claims' are said to have drawn as much as 20 to 30 tons a day, and to have earned anything from £20 to £30 a week"

The earnings quoted were a fortune compared to the average miners wage of £2 10s a fortnight at that time. It should not be construed from the above, despite the mention of hundreds involved, that the activities described benefited more than a small percentage of the workforce. The majority suffered significant deprivation during the strike.

In Evenwood the local paper recorded in June.

> "During the last five weeks an average of 360 children have been provided daily with a substantial free dinner in the Comrades Hall. The funds have been obtained by public subscription and gifts of goods by tradesmen and farmers and from the sale of coal won from 'snecker' drifts. The cooking and serving has been done by a large number of voluntary workers representative of all the churches and other organisations."

At nearby Coundon in early June three hundred children under two years old were receiving free meals daily and, two months into the strike a staggering fifty seven thousand free meals had been provided to school children. The meals were hearty and wholesome as detailed by the local paper.

> "Some days they have soup. On others dumplings, meat and green peas or meat, beans and mashed potatoes. They are given two meals a day breakfast and dinner."

By mid July the strike was over though it would be months before the local mines resumed full-time working. The restart at Randolph Colliery was delayed and by October was only working three days a week. Eldon Lane Colliery was working erratically by October when in one week only one shift was worked. It did not resume a six day working week until the middle of February the following year.

The strike had one other consequence. It warned the Government of the potential economic disruption of such strikes and they made contingency plans which proved an effective counter to the General Strike five years later.

In November 1921, when the depression and the aftermath of the strike was at its severest, the Bishop Auckland Employment Committee, responsible for an area covering Bishop Auckland, Spennymoor, Crook, Shildon, Cockfield, Wolsingham and Weardale reported 18,104 unemployed and a further 373 on short time, the highest figure of any district in the North East.

Fig. 95 Randolph Colliery, Evenwood. Unlike the mines at nearby Ramshaw this was a deep shaft pit with winding gear to lower and retrieve both miners and the coal trucks.

The General Strike

By the next April unemployment had reduced to 11,667 and was down to 4,510 by April 1923. In the continuing improved economic situation of the following year miners negotiated a wage increase with representatives of the Coalowners. The economic improvement was not maintained and by May 1925 there were over 10,000 people unemployed in the District. Those still employed in the mines received unwelcome news in July when the Coalowners announced their proposal not to implement the wage increase but instead to pay reduced wages and impose longer working hours. This time the members miners, railwaymen and transport workers acted in unison and imposed an embargo on the movement of coal. The Government, alarmed by the development agreed to a Royal Commission which would determine how to resolve the situation and in the meantime agreed to subsidise the miners' wages until 1st May 1926. The miners and their allies called off their industrial action on a day which became known as 'Red Friday'.

The subsidy maintained the wages for miners in work but did nothing for the unemployed, nor was it intended to. Consequently the level of unemployment had changed little by February 1926 when 120 Bishop Auckland miners left to work in the Derbyshire mines. The photos in the local paper of their rousing sendoff from Bishop Auckland station were reminiscent of pictures that had appeared twelve years earlier of soldiers leaving to enlist in the Army. The experience was not to every miners liking and 25 returned the following week complaining of the working conditions in Derbyshire including the reduced coal allowance and loss of rent allowance.

On 1st May 1926 the Samuel Report by the Royal Commission was published. Its findings and recommendations were not unexpected but were still a bitter disappointment to the miners. Whilst generally sympathetic to them it stated they had to accept lower wages and longer working hours for a 'temporary period'. The miners leaders rejected this view coining the slogan 'not a penny off the pay, not a second on the day' and sought support from other key industries in a General Strike. This was not intended to bring every worker out on strike but was targeted at strategic industries such as transport and manufacturing. One and three quarter million workers joined the strike in support of the one million miners and most remained out for its duration. The strike paralysed the country.

The Government had learnt from the earlier miners strike. The time taken by the Royal Commission had enabled it, and industry, to make preparations to mitigate the effect of the strike. They controlled the media in the form of the BBC. In a class ridden society strike breaking volunteers, drawn primarily from the middle and upper classes including undergraduates were brought in to drive trains and buses and move goods and even print The Times newspaper. In contrast the Unions appeared poorly prepared and consequently the strike was called off after nine days on 12th May ostensibly after successful negotiations with the Government though in practice no significant concessions had been won. As in the 1922 strike the miners were left to continue their bitter struggle alone.

The Auckland Chronicle made little reference to the issues of the strike but did describe how the mining communities of Evenwood and Ramshaw responded to the hardship caused by the strike. Provision was made to feed the children of the community. In June an article described the feeding of children between the ages of three and fourteen. They received breakfast, and a dinner of potato hash and rice pudding. A tea was provided of cocoa with slices of bread and butter spread thickly with jam or syrup. In the July members of the Evenwood Workmen's Club and Institute provided a tea for over a thousand children from Evenwood and Ramshaw. The following month the children of Ramshaw were given a tea at the local Institute and at the same venue in October a dance was held to raise money in aid of the Children's Boot Fund.

Neither were the old folk ignored as evidenced by a picture in the Auckland Chronicle with the following caption.

> "unemployed miners in the Evenwood District spent the whole of Tuesday working at the
> Old Norwood Drift in search of coal for the aged miners and their wives".

By the end of October the paper was able to report that "the drift back [to work] in the District continues" though those working were often met with stone throwing when leaving the mines. The strike was unsustainable. At the end of November a vote by miners for continuing the strike failed to get the required two thirds majority and the strike came to an end. Apathy amongst the miners was blamed but they had held out for nearly seven months and there was no realistic prospect of their demands being met. They had no option but to accept the lower wages and the extra hour on the working day.

Aftermath of the Strike

The strike had a severe impact upon the economic future of the local mines. In April 1927 the local paper reported that -

> "The industrial outlook in the Ramshaw district is bad, and the employees of Railey Fell
> Colliery have received 14 days notice to terminate their employment."

Two months later a more serious blow fell when it announced that -

> "Whit week-end was somewhat marred by the closing down of Randolph Colliery, which affected
> a wide district including Evenwood, Ramshaw, West Auckland, Ingleton and Toft Hill."

At Leasingthorne Colliery, where Stephen Mattimoe, his sons and his nephew Tom worked, selfless action was taken by the workforce to provide additional work for the men in their community.

> "the quarterly cavils were drawn at the Leasingthorne Colliery on Thursday last. With the addition of another shift made possible by the piece workers agreeing to a reduction ranging from 5 to 10 per cent, more hewers etc. were caviled."

In October 1929 Railey Fell reopened after being closed for three years and at the end of that year the Auckland Chronicle reported more good news–

> "It is officially settled that all hands (1,000 in number) will restart work at Randolph Colliery on Monday, and the cavils will be drawn this week."

This welcome news did not remove the need locally for charitable assistance to alleviate the plight of the unemployed and their families as seen by reports at the beginning of 1930.

> "A quantity of milk, cocoa and sugar were distributed at the Temperance Hall, Evenwood. The food was sent to the Randolph Lodge secretary through the appeal for distressed miners."
>
> "The Salvation Army is to open a soup kitchen at Evenwood shortly for distressed miner's children."

The coal industry limped through the early 1930's. The welcome news of men being reemployed at mines was often followed, barely a few months later, with news of men being laid off, often at the same pit. In June 1930 1,800 miners received notice at Leasingthorne Colliery. From this low point improvement was slow until the outbreak of the Second World War. Government training schemes, often referred to as 'Dole School', trained young men in new skills but did little to stimulate the local economy. John Armstrong, no relation but a life long friend of the family, remembers that the family would pass through his family's farm at Morley on the way to church at Witton Park and pop in to see them on the way back. During the years of the depression Peter Mattimoe's son, Tommy, would help out on the farm. The meal he received was thanks enough in those times of hardship.

Fig. 96

Peter Mattimoe's son, Tommy, second from the right in the front row. He was on a working holiday arranged for unemployed men during the 1930's.

James Moore Retires as Headmaster

In March 1923 James Moore retired as Master of Ramshaw School. He had been in the post for nearly forty two years. He had overseen the development of the school from a Church school funded by the local mine owner to Local Authority funding and from the crowded 'one room' environment of the original building to the 'new' school which the local children still attend. With strict discipline he had ensured that the children in his charge gained a sound grounding in the three 'R's' and developed an understanding of the world and their place within it enabling them to grow into sound members of their community. In his final entry in the school log in which he had assiduously recorded the business of the school for over forty years he noted his departure with the simple words.

"I terminate my engagement as Head Teacher of this school today"

On 9th April William James Weatherley took up the post of head teacher. This heralded a new approach to teaching at the school, encouraging self expression by the children. William's love was music and he quickly shared his passion with the children. Within three years a choir had been formed and had reached a standard sufficient to attend a local music festival as William records in the school log.

"School closed all day as the school choir will be taking part in the Barnard Castle Musical Tournament where they were awarded second prize gaining 179 marks out of 200."

The school improved on this good result when the following year the log notes.

"School choir gained a first and two second prizes at Barnard Castle Music festival. Also won the Dawson shield for highest marks in Classes 7, 8 or 9."

Seventy six years later Irene Welsh nee Burnie, who sang in that choir as a girl still remembered with pride the excitement of that event and the choir's achievement.

The log continued to reflect the economic hardship under which local families lived as in September 1926, at which time the miners had been on strike for four months.

"The attendance has fallen today owing to heavy rain. Many children have been unable to travel to school because of defective boots."

More seriously however a visit in 1928 by the newly appointed School Medical Officer, at a time when both local mines had shut down, identified nineteen children suffering from malnutrition, approximately ten per cent of the school roll. The following year fourteen children were noted as receiving breakfast and dinner provided by the school. In February 1932 the Depression was preventing any significant improvement.

"Dr. D S Buchanan visited the school this afternoon to examine the children being fed and the others. He certified 7 more as suffering from malnutrition. These are to be fed from Monday 17th Feb."

Despite the physical hardships the new approach to teaching in the school was bearing fruit. The school log records the names of pupils who had been successful in obtaining scholarships and the Inspectors noted the following in their report.

"In recent years the progress made in this school is phenomenal. The children display a confidence and a natural freedom of manner which mark a happy blend of thorough and intensive training and a spirit of willing and industrious work. The atmosphere is one of hopeful endeavour, initiative and alertness."

William James Weatherley left Ramshaw School in November 1939 to take up duties as headmaster at the New Seaham Boys School, but the Inspectors report from seven years before his departure makes a fitting tribute to the new spirit and enlightened approach he had brought to teaching at the local school.

Local Difficulties

Alongside the economic difficulties the residents of Ramshaw endured during the years between the wars the weather added its own difficulties. The local paper portrays this period as a time of balmy hot summers contrasting with harsh snowy winters. Within this pattern other extreme events occurred as in August 1927 when it reported the following.

> "Unprecedented scenes were witnessed at Evenwood on Monday caused by the sudden and heavy rainfall.
> Many of the low-lying houses were flooded and fields were inundated with water.
> The bridge allotments near the River Gaunless suffered severely some of the crops being washed out and in one or two cases covered with debris a foot thick so that there is now no trace of a garden.
> At Railey Fell timber and other matter was swept out of the pit yard on to the highway. At the crossing motorists had a difficult passage when the water was running two or three feet deep.
> Here a serious accident was narrowly averted. A girl went into the water to retrieve pieces of wood and a married sister, seeing her danger, rushed in to bring her out. Both were caught by the main stream which was passing at a terrific rate through an archway under the railway, and a bus driver and another man went to their assistance and succeeded in rescuing them.
> A large amount of small coal has been washed down the Gaunless and lodged in the allotments.
> A large pitfall occurred in a field near Oaks Bank, expected, it is supposed by the heavy rainfall.
> A house known as The Ford, the residence of Mr. Weatherley, schoolmaster, was rather badly damaged."

The dangers of pit life were demonstrated locally in two incidents in 1920. In July a man was killed at Randolph Colliery when he was caught between a set of tubs and the cage to the shaft. Then in October nine year old Robert Stone was out brambling and whilst crossing the tub line from Carterthorne Colliery was knocked down by some tubs suffering injuries to his back and head as well as several broken ribs. In April 1929 Stephen Mattimoe, then in his sixtieth year suffered an accident working underground.

> "Stephen Mattimoe of 6, Cambridge Street, Leeholme, a chargeman in the Busty seam, Leasingthorne Colliery, was caught by a fall of stone on Tuesday. He was taken to Newcastle Infirmary and was found to be suffering from a fractured arm and injuries to ribs."

Fig. 97 West Tees (Railey Fell) Colliery taken in the late 1930's after it had closed by Ada Temple who was writing a thesis on Durham Colliery villages for her degree from Newcastle University. Ada's car is parked in the Colliery yard. The disused tramway from the drift beyond Sand Hole still crossed the road leading to Toft Hill.

Whilst reports of the small, often fatal, mining accidents continued to appear weekly in the local paper they began to be matched by motoring accidents reflecting the growth in traffic. A surprisingly high proportion of these involved the single decked, open sided buses of the time and were often accompanied by dramatic pictures of the wrecked vehicles, however fatalities were rare. One incident involved a bus carrying miners returning home from work which left the road and rolled over destroying the coachwork leaving only the chassis and wheels intact. It was clearly a serious accident but the miners walked away with only scratches. Perhaps their work had inured them to all but the most serious injury.

The Auckland Chronicle continued to give good local coverage of incidents in the village through their unknown reporter. In November 1922 a report appeared which succinctly but vividly describes one of those incidents which, though alarming at the time, probably provided much opportunity for later retelling with amusement, and possible embellishment, by those involved.

> "A man, seemingly of the tramp fraternity, insisted on going into a house in Gordon Lane one day last week. A son of the house had just washed after having been on the night shift, their mother had gone to the door to throw out the water when the man rushed the door, but the woman gave him the contents of the tub. The man still persisted, and placed his foot in the doorway. The husband, in rushing downstairs to his wife's assistance, fell down several stairs and received some bruises. It was some time before the intruder could be prevailed upon to go away. He made similar efforts at two other houses."

Descendants of the Carrabine family suffered two tragic losses. In Christmas 1922 the local paper reported the following.

> "The festive season has brought sorrow to the home of Mr and Mrs Carrabine, Oaks, by

the death of their daughter Sarah Elizabeth, aged eight years, which took place on Sunday after an attack of measles."

Seven years later a terrible accident occurred to a descendant of the Carrabines and was reported in sad detail following the Coroner's inquest in June 1929.

"How an Evenwood miner's child received fatal burns when her nightdress caught fire was described at the inquest Darlington, on Monday, on Kathleen Carrabine, aged 7 of Oak House, Evenwood. A verdict of 'Death from burns accidentally received' was returned … Deputy Coroner … added that no blame attached to anyone.
Mrs. Elizabeth Ann Carrabine, mother of the child, said that on Friday morning, Kathleen went up to her sister's room. A few minutes later she heard a scream. She ran up to the room and found the child in flames. She wrapped a mat round her to put the flames out, but the child was severely burnt.. A doctor was called in and Kathleen was ordered to the General Hospital, Darlington where she died during the afternoon. The witness did not know how the nightdress had caught fire.
Mrs. Edith May Stone, the sister of the dead child, who appeared with her hands still bound up, stated that according to her custom her sister, Kathleen, had come into her bedroom on Friday morning. There was a fire in the room.
"She had been in a few minutes when she suddenly screamed" said Mrs. Stone "I saw flames shoot up. When I jumped out of bed I found Kathleen's nightdress ablaze.
"I did my best to put it out and mother came up and helped me. Kathleen was very badly burnt"
Mrs. Stone explained that her hands were burnt when she was trying to put out the flames. The Deputy Coroner … stated that he had a letter from the doctor at the hospital in which he stated that the child, when admitted, was suffering from shock. …
Kathleen was the youngest member of the family, and was a bright and promising child."

In the same edition of the newspaper another descendant of one of the original families of *'Little Ireland'* received news of a sad loss.

"Mr. and Mrs. Gaffney of West Terrace, Evenwood have been notified that their son, Wilfred, has been accidentally drowned in Canada.
Further information has come to hand that he was swimming and was caught in a pool and drowned before his companions could rescue him. The youth emigrated to Canada nearly two years ago and was doing well.
Immediately news of the sad fatality was received at Evenwood a communication was sent to Mrs. Gaffney's mother in Scranton, USA and the funeral took place there."

Even minor accidents could have serious consequences which today we would not expect as shown by the following report.

"A serious accident occurred in the recreation field on Tuesday night. A girl named Margaret Rutter, aged 13 years, daughter of Mr. and Mrs. Jos. Rutter, Rochdale Terrace, was with other children, swinging on the maypole when she lost her hold and fell heavily to the ground, resulting in a fracture of the leg. After being attended to by Dr. Milne she was conveyed to Greenbank hospital, Darlington. It was found necessary to amputate the leg."

Two weeks before the outbreak of the Second World War Mary Ann Mattimoe, the wife of Patrick Mattimoe the eldest son of Thomas and Ann died. The Auckland Chronicle reported the funeral giving a detailed list of those who attended and, a boon to family historians, their relationship to Mary Ann.

"The Rev. father Walmsley, of Witton Park, conducted the service at Evenwood Cemetery of Mrs. M. A. Mattimoe aged 73 years of Gordon Bank, Ramshaw. The chief mourners were Mr. and Mrs. S. Mattimoe (son and daughter-in-law); Mr. and Mrs. J. Peacock (daughter and son-in-law); Miss P. E. Rutter (sister); Mr. H. Rutter (brother); Mr. and Mrs. T. Rutter (brother and sister-in-law); Mr. and Mrs. E. Rutter (brother and sister-in-law); Mr. J. Rutter (brother); Mr. and Mrs. L. . Mattimoe, Leeholme (sister and brother-in-law), Mrs. P. Mattimoe (sister-in-law); Mr. and Mrs. H. Mattimoe, Mr. and Mrs. N. Bussey (grandson and granddaughter); Mr. and Mrs. H. Rutter, Mr. J. Rutter, Mr. and Mrs. J. Hannon, Mr. Joseph Hannon, Mr. F. Hannon, Mr. T. Hannon, Miss S. Hannon, Miss K. Hannon, Mrs. Finlay, Mr. and Mrs. Upton, Mr. P. Mattimoe, Mr. Pat. Mattimoe, Miss E. Mattimoe, Misses L. and E. Mattimoe, Mr T. Mattimoe, Mr. T. Mattimoe Leeholme, Mr. J. Mattimoe, Mr. S. Mattimoe, Anfield Plain (nephews and nieces)."

Ramshaw – A Resilient Community

Despite hard times and personal tragedies the population of Evenwood and Ramshaw continued to celebrate local events in style

Visits to nearby Bishop Auckland by Lord John Sangster's Circus, with bareback riding, acrobats, clowns and his performing sea lions regularly provided an entertaining diversion. There was also a visit from Bronco Bill's Circus which proved to be more exciting than planned when horses pulling one of the wagons bolted, fortunately not causing any injuries other than to an 'actress' who was treated for shock.

Through all the hardships brought about by high unemployment, low pay and poor working conditions the miners showed great resilience. The Evenwood Annual Leek and Vegetable Show took place throughout the period and was usually "an unqualified success" drawing a "large entry [with]... exhibits of good quality". In 1919 John Mattimoe, though now living in Coronation but probably retaining a vegetable plot on his brother-in-law's field, won first prize in the trench leeks (open) class. There is no mention of a second place winner so he may not have faced much competition. His brother Peter won second prize in the heaviest potato class.

St. Patrick's Day continued to be celebrated by the congregations of the local Roman Catholic churches who demonstrated both their ability to have a good time and their love of Ireland which many regarded as the Old Country. The Priest would hand out a shamrock to every child and adult attending morning service. In later years the children had a harp, a shamrock and the Irish Colours pinned to them to go to school. They would go to Mass and the shamrocks would be blessed. There was always a whist drive and dance in the evening as in March 1923.

> "Members of St Chad's [Witton Park] held a whist drive and dance on Monday night. There was a great company present. The Rev. Father Kearney conducted the whist drive ... Dancing was indulged in till the early hours of the morning to music supplied by Ross's Band."
>
> "An excellent concert ... in aid of St Wilfred's Mission [Bishop Auckland} was given in the Town Hall on Monday evening ... Included in the programme were many old Irish favourites."

Closer to home in July 1924 the local Roman Catholics, of which the Mattimoes and Hannons would have been well represented, held a whist drive at the Railey Fell Institute in aid of the new Witton Park Presbytery. Miss Mattimoe won first prize amongst the ladies.

A more ambitious event in February 1925 saw the Hannon and Mattimoe ladies again prize-winners.

"A whist drive and dance, promoted by the Evenwood Catholics in aid of the new presbytery at Witton Park was held in Railey Fell Institute on Friday night. The MC was Mr. T. Cooper. The prize winners were:- Ladies: 1, Miss K. Hannon; 2, Miss A. Doyle; 3, Miss M. Mattimoe ... Dance music was supplied by Mr. Ross's Band. Messrs A. Hutchinson and Mr. J. Hannon officiated as MC's".

Not that whist was the only activity for which the adaptable Mattimoe ladies showed an aptitude. In August 1926 at a Field day for the residents of the Oaks Mrs F Mattimoe won the wheelbarrow race.

The resilience of the local community was shown by the following reports, which appeared in the Auckland Chronicle of June 1927, the same edition which announced the news of the closure of Randolph Colliery, demonstrating that people could put their troubles to one side and enjoy themselves.

"There was a large number on Monday on holiday bent, and many journeys by train to Appleby and Barnard Castle. Motor buses were kept busy all day conveying passengers to and from Barnard Castle."

"The annual tea and social held in connection with St Chad's R.C. Church, Witton Park, on Monday was well attended by the parishioners. Games and competitions, for which prizes were awarded, were indulged in by the children, and there was much keenness shown. A good number sat down to the tea which followed, and the event concluded with a dance in St. Chad's Hall which was well patronised."

Fig. 98 This group photograph taken in the 1930's was the only one in Sally Hannon's album but its significance has been lost over time though it remains in interesting picture depicting the dress of the time. It appears to be a an outing for retired people though this does not explain the presence of the young boy on the right of the front row.

In July 1938 the Catholic Women's Guild held a successful garden fete and sale of work in the grounds of St Chad's, Witton Park followed by a social in the evening, and in the same month the Roman Catholics of Coundon were enjoying their annual excursion when 230 children and adults travelled to Redcar by motor buses.

The local band often played to raise money for the needy. In Early April 1925 they paraded the village to raise money for the Scotswood Pit Disaster Fund and collected the sum of £8. The disaster had occurred at Montagu View Pit at Scotswood, 3 ½ miles west of Newcastle, at 10.30am on 30th March. A Deputy, working at a flat by the Brockwell seam, at almost the lowest point of the mine, set off three shots which caused water to break through in a sudden inrush from the Paradise Pit which had been abandoned in 1848. Thirty eight miners perished. All the bodies were retrieved but new pumping equipment had to be installed and the last body was not retrieved until 19th October. The Mayor of Newcastle set up a Relief Fund. A memorial to the men lost in the disaster was erected in Elswick Cemetery near Newcastle.

On August Bank Holiday 1933 the Evenwood band played in Gordon Gill. There is no mention of the reason why they chose to play in *'Little Ireland'* but it must have been a lovely event with the families who lived there joined by friends and relations who had walked up from Bowes Close, Ramshaw and Evenwood and down from Gordon Bank Top to listen to the band. Perhaps some brought picnics and sat on the grass by the beck as the children played in the water and explored the nearby woods.

Unemployed miners were not content to stay idle. The rural location of Evenwood and Ramshaw helped and the local paper carried a picture of unemployed miners helping a local farmer bring in the hay. They seem to be enjoying the activity but are dressed in trousers and waistcoats with sleeves rolled up almost as if they had chosen to wear their Sunday best clothes. Their miner's working clothes would certainly not have been suitable.

Fig. 99

The Railey Fell Incline Engine House. This was probable situated at the top of Gordon Bank and was used to haul the empty coal trucks up to that drift mine and lower the full trucks down to Railey Fell bank head in a controlled manner. At the end of the 19th century a big horse was used to pull the empty trucks up a smaller incline beyond the Old Norwood Colliery, the full trucks being allowed to descend unchecked

Courtesy of Beamish the North of England Open Air Museum

Unemployed miners from the congregation of St Chad's, Witton Park put their time to good effect as was reported in the Auckland Chronicle of September 1933.

> "The unemployed members of St Chad's Church, Witton Park, have at various periods carried out much valuable work in improving and beautifying their church and its grounds.
> During recent weeks under supervision of the Parish Priest the Rev. Father Walmsley they have laid out a waste piece of land as a flower garden and facing the east door of the church they have built a grotto.
> In the grotto a statue of Our Lady of Lourdes, given by a parishioner, has been placed. The ceremony of dedication and blessing the grotto and statue was carried out by Father Walmsley in the presence of a large congregation."

An interesting development was announced in April 1936 when the local correspondent of the Auckland Chronicle noted the following at Evenwood.

> "The Newcastle Electricity Supply Co. have started to erect the poles which are to carry electricity into the village. The streets will continue with gas lights but most of the houses are having electricity installed."

Royal events had always drawn a positive response from the villagers. After the sixty three year settled period of Queen Victoria's reign there were four kings crowned during the following thirty five years. There is no evidence that the residents of Ramshaw celebrated these events with dulled enthusiasm. Houses were decorated for the coronation of George V in 1910 whilst in 1937 the Auckland Chronicle was able to report the following.

> "Despite the dispiriting weather Wednesday there was a good parade of children from the schools of Evenwood CE and Ramshaw Council Schools when, headed by the Evenwood Silver Band they marched from Ramshaw Railway Bridge to St Paul's Church ... The children retired to their respective schools for tea and each was presented with a souvenir mug."

The following year the prospect of another war concerned the local community. The Auckland Chronicle dedicated a whole page to photographs and captions concerning the speeding up of air raid precautions in Co. Durham. In February 1939 collections were made locally in aid of Spanish refugees. That July an ARP Evacuation Meeting was held at Evenwood.

War was declared on 3rd September 1939 and soon after 150 children mothers and babies from Newcastle-on-Tyne and Hebburn-on-Tyne were evacuated to Evenwood.

The following month saw the first reports in the local paper of soldiers and battles. The battleship Royal Oak was reported sunk with local men amongst the crew. The period of peace was over.

15   John Mattimoe's Family

John Mattimoe's latter years were spent in comfort, amongst friends and family. Before retiring he had progressed to the position of Deputy Overman and had the respect of his workmates who he would have still seen regularly. He lived close to his daughter and her young family and had contact with them daily. His sons visited Coronation frequently to see their father and sister. John's nephew ran the 'Top House' in Eldon Lane, the other side of the railway bridge from Coronation. His brother, Stephen and his family lived not far away. His other remaining two brothers and his sister lived not far away in Ramshaw and Evenwood. We know that John was a regular visitor to Ramshaw and helped his sister's family with their smallholding. The trees he planted adjacent to the river can still be seen. He was the eldest member of the extended Mattimoe family and the sole surviving member of the family group who had journeyed from Ireland sixty years earlier. He maintained a position of seniority in the extended family and, through wise management of his own finances, was able to provide help to get them started in life. John had become comfortably off owning several properties in Evenwood and Coronation. His Grandson Jack remembered accompanying his Grandfather to collect rents.

John's third wife, Sarah, died in June 1920. John was not a man used to living on his own and he had met a woman whom he hoped to make his fourth wife but he died before this could happen. No information has survived regarding this woman with whom John wished to spend his last days. The Auckland Chronicle recorded the circumstances of his death in July 1922.

> "The death occurred under somewhat tragic circumstances, on Monday night, of Mr John Mattimoe, aged 67, of 6, Mary Terrace, Coronation. Mr Mattimoe, who was a widower, lived alone and had complained to his daughter of not feeling very well on Monday morning. She called to see him again at 6.30pm, when he was apparently alright, but on making another visit at 9.30pm she found her father dead in bed. Dr. Thorpe certified death as due to heart disease."

With his death the Mattimoe family lost their last direct link with Ireland. John left a will which, split his estate equally between his children. However, in advance of his death he allowed various members of the extended family to have use of the properties and they were required to pay into the estate a sum equal to their value in order that the estate could be shared as willed by John. Copies of the solicitor's final correspondence still exist. John's house that he occupied in Coronation was unencumbered and sold at auction on 18th August generating the following entry in the local paper.

> "At the South Durham Hotel Eldon Lane on Friday Mr A. E. Morgan offered for competition 6, Mary Terrace (Brookfield House) Coronation near Eldon Lane lately occupied by Mr John Mattimoe deceased. Bidding began at £150 and the property was knocked down to Mr Oliver W Hedley for £260 …"

John was able to spring one last surprise on his children after his death. Stephen, Frank and Molly were clearing the house after their father's death when Stephen reached under the bed, pulled out a box which he opened and quickly called his brother and sister to see what he had found. The box was full of gold sovereigns.

John Mattimoe's family

John Mattimoe/Mary Redfearn Parmley
b. 1858, Ireland   b. c.1854, d. 21.4.1883
d. 17.7.1922   m. 18.11.1882, St Wilfred's

/Hannah Donlan
b. 1858, Ireland, d. 14.2.1914
m. 22.11.1884, St Wilfred's

/Sarah Wilson
b. c.1870, d. 22.6.1920
m. 12.4.1915, St Wilfred's

Thomas 'Tom' Henry Mattimoe b. 15.4.1883, d. 8.3.1956
   m. Caroline 'Carrie' Dora Sams 21.10.1907, St Chad's
— Stephen Mattimoe b. 22.9.1885, d. 12.7.1952

— John 'Leo' Mattimoe b. 14.9.1888
   m. Jane 'Ginny' Haws c.1914
— Francis 'Frank' Austin Mattimoe b. 11.9.1890
   m. Mary Ellen 'Nellie' Welsh 25.4.1914
— Mary Ann 'Molly' Mattimoe b. 14.5.1894, d. 28.12.1939
   m. John William Gray 11.10.1913

John also had much good furniture which was auctioned, his children having more need of additional finance than additional furniture.

Later that year Molly wrote to her Aunt, her mother's sister, living in Denver, Colorado giving family and local news including the death of her father. She also enclosed a family photograph. Her Aunt replied in a letter written on Boxing Day that year. From the style of its writing it is clear Molly's Aunt retained a strong Irish accent.

> "Dear Mary
>
> We received your letter and were indeed very glad to hear from you. We had lost your address and were unable to continue writing to you. We are very sorry to hear your father is dead may he rest in peace. I suppose you have not heard of Uncle Pat's death he died two years Dec. 1 poor Uncle may he rest in peace.
>
> We are very glad to hear that all the children are doing so nicely. Mary and Jack are surely cute. Ellen is now going to high school and she will graduate in another year. Dad is still fine and is feeling fine.
>
> You said you were going to write to Uncle Martin have you his address. Is he still living why we all thought he was dead. We haven't heard from him in years if you have his address and know where he is please write and let us know so we can write to him too.
>
> Things are very hard here too a person is not safe out of the house after eight o'clock with all the hold-ups that are taking place. Have you heard of the big mint robbery that took place here a week ago yesterday? $200,000.00 was stolen from the mint. All this money was in $5 bills and the newspapers offer a reward of $50.00 (10 pounds) to any one who can produce one of the bills.
>
> I had an operation for my troubles last April and am feeling fairly good now but am not altogether well. We are glad to hear your brothers are well and working. Your Aunt, Uncle and cousin in San Francisco would like to hear from you once in a while.
>
> Well I don't know any more news this time, Mary I will close hoping to hear from you soon. I am enclosing the address of your Aunt & Uncle & cousin in 'Frisco as I think they would be glad to hear from you too. Give my love to all the children your brothers and yourself. I close hoping to hear from you.
>
> Your Loving Aunt
>
> Mrs J Ryan
>
> Love to the children from Ellen"

Great Uncle Martin

Molly was not able to make contact with Martin, who was always referred to in the family as Great Uncle Martin, as much for his height being 6ft 7½in tall, as for his relationship to my own Aunts and Uncles. Perhaps she tried but he had moved.

A few years later, however, in May 1928 Great Uncle Martin, unaware of the death of his brother-in-law sent him the following letter which Molly opened. Like his sisters he retained his Irish accent and reading the letter with such in mind adds colour to both the content and the writer.

> "Dear Brother
> Just a line hoping you ar' all well as the Lord leaves me.
> I am very sorry for not writing for so long.
> How is all the boys and Mary and how is Pete, Stephen & Frank.
> Ar' they still living in the same old place? Tell them I was asking for all.
> I would like to see them all once more. How do you feel anyhow?
> What about coming out here for a while & then we will go back together & have a good time. Please write soon.
> There is all kinds of work here with big pays. I hold a good job here in a bank as special officer. Two thousand dollars a ye'r.
> If only I could hold all the money I handle in a day I would go back to England, buy out Durham County and then we could have a good time.
> John please send a copy of that picture of mine.
> Please I haven't got one wit' that uniform.
> I would like to have one John if you don't mind
> I must close this time hoping to hear from you soon xxx
>   Martin Donnelly"

Fig. 100   Great Uncle Martin

The photograph he refers to in the letter may be either one of him in police uniform or that of him in his bank special officer uniform. Copies of both remain in the possession of John Mattimoe's descendants and serves again to illustrate Martin's exceptional height.

Great Uncle Martin did return to England for a visit, probably in 1929/30. His great niece, Nora remembered him visiting the house in Bushey, his towering presence and outgoing character making quite an impression. He returned to America but was killed in an accident when he was tragically decapitated whilst leaning out of a train window.

Tom Mattimoe's Family

On return from the First World War John Mattimoe's eldest son Tom by his first wife, Mary Ann, resumed work at Leasingthorne Colliery. Tom and his wife Carrie had lost their first born but, on his return, Tom was greeted by five surviving children. Tom and Carrie went on to have five more children together but their next child a daughter, and later twin girls died when each was a little over six months old. Their eldest child had been born in

Fig. 101 Great Uncle Martin in the uniform of the special officer at the bank in New York.

1909 and the youngest, Julia, was born in 1933. My mother, father and I were very pleased when we made contact with Julia and her husband John. Julia was able to tell me about her father. Julia was a lovely woman and, like all the family very welcoming and interesting to talk with. Watching my mother and Julia talking together reminded me of my childhood when I would sit listening to my mother and my Aunts talking yet she had only just met Julia for the first time.

Julia sadly died during the writing of this book and is sorely missed by those who knew her. Her husband, John Bell, was born and brought up in the cottage next to the school in Lynesack. When John was at Grammar School he took the bus each day to Bishop Auckland. The bus driver always stopped outside a cottage on the Lands Road to pick up his 'bait' and a pop bottle of tea. His wife would lift up a little girl, their niece, to hand over the tea. This little girl was Julia. She married John just before her eighteenth birthday and they were devoted to each other for the fifty two years until her death.

Bringing up a large family such as Tom and Carrie's during the Depression was far from easy although Tom always worked. Unexpected events however could stretch the family's finances. One incident illustrates this but also demonstrates that whilst having been taught in a village school with 130 pupils organised into five classes in one large room Tom achieved a good command of the written word and was well able to express himself in an erudite manner. The following letter sent from Tom to the local shopkeeper was found by the descendant of the shopkeeper when sorting through the shop's contents following the death of her parents.

"Dear Sir

Our Mary was at your place this morning & she thinks that our groceries are not being given with a very good grace. Of course it may only be her thoughts. I am fully aware that we have not paid as per bill but if I am allowed I might say that I have had a little ill luck, moreover I was put in queer street with our Jack coming & he had almost an empty pocket to come home with, consequently I could not do what I intended as regards you. I do not know how much we have had this week, but if we have run that £1 ticket out say so & we shall ask for no more. I intended coming along on Friday & seeing you personally & getting the prices of absolute necessities, say about 25/- worth so that we could give you a shilling or two each week but Mary's thought put into words knocked the stuffing out of me. Now I am not a bit vexed about anything so just sit down & write me a straight forward note as to how we may proceed for the benefit of us both & believe me to remain

Your Grateful Friend

Thos Mattimoe

ps
understand I do not lose sight of your goodness to me"

The letter appears to have been written around 1930 as Mary, who married in September 1931, was still living at home. It would be difficult to write a better letter on a sensitive subject and make ones point clearly without alienating or offending the recipient. We will never know the outcome but it is significant to note it made such an impact upon the shopkeeper that despite all the other correspondence, invoices and receipts he received in the intervening years he chose to keep Tom's letter.

It also suggests that Tom, like many others of his generation, possessed an intellect above that which might be indicated by his occupation and which remained unfulfilled due to the lack of opportunity and the immediacy of providing for his family in the best way available.

Tom was not only an able writer but also possessed musical talent. He was an accomplished violin player. All the Mattimoes seem to have been musical but Tom's particular

Fig. 102 Tom Mattimoe's youngest daughter, Julia.

Fig 103

Sergeant Stephen Mattimoe in the early 1930's showing his presence at a local event in Anfield Plain. He was a popular man locally. The dress of the members of the public and the char-a-banc in the background date the photograph as clearly as Stephen's police service record.

talent would have also been influenced by his Parmley ancestry as they were accomplished musicians. Edith Parmley is today organist at the Chapel in Gordon Lane. Tom was also a smart dresser and known for his spats which he always wore.

Tom Mattimoe worked underground until he retired at sixty nine years of age, following which he became a nightwatchman. He worked as a nightwatchman for five years when he had an accident receiving a terrible electric shock which threw him back. He was lucky to survive but his condition deteriorated after the accident and he died not long afterwards.

Stephen Mattimoe

Stephen rejoined the Durham Constabulary on release from the Army and was stationed back at Consett. In July 1920 he was promoted to sergeant and the following year moved to Anfield Plain where he served until his retirement in December 1934 on an annual pension of £195.10s.9d. Sergeant in a village police station was a position of some status and not a little autonomy well away from Superintendent who would be based in the town a good few miles away. Five years after retiring Stephen was readmitted to the First Police Reserve two days before the outbreak of the Second World War, resigning at the end of 1945.

His brother Frank's daughters Mary, Ronnie and Anne remember Stephen as a nice man, full of fun and always very smart and dapper. He would wear plusfours when they were in fashion and beautiful shoes. He joined an amateur dramatic group and landed a part which involved him wearing a cloak which he enjoyed showing off to his nieces swirling it round with dramatic flourishes.

Stephen liked a drink and also liked to treat his nieces. On occasions these two pleasurable activities could be combined. He would take Mary and Ronnie to dinner in Newcastle then on to the theatre. When

Fig. 104 Stephen Mattimoe with his nieces Mary, Betty and Monica

they were settled and comfortable he would tell them he had to pop out for a little while but not to tell their father when they got back. He would return before the end of the performance obviously having spent the intervening period in the bar or a pub and remind the girls not to say anything to their father.

On another occasion Stephen took Mary to the wrestling. She enjoyed it so much it became a regular outing

Mary joined the RAF and when she was abroad her Uncle Stephen, who had beautiful writing, would send her letters full of sayings and quotations.

Stephen lived with his brother Frank's family once he retired. One evening when he arrived home from the ballroom somewhat worse for wear Ronnie was asked by her father to stay up to keep an eye on Stephen in case he dropped a cigarette. Ronnie was up until nearly three in the morning.

Stephen was a ladies man but always was true to one woman in particular, Maggie Manley. She was a schoolteacher at Thistledown school and lived near Stanley. She was always beautifully dressed. Her father allegedly refused to allow her to marry Stephen so they would travel separately from Stanley where they both lived before meeting. Stephen and Maggie used to write to each other regularly.

Stephen was tragically killed in an accident, knocked down by a car when walking home one night in July 1952.

Leo Mattimoe's Family

John's son Leo married Ginny Haws and they had four children Katy, Annie who married George Weber, Jean and John. Ginny had been married before. It was perhaps for this reason that Leo's family moved away from the Catholic Church. Ginny had suffered a serious problem in giving birth to one of her children which affected the left side of her body leaving her slightly paralysed down one side. Her nieces and nephews, like children everywhere, would sometimes make fun of Aunt Ginny behind her back but they all loved her and her set countenance betrayed a kind-hearted woman. Leo's brother Stephen on visits to his brothers and sister from Anfield Plain always detoured via Ferryhill to see Leo. Some times

Fig. 105 (right) Leo Mattimoe's wife Ginny Haws

Fig. 106 (below) Leo and Ginny's children Katie and John

Leo would be in bed having worked the night shift but Ginny would insist on getting him up to see his brother saying "He'd never forgive me if I told him you had been and I had not woken him".

Frank Mattimoe's Family

John's youngest son, Frank served at Chester-le-Street police station from May 1914 till his retirement in November 1945. He was known for his beautiful copperplate handwriting so was based at the station most of the time. He was given the job of writing up the reports for the Assizes. He would bring them home and Nellie had to heat up slabs of material which turned to jelly and smelt fearful, to enable copies of the reports to be taken.

Frank was responsible for organising the annual ball which was held in the big hall next to the police station. There was a whist drive as well as dancing. He acted as Master of Ceremonies though his wife Nellie never attended.

He was never promoted beyond constable despite being told by his Superintendent that he had regularly been recommended for such promotion. His Superintendent told Frank his Irish ancestry prevented him progressing in the force. At that time the Irish Republicans were active.

Frank was well respected in Chester-le-Street and knew everyone. His daughter Mary remembers walking down the street with him when he was out of uniform wearing the bowler hat off duty policemen were required to wear at that time. He greeted everyone they met with a cheery hello and a half salute, touching his hat.

Frank, like his brother, was a tall man. Kathleen McRory who married Frank Hannon remembered being at Gordon Lane, Ramshaw one day when he visited. She went out the back and had bent down to open the gate when he arrived and she turned to look up at him and told me "I started at the bottom and I thought I was never going to reach the top". Like the other Mattimoe men he was larger than life, loud and full of fun.

Frank and his brother Stephen, like their uncles, both had good singing voices and were good dancers. Frank's daughter Mary remembers her father singing Irish ballads that all seemed to be about a Mary. He would also sing Irish rebel songs one of which she could still sing fifty years after his death.

Frank married Nellie Welsh from Ushaw Moor. Nellie's father had married a woman who had money but was in poor health. They ran a pub in Ushaw Moor. When his wife died the children were farmed out to various relatives. Nellie was only thirteen and went to live with her Uncle Ned. Her father married again to a woman he had allegedly been seeing when his first wife was ill. His new wife had a daughter who had emigrated to Chile so he used his money to first buy a house in Alderley Edge then to emigrate to Chile.

Kathleen McRory remembered Nellie. She was a large woman, but a lovely woman who like her husband was always full of fun. Nellie would visit the Hannons at Ramshaw and Kathleen remembers vividly the tragi-comic incident when on one such visit poor Nellie accidentally trod on the family cat and killed it. One can only imagine the turmoil that ensued as a much loved relative, no doubt mortified by the accident, was reassured and comforted by the Hannon family who tried to make light of the matter. Years on Angela and I could not help but laugh with Kathleen as she described the incident.

Nellie's daughter Mary said that her mother rarely went shopping. The butcher and the baker came to the door. Groceries were delivered. The girls were sent to the shoe shop and clothes shop for items which had been ordered. Whenever Nellie did go to the grocers shop nearby she received immediate attention

Fig. 107 Frank Mattimoe's wife Nellie Welsh

Fig. 108 PC Frank Mattimoe

from the grocer. If the girls went unaccompanied the grocer would enquire after their mother and hope she was well. Nellie always bought the best quality food. Mary remembered one time she and Ronnie were sent shopping with a five pound note, a lot of money in those days equivalent to a months groceries. Ronnie lost the money and they dared not go home. Mary thought the money was stolen from Ronnie whilst they were in Woolworths.

Molly Mattimoe and Willy Gray in Coronation

The youngest of John Mattimoe's children, Mary Ann (Molly), married John William 'Willy' Gray in October 1913 and initially lived in Mary Terrace up until her father's death in 1922 then moved to Richard Terrace, Coronation.

Coronation was created in 1901 by James 'Jimmy' Moore. The terraces he built were named after himself, his wife Mary and his children David, Margaret, John and Richard. James himself had started out as a lead miner then became a seedsman before branching out into property. At this time Pease and Partners the Quaker family that owned the mines was encouraging miners to become homeowners by guaranteeing their mortgages in Coronation that were paid back at 5s per week.

Each pair of Terraces backed onto an alley. There was an outdoor 'privy' at the bottom of each yard with a hatch opening onto the alley to allow the 'night-soil man' to collect the waste.

One of the houses on the terrace nearest the school is double-fronted and was intended for a doctor.

The Coronation house was lit by gas downstairs but upstairs it relied on candles. Molly's daughter Betty remembered when the family lived in Richard Terrace they would take one of the trays from the oven by the fire, wrap it in a cloth and use it as a bedwarmer. It was very effective but if the wrapping came off you could burn your feet. At least four of the daughters would have shared the same bed with two at each end and four sets of toes fighting for a share of the betowelled tray.

Willy Gray and Molly Mattimoe had seven children; John James 'Jack', Mary, William Laurence 'Laurie', Nora, Monica, Margaret 'Peggy' and Betty. All the children were baptised in St Wilfred's Church. Sponsors (Godparents) for Jack were Joseph Mattimoe and Ann Mattimoe; for Mary, Stephen Mattimoe and Ann Mattimoe; for Laurie, Leo Mattimoe; for Nora, Alice Wilson; for Peggy, Sally Hannon; for Betty who was christened Elizabeth but not registered as such by her father much to her mother's annoyance, Elizabeth Gray.

Willy Gray's Accident

Willy Gray worked in the mines and progressed to a Deputy Overman at Eldon Colliery responsible for the deployment of men underground and for checking the underground workings to ensure they were safe before the men entered the tunnels. On a fateful day in April 1927, at Eldon Colliery, only four months after the end of the General Strike Willy was working underground when he met with a fatal accident. The Auckland Chronicle of 28 April 1927 records details of the inquest into the accident.

> "A verdict of 'Accidental death' was returned at an inquest on William Gray, aged 42, a deputy-overman at Eldon Colliery, of 12, Richard Terrace, Coronation, who was killed by a fall of stone on 22 April.
>
> Joseph Woodward stated that he went to the colliery at about 5 o'clock on Friday night to inspect a chain which had become fouled by a broken prop. Four experienced Deputies were working when the fall of stone occurred. Gray was caught by his right arm, head and shoulders between some heavy pieces. He only lived a few seconds, and his body was not got out until seven hours after the accident.
>
> Another man, John Wood, was able to extricate himself, and although bruised, walked

John Mattimoe and his family 189

Fig. 109 Willy and Molly Gray with their first three children, Jack, Laurie and Mary.

home. Gill and Constantine, the other two men, escaped injury.

Gray was a married man, aged 42, and leaves a widow and six children. In an effort to recover the dead man, a rescue party had some dangerous work, and they had cleared the stone away from the body when another large fall occurred and they had to recommence operations."

I met John Wood's son, Tommy, seventy five years after the accident and his recollection of that traumatic day was still crystal clear. When a young boy he would often be sent on errands. On the Friday afternoon when the accident occurred he was on an errand in the fish shop situated on the edge of Eldon Lane within view of the colliery, when someone came rushing in and said that there had been an accident at the mine and John Wood had been killed. Tommy remembers hearing this news, dropping his money and dashing out of the shop, running all the way home to find his father alive but badly bruised down his side, sitting in front of the fire. Molly and her young family had no such reprieve from their shock and grief.

Willy was buried in Bishop Auckland cemetery, in the area reserved for those of Roman Catholic faith. Tommy Woods remembered that Willy Gray was a well regarded man, liked by all and "would do anything for anyone". His funeral was consequently well attended by friends and workmates. His headstone can still be found in the cemetery.

The Arbitration Committee of the Durham Colliery Owners Mutual Protection Association and the Durham Deputies Mutual Aid Association awarded the family the sum of £600 to be invested in the Newcastle Savings Bank, the amount and its interest to be used to generate a weekly income for the family of £3 5s per week.

Mary Mattimoe, daughter of Frank, remembered her Aunt Molly as being a tall distinguished woman but a very lovely woman who was easy to talk to. Her brothers Frank and Stephen visited her frequently. When Molly's husband Willy was killed Mary remembered the upset and her mother crying. Her father and his brother Stephen were away for days helping Molly after the incident. When Molly moved her family south Frank and Stephen were very upset and Molly and Nellie were crying together. They visited Molly and her family in their new home several times.

Mary Ann Mattimoe did not get on with her husbands family therefore following his death there was little contact between them though Nora remembered meeting 'Grandma Gray' on her way home from school and talking to her.

Fig. 110 Nora and Mary Gray. Judging from the chalk lettering on the table this photgraph could have been taken in August 1922 when their Grandfather's (John Mattimoe) effects were being auctioned after his death.

John Mattimoe and his family 191

Fig. 111 Grave of Peter Gray, Mary Gray nee Conway and their son James Gray.

Fig. 112 Grave of John Mattimoe. The base to the cross mentions his wife Bridget Hannah and his son-in-law John William Gray but they were both buried elsewhere in the cemetery.

Bishop Auckland Cemetery

1. John William Gray d.1927
2. Elizabeth Ann Gray nee Haigh d.1936
3. Peter Gray d.1898
   Margaret Gray nee Conway d.1910
   James Gray d.1888
4. Mary Gray d.1911
5. Hannah "Bridget" Mattimoe nee Donlan d.1914
6. John Mattimoe d.1922

Fig. 113 Bishop Auckland Cemetery indicating locations of members of the Mattimoe and FGray familes. Most graves marked do not bear a headstone.

16 Stephen Mattimoe's Family

John Mattimoe' brother, Stephen, who had left the Gill with his family at the same time as John, lived initially in Eldon but soon moved to Leeholme where a model village had been built to house the workers of the nearby pit. Stephen and his sons, apart from Frank, worked in Leasingthorne Colliery. Joe was ambulance man so only went underground if there was an accident. Cornelius 'Con' was a foreoverman working underground. Tommy was an onsetter, who controlled the movement of the cage in the pit shaft when they 'rapped' it away from the top to the bottom so he didn't work underground. They were traumatic days. Leasingthorne Colliery was nearby. There were different seams that they used to talk about. There were three shifts a fore shift 2.30 to 10am, a back shift 9am to 5pm, afternoon shift 3pm to 11pm and a night shift.

The pit was always working including weekends. There was a lot of water so they were always pumping.

Mary Ellen Hagan

Stephen and his wife, Mary Ellen, had a large family though, as for his parents before him, things would have been eased by the sons working different shifts. Some would be getting out of bed as others were getting ready to get in. The family had a 'desk bed' in the downstairs room which looked like a cupboard but opened up into a bed. With Stephen and his sons working the household had a good income. Mary Ellen was as small in stature as her husband was tall. She was a good manager of the family's finances and was generous to others. Her grand nephew, Jackie Moran, remembered that Mary Ellen was always very good to his family. Every Easter and Christmas Jackie and his brother were rigged out top to bottom by Mary Ellen. Jackie's father was a painter but they never went short of coal as Mary Ellen's family were all miners. Jackie would go down with an old bike and bring a sack of coal back slung through the frame so the family always had a fire and hot water from the boiler next to the fire.

The tradition of providing visitors with something to eat, anything from a snack to a full meal, was and still is, such an accepted practice that it is rarely commented upon. Therefore for both Jackie and Mary Ellen's grand-daughter, Mary, to separately make mention of the spreads that Mary Ellen would leave for those that might visit is an indication of how extensive they were. A white table cloth would be left covering the food and a kettle left boiling on the hob. Anyone visiting would help themselves.

Jackie Moran, himself a good and generous man became a successful ham and bacon butcher in Bishop Auckland and would always ensure the Mattimoe and Hannon families had gammons at Christmas. Jack undertook many good works through the Church. Mary Eales once told him "You know Jackie, I'll never forget you for as kind as you've been". Jackie replied "No, and I'll never forget Aunt Mary Ellen. The times she used to come down our house and say "Get them bairns ready" and she would take us and rig us out. That's why don't say I've been good, it's just repayment".

Tragedy was never far away from the Mattimoe families and sadly Stephen and Mary Ellen's was no exception. In addition to the three children who died young and Frank who was killed in action in the First World War they were to lose three children who died in the prime of their lives, Mary Eveline died in

Stephen Mattimoe's Family

Stephen Mattimoe / Mary Ellen Hagan
b. 25.12.1869, Bishop Auckland   b. c.1870
d. 3.2.1950   m. 11.10.1889, St Wilfred's   d. 7.2.1948

- Thomas Edward Mattimoe b. 11.10.1890, d. 4.3.1896

- James Frances 'Frank' Mattimoe b. 12.4.1892, d. 18.12.1918
  m. Hannah Smith 14.7.1917, St Patrick's, Middlesbrough, d. 22.6.1974

- Annie Mattimoe b. 5.1.1894, d. 15.3.1918

- Teresa Demelda Mattimoe 23.3.1895, d. 27.4.1895

- Mary Eveline Mattimoe 12.9.1896, d. 9.6.1915

- Joseph 'Joe' Mattimoe 6.1.1898, d. 8.8.1958
  m. Elizabeth 'Liza' Dent 22.2.1919, St Wilfred's

- Cornelius 'Con' Mattimoe 17.6.1901, d. 6.5.1978
  m. Olive Thompson 8.2.1922, St Wilfred's, d. 29.4.1936
  m. Kathleen Ann Wigley 27.5.1939, St Joseph's, Coundon

- Timmy Mattimoe b. 19.2.1903, d. 26.3.1927
  m. Jean Hay 16.2.1926, Penshaw, Tyne & Wear

- Tommy Mattimoe 31.12.1904, d. 1.6.1973
  m. Minnie Smith 1929, d. Nov 2002

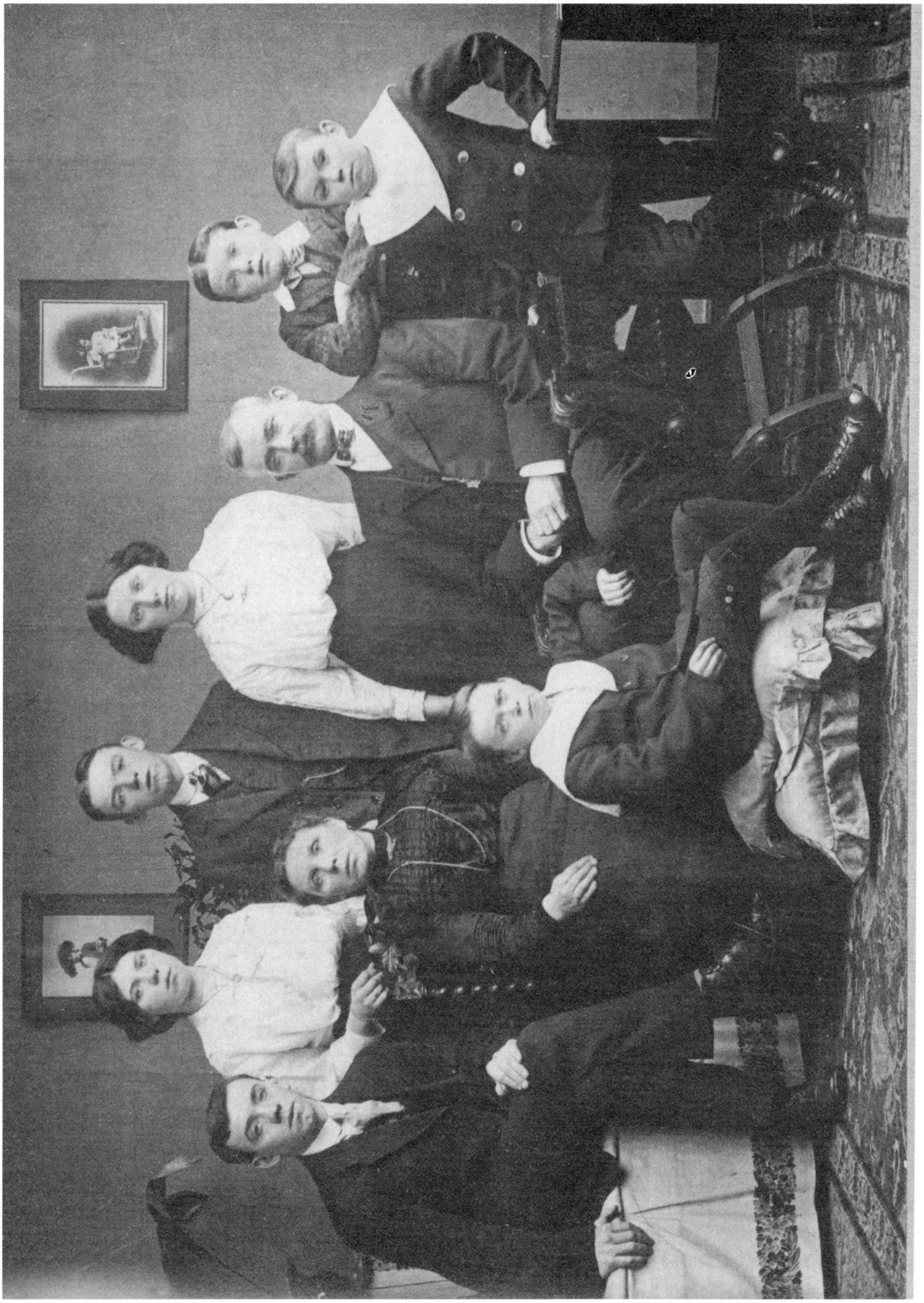

1915 aged eighteen, Annie died in 1918 aged twenty four and Timmy died in 1927 aged twenty four leaving a wife and son.

Mary Ellen, when elderly, fell from a table which she was standing on to put up the black out curtains. She broke her hip, an injury from which she never recovered and spent the last seven years of her life in bed in the front room. She died in February 1948.

When he retired from the pit Stephen became a 'knocker up' banging on the windows of those who were on the fore shift at three thirty in the morning. He also became the lamplighter at Leeholme lighting the gas street lights at dusk and putting them out the following morning. His grand-son Thomas remembers accompanying him on his rounds in the evening. Thomas remembers his grandfather as being very strict, a smart man with good posture. He was a good man and very religious. Jackie Moran remembers him in later life sitting in the chair quietly with his rosary in his hands. Stephen died almost two years to the day after Mary Ellen in February 1950.

Joe Mattimoe

Stephen and Mary Ellen's son Joe initially worked at Eldon pit as a Deputy until it flooded and closed when he went to work at Fishburn Colliery. It was while he was working at that pit that he was seriously injured. He was caught by a fall of stone which fractured his spine. He was in a plaster cast for several months but was eventually fit enough to go back down the pit when he went to work at Auckland Park. The after affects of his injuries forced him to give up working underground so he became an Ambulance Attendant at Leasingthorne Colliery.

He then became Steward at the Close House Club for three years following which he became landlord of the South Durham Hotel at Eldon Lane, locally referred to as the Top House, where he remained for seven years. Thomas's eldest son was born in the Top House.

Joe was a popular man always willing to help people. He was in the St John's Ambulance. He took a course on SAME instruction, a form of Swedish massage. Local Doctors referred people to him. Thomas particularly remembers one man who could not raise his head from its position leaning on to one of his shoulders. After each session there was significant improvement until finally he was cured.

In an indication of the seriousness with which the local community viewed the threat of war Joe sat and passed the ARP examination for the Ambulance Brigade in January 1939.

Whilst he worked in the colliery he used his skills to help train people for running. He ended up training the local youth football team in Eldon. During the Second World War when units of the Army were based at Eldon the Officer came to Joe and suggested a match be organised between the team and one from the army. Joe agreed and the match duly took place to be followed by several more whilst the army were in Eldon. The Officer was Matt Busby who went on to become the most famous manager of Manchester United.

Tommy Mattimoe

Stephen and Mary Ellen's son Tommy inherited the Mattimoe talent for dancing and he and his wife Minnie would take the lead in Old Time dance.

Fig. 114 Stephen and Mary Ellen's family taken around 1912. From left to right they are Frank Mattimoe who was to die in the battle for St Quentin eight weeks before the Armistice was declared; Annie who died in March 1918; Mary Ellen Mattimoe nee Hagan, sitting; Joseph 'Joe'; Tommy, sitting; Mary Eveline who died in 1915; Stephen Mattimoe; Cornelius 'Con'; Timmy.

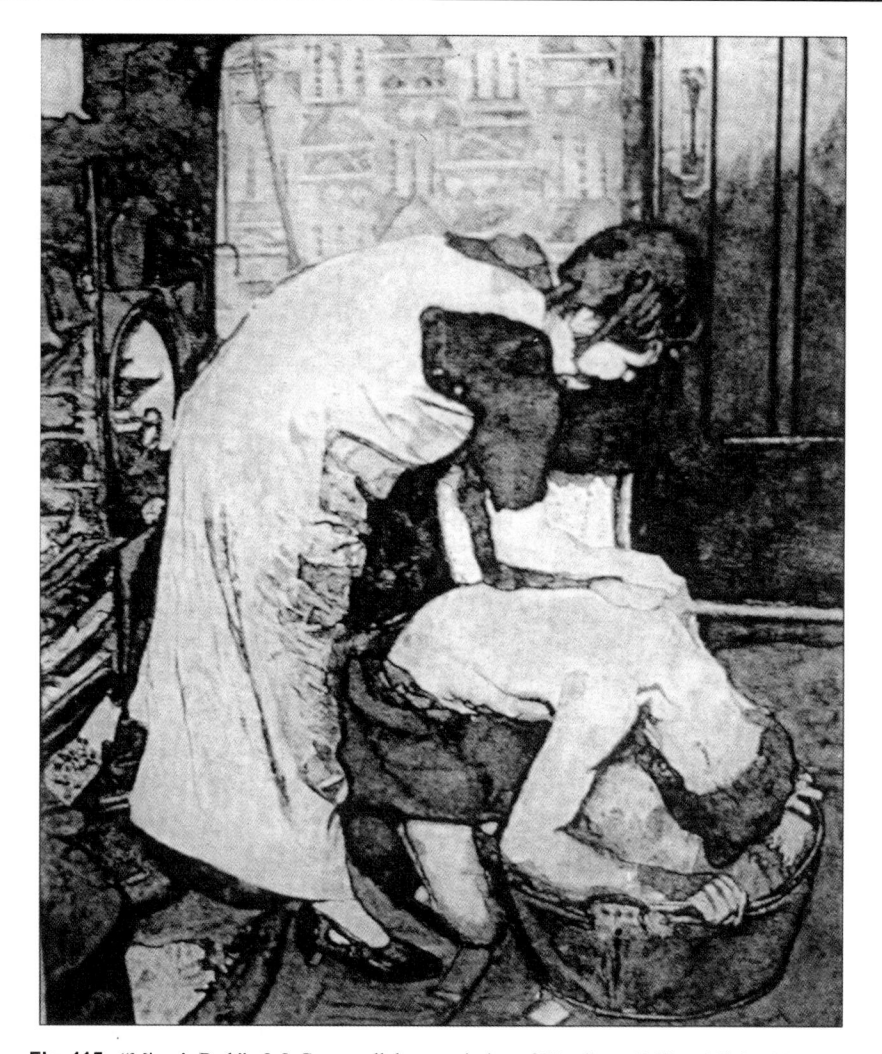

Fig. 115 "Miner's Bath", J. J. Greenwell by permission of Woodhorn Colliery Mining Museum

Life for a Pitman's Wife

In later life Stephen and Mary Ellen lived with their son, Con, and his family. Con's first wife died young and his young daughter, Mary, looked after the house. Mary remembers it being hard work for a young girl, the black leading and the baking of the bread. Con still worked down the pit so the house was always full. The desk bed in the front room was the domain of Stephen and Mary Ellen. Mary spoke of her tasks which were strongly reminiscent of those her father's Aunt Annie had to undertake as a young girl for her family.

> "When the men returned from the pit the tin bath had to be dragged in and the water boiled. There was a boiler beside the fire in the living room so there was always hot water. The fire never went out even in the night. You had to fill two pails of coal, one for the fire and one for the back. That's what was known as backing up the fire. Before you went to bed you would pull down the coal at the back. You did not need central heating the fire would heat

the whole house. You would come down in the morning and it was still warm. You always had hot water and the back kitchen had a set pot. On washday you would get the fire in the back kitchen set away and heat water in the set pot. Then you would boil clothes in it. The miner's clothes were washed once a week. You did not wash them more frequently because you could not get them dry. Cornelius was a fore overman, they had to go particular. When he got in you had to bash his pants and that against the wall to get the dust out of them. His kneepads had to be blackened with boot polish, for wear and appearance. He wore leggings. He used to polish and do his helmet. He left home dressed in his work clothes. There were no changing rooms at the pit and not until very late on were there showers."

Christmas time was a time for a get together but the best of all was New Years Eve when all the family would get together. Mary said "You go out for entertainment? You never saw such entertainment as we saw in here. Father was a canny singer and Tommy. Tommy played the mouth organ. We had some good times. The Mattimoes were musical a musical family and good dancers. They would say that you couldn't waltz unless you could waltz on a sixpence and not take the floor."

Throughout the rest of the year the families would receive frequent visitors. Sometimes this was for a particular activity such as the making of 'proddy' mats. The prodded mats which the Irish families and their descendants made were on a canvas backing which would be set up on a frame. Two holes would be made with the prodder and a strip of material pushed through and knotted on. This process would be repeated until the mat was completed. The mats reused the old clothes which were cut into strips (clippings) using scissors. Cutting the clippings was a job for the children. At the beginning the mat would be quite loose so the frame would have plugs to keep the canvas taut but as the mat progressed it would tighten naturally so the plugs would gradually be removed. The women would help each other out with their mats. On such visits the children would be made toffee. The mats were made in designs often with an Irish theme such as the shamrock. They would sell one or two at Christmas but even a large mat would only fetch fifteen shillings (75p).

Fig. 116

Fireplace in Miner's terrace.

17 Peter Mattimoe – A Pillar of the Community

A Big Loss to the Village

Peter Mattimoe played a full part in the community life of Evenwood and Ramshaw. The respect in which he was held was shown by his serving for thirty three years as checkweighman, a position demonstrating the trust and confidence he enjoyed of his work mates. He had served on the Parish Council becoming Chairman for a period. He also sat on the Burial Board, the Randolph Lodge Welfare Committee and the Board of Governors of the local school where he and so many other Mattimoes had been educated. He had been at the heart of village life through time spent as licensee of the Bridge Inn, Ramshaw and as Secretary of the Evenwood Workmen's Club. Over a period of nearly thirty years the local paper carried frequent mention of his active participation in all aspects of village life which had one common theme, the helping of others. It was therefore a great shock to the community when in January 1931 they learned of Peter's sudden death. The Auckland Chronicle recorded the news as follows.

> "A painful sensation was caused in the village on Sunday evening when it became known that Mr. Peter Mattimoe had died. The end came with tragic suddenness. He had just finished his tea and sat down in a chair and expired. Aged 63 he was checkweighman at Randolph Colliery, secretary of the Workmen's Club, a member of the Parish Council, a member of the Burial Board and he held other offices. He was held in high esteem by all classes, and will be a distinct loss to the village. Sympathy is felt for his widow and large family."

Fig. 117

The Bridge Inn at Ramshaw where Peter Mattimoe was landlord in the early years of the 20th century leading up to the First World War.

This photograph, taken in the 1950's shows the landlady, Mrs Banks, in the foreground together with a large gathering of customers who have brought their drinks and the tables outside for the benefit of the photographer.

Joe Hannon is the man in shirt sleeves standing second from the right.

Courtesy of Beamsih the North of England Open Air Museum

Peter Mattimoe's Family

Peter Mattimoe/Elizabeth Ann Kelly

b. 4.8.1867, Bishop Auckland   b. c.1876

d. 11.1.1931   m. 13.4.1904, St Chad's   d. 25.6.1957

- Jane Mattimoe b. 4.3.1905, d. 20.7.1967
  m. James Ward 30.11.1935, St William, Darlington
- Ann 'Annie' Mattimoe b. 16.04.1906, d. 9.9.1968
  m. William Armstrong 26.9.1936, St Augustus, Darlington
- Elizabeth Mattimoe b. 7.7.1907
- Mary Mattimoe b. 7.7.1907
- Esther Mattimoe b. 28.2.1909, d. 5.8.1984
- Peter 'Pete' Mattimoe b. 9.6.1910, d. c.1946
  m. Violet Tervit 28.7.1945
- Patrick 'Pat' Mattimoe b. 19.6.1912, d. 17.10.1977
  m. Irene Smith c.1946
- Thomas 'Tom' William Mattimoe b. 25.2.1914, d. 11.7.1974
- Evelyn Mattimoe b. 19.9.1915, d. 7.11.1974
  m. Harry Fearnley 31.10.1942, Leeds

There was a large gathering for Peter's funeral. The funeral procession was headed by representatives of the Randolph Miners Lodge who also sent a globe. Other organizations represented included the Parish Council, the Burial Board, the Miners Welfare Association, the Workmen's Club and, in an indication of his political affiliation, the Labour Party

"THE INTERMENT took place at the Evenwood Cemetery on Thursday of Mr Peter Mattimoe, of West Terrace, Evenwood. Mr Mattimoe who had reached the age of 63 years was held in high esteem in Evenwood and the surrounding district, having been a checkweighman for the past thirty years, nine years being spent at the Evenwood Randolph Colliery. He had served as a parish councilor, workers compensation hon. Secretary, member of the Burial Board, Court of Referees (representing miners), vice-president of Evenwood Miners' Welfare, and had held the office of hon. Secretary of the Evenwood Work Men's Club for the past 16 years. The cortege was headed by the Randolph officials, including Mr T H Blacklock (manager), and the Randolph Lodge Miners' Union. The service at the graveside was conducted by Father Walmsley, Witton Park. Principal mourners were :- Mrs Elizabeth Mattimoe (widow), Misses Jane Mattimoe, Esther Mattimoe, Elizabeth Mattimoe, Mary Mattimoe, Evelyn Mattimoe and Annie Mattimoe (daughters); Peter Mattimoe, Patrick Mattimoe, Thomas Mattimoe (sons); W F Mattimoe (brother), Mr and Mrs T Kelly, Esperley Lane; Mr and Mrs G Kelly, Esperley Lane; Mr and Mrs A Bainbridge, Cockfield; Mr and Mrs T Merryweather; Hannon family, Ramshaw; Mr and Mrs F Hannon, West Auckland; Mr and Mrs Mattimoe, Leeholme; and Mr W Armstrong. Others present included Alderman J Davis, J. P. (Cockfield), Councillors E Liddle, G Parkin, J Gent and D Carrick; Capt. J R Lowson Mr R Place, Mr H L Raines, Mr G Heaviside, Mr J Sowerby, Mr R Hodgson, Mr J Turnbull, Mr R Parkin, Mr G Hollis, Mr J Welch, Mr and Mrs L Corner, Mr Morland, Mrs T Dixon and Mrs H Robinson. The committee members of the Workers' Club acted as pall bearers, Messrs R Hesiltine, J Walton, R Race, J Gaffney, G Howe, T H Parkin, J Hewitt and T Young."

Fig. 118 Peter Mattimoe

The sudden, unexpected nature of Peter's death is demonstrated by the record of his attendance at the meeting of the Burial Board in December 1930, a month before his death, where he and another agreed to arrange purchase of a waterproof cover for use by the Caretaker when mowing grass in bad weather. At the annual meeting of the Randolph Welfare Committee in the Temperance Hall, Evenwood the chairman, Mr G Holliss, referred to the loss they had suffered in the death of Peter Mattimoe and a vote of sympathy was passed.

Seventy years after his death descendants of his family and friends still spoke about Peter with great fondness and respect.

Peter's wife Lizzie died in June 1957 in Evenwood, the last representative of that generation.

Peter and Lizzie's Children

Peter and Lizzie had a large family. The eldest was Jane who married James Ward. Jane did not enjoy a happy life but had three children the eldest of whom, Peter was born on the day before the Second World War was declared and went on to become a butcher in Evenwood with many an interesting tale of his time helping on the rounds of the villages in all weathers. Their second child, Annie, married William Armstrong and they had a son Brian who was born on the day after the Second World War was declared. Elizabeth and Mary remained single, Mary becoming a nurse. The fifth child, another daughter Esther progressed to become a Matron at the local hospital. Her nephew Brian remembers calling to pick her up from the hospital not knowing that she was the matron and being surprised at the reverent response from nurses in the hospital when he enquired about his Aunt.

The sixth child, a son Peter, followed in his father's footsteps becoming an active member of the community. He lived in difficult times and in January 1937 had to move away to find work. The Auckland Chronicle recorded the sad loss to the village.

Fig. 119 Esther Mattimoe

> "Mr Peter Mattimoe eldest son of the late Mr P. Mattimoe, Colliery Checkweighman, has left the Evenwood district to take up work at Willington Quay.
> Mr. Mattimoe has been a very active worker and rendered valuable service to the public life of Evenwood. He will be a big loss to the district. He has been secretary of the Evenwood and District Social Service Centre, secretary of the Gardens' Guild, secretary of the South West Durham SSC Club and representative of a sub-committee of the Community Service Council Ltd. He has always taken an active part in sport having been secretary of the Evenwood Crusaders and the Gaunless Valley League. He will have the best wishes of the people of Evenwood and district."

Peter sadly died when aged thirty five leaving a widow, Violet.

The seventh child Patrick married and had a daughter but also had to move away to find work. Sadly Patrick's wife and daughter both died of tuberculosis and he was to return to Evenwood and spend his latter years living with his sister Esther.

The eighth child Thomas William remained in Evenwood all his life and never married. He initially worked on the railway as a guard then become a storekeeper at Randolph, Shildon and Dean and Chapter Collieries before ill health brought about his semi-retirement. He was a religious man and was closely connected with St Chad's Roman Catholic Church, Witton Park.

The last child, Evelyn, married Harry Fearnley, and they had three daughters one of whom died in childhood.

Little Ireland

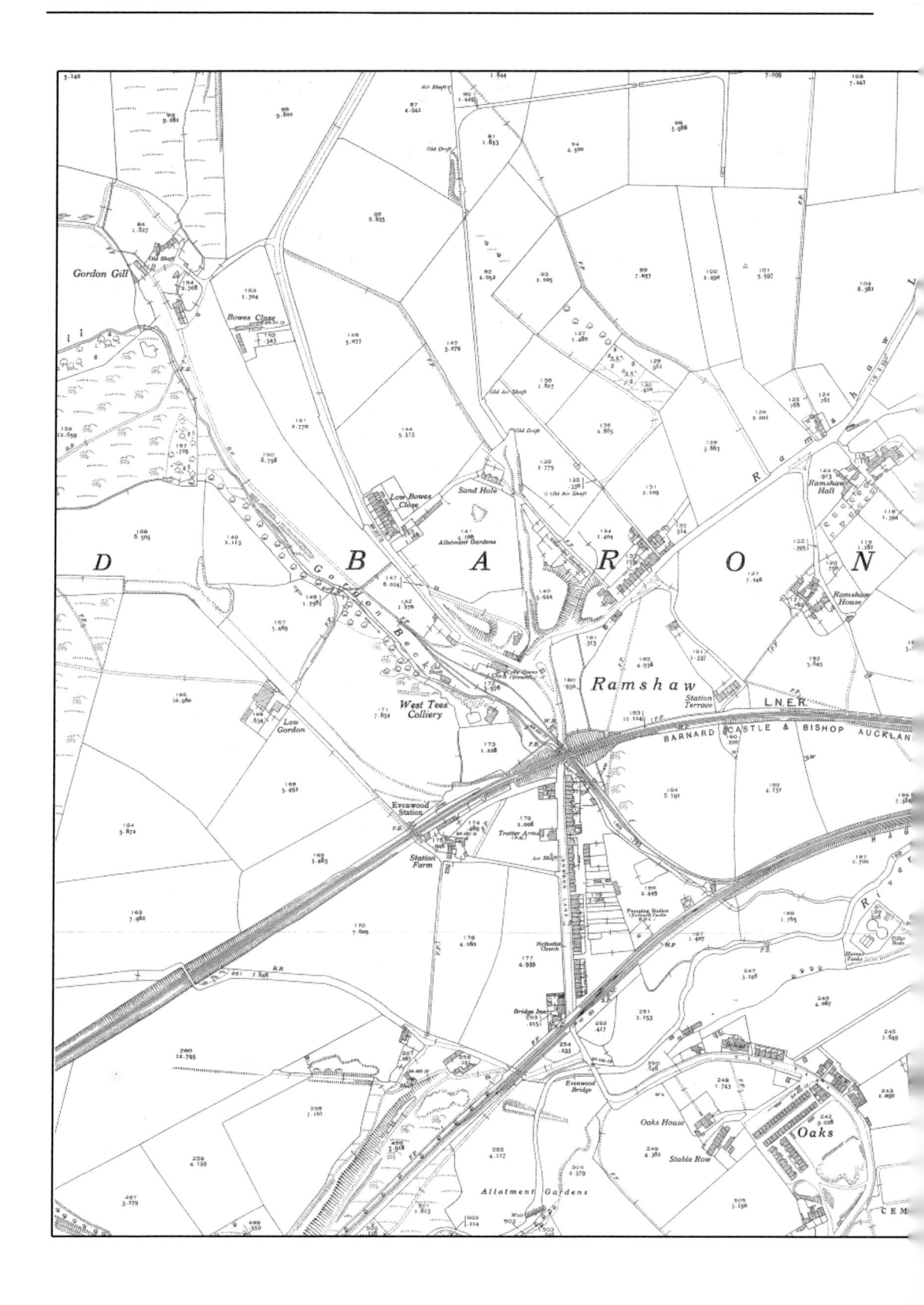

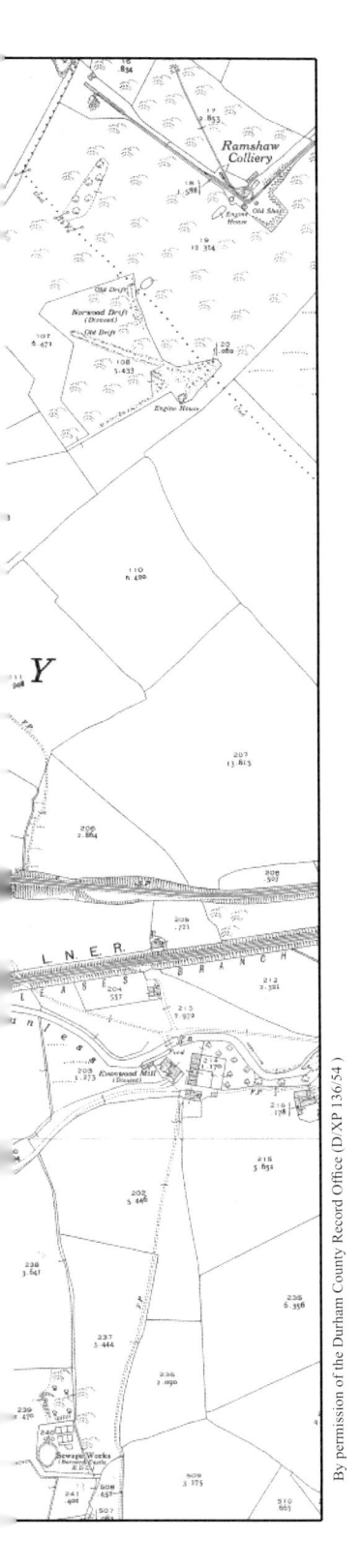

Fig. 120

This Ordnance Survey map of 1939, scale 1:2500, shows Ramshaw as it stood at the outbreak of the Second World War. West Tees Colliery is shown though by this time was not operational, its coke ovens disused and the tramway and rail links shown on the 1921 map much reduced. Randolph Colliery in nearby Evenwood was the main colliery in this area at this time. Other collieries in the Gaunless Valley seemed to be thriving however as the Haggerleases line had been widened from the single track shown in 1921 to two tracks shown on this map. New drifts had been opened up above Ramshaw. A Norwood Drift had been opened up north of Ramshaw Hall but it had a short life and had been abandoned by 1939, only the entrances to the drift and the engine house remaining. North of this drift a Ramshaw Colliery had been established with several tramways leading to drift workings in that area. Tom Hannon worked at this colliery, walking to work up the long hill from Gordon Lane to the colliery at Ramshaw Heugh.

In common with the rest of the country Evenwood and Ramshaw had set land aside to be divided into allotments to encourage working men to improve their health through exercise in the growing of fruit and vegetables. The regular reports of the Evenwood and Ramshaw Vegetable shows indicates that such encouragement was not needed locally but the allotments were eagerly taken up, providing a valuable additional source of fresh vegetables for local families. The allotments in Ramshaw lay in an area bounded by the houses of Bowes Close and Sandhole and by the Institute, previously Ramshaw School. Further allotments can be seen west of the Oaks.

Gordon Gill remained little changed though the cottages previously occupied by the Mattimoes, Gaffneys and other families of Irish descent which gave the area its name *'Little Ireland'* were soon to be abandoned. However, even at this date, a Grandson of Thomas Mattimoe, John Hannon, was living in the Gill with his young family. They were soon to move to Gordon Bank Top next to Jane Peacock, niece of Thomas Mattimoe.

The pumping station, behind the houses in Gordon Lane, belonging to Barnard Castle Rural District Council indicates that mains water and drainage had now been provided to these houses including the one where the rest of the Hannon family lived together with Thomas Mattimoe's youngest son, Frank.

18   The Hannon Family

By 1920 Annie and Thomas Hannon and their family had moved to the end house in Gordon Lane. The Haggerlease Branch line ran between the house and the River Gaunless. A level crossing by the bridge stopped the traffic when the steam engines pulling the trucks of coal and coke from the bankhead of Railey Fell and the other pits further up the line. The houses at this end of Gordon Lane did not have gardens, instead the 'green' between the backs of the houses and the railway were used as a communal area for the women of the houses to hang out their washing to dry, providing the opportunity for social exchange during their working day. The enginemen would take advantage of the proximity of the line to the houses and ask the women for hot water to make tea in their cabs. No doubt in return the drivers would take extra care on wash days to ensure the engines did not belch too much smoke and soot smuts as they passed. The young boys of Gordon Lane viewed the trains and their wagons as playthings and regularly had to be chased out of the stationary wagons that were about to be coupled up to the engine and taken away. One time a lad escaped detection and was not found until the train reached Barnard Castle.

The Hannon family had the use of the fields which lay either side of Gordon Lane between the railway line and the river. These were run as a smallholding. They had goats which were relatively easy to keep and could be fed on vegetable waste from the kitchen and allotment, weeds such as dock and dandelion and even hedge trimmings. If the diet was supplemented by a little bran, oats or cattle cake a good milking goat could yield one hundred gallons of milk a year. This was a useful supplement to the diet of the Hannon's large family. The milk was not to the taste of all the visitors to the Hannon household. Frank Mattimoe from Chester le Street was one who refused to drink it knowingly, but as there was no alternative he drank plenty of it unknowingly.

Living over Mine Workings

The tunnels of the drift mines of Railey Fell were often close to the surface. Miners would say that the workings under Gordon Lane were so close to the surface that on wash days, when the women gathered together on the green behind the houses to pound their washing in tubs with possing sticks the sound could be heard clearly in the tunnels. Tom Seagrave told me that in the 1970's he and another man were excavating and extending an abandoned drift in the land behind the Bridge Inn towards Lands. At times the seam was only fifteen feet below the surface but as they excavated toward the old railway line it became very near to the surface to the extent that a tap on the roof of the tunnel brought down the roof to let in daylight.

Tom told me that the workings beneath the houses in Gordon Lane were very extensive "like a ballroom with pillars of coal left to hold up the roof". Not surprisingly these workings were to give rise to major subsidence problems in later years. The large tree, some fifty feet high, opposite the houses in Gordon Lane, and shown in the postcard dated 1913 in Fig. 81, disappeared entirely when the land around it subsided. Some years later when Tom was in the old workings beneath Gordon Lane, some eighty feet below ground, he came across the roots of that tree hanging from the roof of the tunnel. Bizarrely this 'landmark' enabled him to get his bearings underground and find his way back to the mine entrance.

Annie Mattimoe's Family

Annie Mattimoe / Thomas Hannon
b. 14..1872, Gordon Gill, Ramshaw   b. c.1878
d. 5.6.1928   m. St. Chad's   d. 1928

- Ann Mattimoe b. 19.11.1900, d. May 1901

- John Hannon b. November 1901, d. July 1980
  m. Lucy Holmes

- Mary Jane Hannon b. 14.12.1902, d. July 1922

- Sarah Jane 'Sally' Hannon 15.12.1903, d. 26.5.1974

- Elizabeth Ellen Hannon b. 7.3.1905, d. November 1921

- Joseph 'Joe' Hannon b. 23.3.1906, d. May 1983

- Thomas 'Tom' Hannon 12.5.1908, d. 27.5.1965
  m. Alice Bradwell c.1937

- Matthew 'Mattie' Hannon b. 1909, d. August 1915

- Francis 'Frank' Hannon b. 6.1.1911, d. 9.11.1987
  m. Kathleen McCrory

- Nora Hannon
  m. Lesley Finlay

- Catherine 'Kitty' Hannon b. 9.12.1913

Annie and Thomas Hannon Pass Away

Annie and Thomas suffered poor health. Annie had led a hard life since a young girl and now in later life suffered strokes that weakened her and eventually robbed her of speech. Her last years were spent sitting in the house in Gordon Lane. She died in June 1928. The report in the local paper read as follows.

> "Mrs Annie Hannon, wife of Thomas Hannon, Gordon Lane, Ramshaw, who had been in failing health for a long period, died on Tuesday of last week. There was a very large gathering at the funeral which took place on Friday. Father Walmsley, Witton Park, officiated. Mrs Hannon was 56, and much sympathy is extended to Mr Hannon who is in a delicate state of health, and the large family of sons and daughters."

Annie's husband Thomas had also suffered failing health for some considerable time. He had tuberculosis that had prevented him working and he had spent time in sanatoriums. His family felt the social stigma attached to the disease and never spoke of it though in reality the disease was far too common and though often linked to poor living and working conditions was no respecter of social position.

Thomas Hannon had never been the easiest of people to get on with but when, some nine months after his wife had died, he lay dying, with his children gathered round him, he called his son Joe to his bedside and said, talking of his two grandchildren from his eldest son John, "Joe, when I am gone look after the bairns in the Gill. If you have a loaf, give them half." then he died.

John Hannon

Annie and Thomas's eldest son, John, was born in *'Little Ireland'* and went to the local school. He left school at fourteen and started work at Railey Fell Pit as a pony putter leading the horses underground as they pulled the tubs of coal to the place from where they would be pulled to the surface.

John Hannon was a devout man to whom his Roman Catholic religion was very important yet he married Lucy Holmes who was from a Salvation Army family. Lucy converted to Catholicism and, as is often the case with converts, adhered strongly to her new religion. Her family were not overly happy at her marrying a Roman Catholic of Irish descent but there was no family rift over the issue. However when their first child Pat was born one of Lucy's family, when visiting the new born said of the baby "Look at those eyes, straight from the bog" thus in one sentence dismissing both the child's ancestry and religion. John and Lucy lodged for a time with Frank and Nellie Mattimoe in Chester le Street where Pat was born.

The family then went back to Ramshaw living in Gordon Gill where their son, Bernard,

Fig. 121 John Hannon

Fig. 122 and 123   Aunt Jane and Joe Peacock.

This image of Jane, daughter of Patrick and Mary Ann Mattimoe, has been taken from a novelty photograph taken at the seaside resort of Redcar before the First World War. The original photograph was a mere 3/4"x1 1/4" (2 1/2 x 3 cms) but the image is extremely clear. Joe died in April 1955 and Jane died three years later in May 1958. They are buried together in Evenwood cemetery.

was born. Later they went to live at Gordon Bank Top in the same row as Joe Peacock and his wife Jane, daughter of Patrick Mattimoe.

Everybody loved Jane but did not appear to have much time for Joe. Apparently in her youth Jane was considered a beauty and could have had her choice of men for a husband. It seems the family thought she could have done better than Joe. While John Hannon's family were living next to Joe and Jane in early 1940 the following incident occurred which seemed to confirm the family's view of Joe.

Air Raid on Ramshaw

During the Second World War German bombers would drop flares over Ramshaw and Evenwood on the way to their targets. A German Company had built the big chimney at Randolph Colliery, Evenwood before the War however the aim of the bombers was not to bomb the pits but instead to provide markers for the return journey to Germany. In June 1940 a flight of German bombers on their way to Newcastle were intercepted by fighter planes sent up from the nearby airbase at Catterick and turned back. Unable to drop their payload of bombs on the intended target and no doubt anxious to lighten the aircraft to better make their escape they deposited their bombs over Ramshaw and Cockfield.

There had been an air raid warning the previous day which proved to be a lone British plane returning to its base thus when the sirens sounded this day no one reacted. The danger was real though and as the bombs were dropped some fell close to Gordon Bank Top.

Aunt Jane had made precautions for such an eventuality. Hers was the only house in the short terrace with a cellar and she had equipped it with chairs and large oil lamps each with a big glass cowl. One lamp had been hung over the steep stairs leading down to the cellar from the joist of the floor above to light the way.

When the bombs started dropping Lucy Hannon hurried her young family next door to Aunt Jane's, her

Fig. 124

An agitated Joe, minus his trousers, appeared at the top of the stairs leading down to the basement. "There I hope you b*****'s are happy", he blurted before knocking the large oil lamp, bringing the glass cowl crashing down onto his head.

Illustration by Stewart Lees

husband, John, was out on duty as an air raid warden. The other neighbours followed suit except for one old gentleman who refused to move and remained sitting in his chair in the kitchen of his house. John's young son Bernard could recall the whole incident vividly over sixty years later and remembered the eerie whistling sound of the bombs as they fell and the tremendous explosions that followed when they landed nearby as he made his way to the safety of the cellar. In all some fifty bombs fell.

Once the explosions stopped those gathered in the basement waited nervously to see whether the raid had truly finished. Suddenly the door to the basement at the head of the stairs flew open and Joe Peacock, in a somewhat agitated state, began to descend the stairs. Joe was a Special Constable at the time in addition to his job as a coal miner and appeared in full uniform from the waist up including tin hat but, possibly because he had been in bed due to working night shift that week, he was minus his trousers. He looked down at the sheltering families and they looked up at this wild-eyed half dressed figure of authority. Joe blurted out "There, I hope you b*****s are happy now, you've got what you wanted!" No one to this day was certain of what he meant though he was a bombastic man, full of his self importance in his role as a Special, and would often castigate others for sitting around doing nothing at a time of war. No sooner had he spoken than the drama and impact of his words were instantly dispelled as he banged his head against the suspended oil lamp dislodging the large glass cowl which fell onto his head and smashed. Through serendipity Joe's decision to put his tin hat on rather than his trousers saved him from serious harm but the shock of the crash appeared to make him think the raid had resumed and he scuttled down the rest of the stairs, fell into a chair and sat in stunned silence amongst the equally stunned spectators of the bizarre event. One can only imagine the looks they gave each other but it was a story that was told many times over the years, with humour and without the need for embellishment.

This moment of high farce belied the fact that the danger they were sheltering from was very real. When the families eventually emerged from the basement they found that the houses had luckily not been hit, but bombs exploding in nearby fields had blown the glass out of the windows. Happily the old gentleman who had insisted in staying seated in his kitchen chair escaped injury from flying glass. John Hannon's wife Lucy had a beautiful statuette of Our Lady of Lourdes in a blue cloak which drew many admiring comments from visitors for its beautiful serene face. This statuette was always kept in the window of the front room. On inspecting the damage after emerging from the basement the statue was

Illustration by Stewart Lees

Fig. 125 Mr Quadrini, the ice-cream seller, was found sheltering under a hedge, holding a biscuit tin on his head for protection

found still standing in the window, totally undamaged, not even a scratch. The statuette still stands in her daughter, Angela's, house.

Another lucky escapee of the raid was Mr Quadrini. He was an Italian ice-cream maker who lived at Witton Park where his family had an old fashioned ice-cream shop with booths. The Quadrini family were well known to the Hannons as they all attended mass at St. Chad's Chapel He had a horse and a two-wheeled cart in which he would travel round the local villages selling his ice-cream. On this day he was riding his horse and cart down Gordon Bank from Toft Hill when the bombs started to drop. Mr Quadrini quickly tied his horse to the cart and took shelter in a hedge. It was there he was found after the raid looking understandably ashen, still holding the biscuit tin on his head, the only meagre means he had found to protect himself.

There was only one casualty from the raid, a young lad in Cockfield, by sad irony an evacuee from Newcastle, who had walked out into the street to see what was happening and was killed by the blast from an explosion.

Most of the bombs fell into fields where grazing cows caught the force of the blasts presenting a horrific spectacle of gore and mutilation to the local villagers.

John Hannon and his family suffered no ill effect from the raid, and although it took several months for the windows to be reglazed there was little discomfort during that Summer and the house was secure from the weather before Winter arrived.

Thus it was that John Hannon gained the dubious honour of having been "blown out" of his home in the little village of Ramshaw in both World Wars, firstly by Zeppelin L16 in April 1916 and then by the Luftwaffe in June 1940.

John Hannon's Later Life

John Hannon loved the Lake District, though he had never seen Ireland the scenery would have similarities with the Loughs of Co. Sligo. Visits there on a Sunday were no excuse for missing Mass. He would say to the Family on a Saturday "Early start tomorrow, first Mass in Barnie". The next morning they would get up early load the car with food, water and the primus then head off to Barnard Castle for the 8am Mass then drive to the Lake District. Another Saturday he would say "Early start tomorrow, second Mass in Ambleside" and the next morning they would load the car in the same way and head off to the Lake District stopping at the little corrugated tin Roman Catholic Church in Ambleside for Mass.

John took the family to Walsingham in Norfolk one time. They stayed in a convent. Before returning he went in to the Church to say three Hail Marys so that the family would complete the journey home safely. He would always raise his cap when he passed a church.

He joined the Leeks Club. Determined to win a prize with his leeks he buried a religious medal where the leeks were planted and the children had to pray to the Saint each night to help the leeks grow.

He shared the fear of forebears that his children would be tempted away from the Roman Catholic faith. There was a Methodist Chapel in the village and his daughter, Angela, was invited by one of her friends to the children's Sunshine Club. Thinking that it sounded like fun she asked her father if she could go and poor John nearly choked on his tea. Needless to say Angela never found out whether the Sunshine Club lived up to her expectation.

John was a quiet man but worked on behalf of the Miners Union and fought to get what was due to members particularly in the way of pensions or compensation for widows whose husbands had been killed in the mines. One time the son of a miner who had been killed in an accident at the pit came to see John to seek his help in getting a pension for his mother. John had to tell the man that his father had only paid into the pension fund for himself and not his wife. Sadly the man had not lived long enough to draw his pension and left his widow destitute. John was unable to help in the circumstances and had to give the son the bad news but it left him feeling he had let the family down even though it was not his fault.

Uncle Frank Mattimoe

Frank Mattimoe, brother of Annie Hannon, had always lived with the Hannon family both in the traditional home in the Gill and once they moved to Gordon Lane. He never married and, following the death of his sister and her husband, Uncle Frank became a surrogate father to those nieces and nephews still living at home. His position became so unquestionably accepted by his nieces and nephews and their children they assumed he was a Hannon. Senior of these was Sally, the eldest surviving daughter who also never married but became the female head of the house and was proved an excellent cook and manager of the families limited finances.

Uncle Frank was a very good, selfless man. His grand niece, Maureen, remembers sitting with him at the back of the house and being comforted by him as a steam engine went by, something that terrified her. When John Hannon and his brother Joe had one of the scavenging contracts for Evenwood, which involved cleaning out the middens at the bottom of the terraces of houses which were used both as toilets and depositories for the household rubbish, they would retrieve any jam jars that had been thrown away. These would be taken home to Uncle Frank who would carefully wash each one, a not very pleasant task, then sell them. The money he raised he gave to the Catholic mission.

Uncle Frank retained a sense of fun and Sally, whom he loved dearly but who could sometimes be rather unbending and lacking in humour, was occasionally the unwitting object of his gentle amusement. Maureen tells the story of one dinnertime when Uncle Frank sat opposite Sally chewing and chewing on

Fig. 126

Frank Mattimoe, brother of Annie Hannon, who lived with his sister's family all his life. This photograph was taken at the back of the houses in Gordon Lane on 'The Green' where the women of the families hung their washing to dry. Behind Uncle Frank can be seen the sidings where the railway coal trucks were stored either awaiting filling or, when full, to begin their journey down the Haggerleases line.

a piece of meat with Sally watching him with increasing agitation. Eventually, when she could contain herself no longer, she asked "Is it tough?" Frank chewed a bit longer, pondering the question, then said "Oh aye" sending Sally into a huff.

Towards the end of his life Uncle Frank suffered from breathing problems as did many men of the family. Perhaps this points to an inherited weakness but if so it would certainly have been aggravated by a working life spent working down the pit, breathing its damp air, laden with coal dust.

Uncle Frank loved his nephews and nieces and their children. He also loved Stephen and Jane the offspring of his eldest brother Patrick. When in December 1939 he lay close to death, he asked "Where are the boys?" referring to his nephews Joe and Tom Hannon. He was told that they were out. In fact they were attending the funeral of his nephew Stephen Mattimoe. Even as he finished asking the question the horse drawn hearse bearing Stephen's coffin from his home in Bowes Close to the cemetery on the other side of the Gaunless passed the house and those at the bedside could hear the noise of the horse's hooves on the road beneath the bedroom window. Uncle Frank died three days later and was buried in the same cemetery, four graves along from his nephew.

Sally Hannon

Sally assumed the role of the 'mother' to the family when her own mother, Annie, became too ill to manage the house. In an echo of her mother's own life this would have happened when Sally was barely a teenager. Sally was an excellent manager of the families affairs and all benefited from the start in life her efforts gave them. Sally dedicated herself to the family and never married though her combination of good looks and domestic management skills would have made her quite a catch. Her Faith was a very important part of her life and she imparted this to her brothers and sisters and their children. Her efforts were rewarded by the love she received from her family and the enduring friendship of those in her community.

Joe Hannon

Joe Hannon, who never married and remained living in the family home in Gordon Lane, worked at the pit in an above ground job and assumed responsibility for the animals in the

Fig. 127 Sally Hannon

family's fields though was not comfortable around them. The horses would be allowed to feed in the woods on the other side of the river. His niece, Maureen, remembers walking in the wood on the other side of the Ramshaw bridge. The wood was littered with old mine shafts. At the bottom of one of the shafts was a skeleton of a horse that had fallen in and could not be rescued. The horse's skull could still be seen with a round hole where it had been shot to put it out of its misery.

Joe's nephew Bernard remembers having to feed the goats when he got home from school and being told by Joe not to put his hand in the feed bucket. Being a boy and not keen on the task of feeding the goats he put his hand in the bucket when his uncle was not looking and stirred the food around. The goats refused to eat and consequently Bernard was not asked to feed them again very often.

Joe was a good public spirited man and served on both the Parish and the District Council.

Tom Hannon

Thomas and Annie Hannon's son Tom Hannon married a very pretty woman named Alice Bradwell and they had a daughter Ann. They lived next door to Sally and Kitty in Gordon Lane. Sadly Tom and Alice separated after two years and eventually divorced. Tom fought a custody battle for his daughter but lost. He never saw his daughter again but he sent her mother a postal order every week.

Frank Hannon

Frank Hannon left school in 1925 at the age of fourteen. His father told him "There's a boy wanting at the store" and Frank went to the store in Evenwood to see about it. In those days all those interested in a job put their names in a hat. Frank's was the last name in the hat but first out and he became a butcher boy. He stuck with the job which was to provide the foundation of his working life. The early days were not easy for Frank and he found the slaughtering of the animals traumatic and suffered nightmares following the days the killing took place. He went to work for a butcher at Butterknowle, travelling there on the bus then taking a horse and cart round the villages selling the meat.

Fig. 128 Annie's son Frank Hannon at Blackpool in the late 1930's.

Fig. 129 (above) Class 6, Ramshaw School in 1920. Kitty Hannon second from the left of the middle row. Esther Mattimoe, daughter of Peter Mattimoe, fourth from the left in the front row.

Fig. 130 (below) Class 1, Ramshaw School in 1920. Nora Hannon fifth from the left in the second row back. Somehow Esther Mattimoe also appears in this photograph fourth from the right of the front row. These photographs were taken in the new school. The houses on the Oaks can be seen in the distance.

Fig. 131 Ramshaw School Cookery Class c.1920. The school building could not accommodate these classes so the children walked to the school at Toft Hill for cookery lessons. Charts on the wall describe the various cuts of meat. The long scrubbed table and metal wash tubs hint at the hard physical work involved in these lessons which would have come as no surprise to these young girls who were used to helping their mothers and elder sisters at home. Nora Hannon is standing at the back of the group sixth from the right.

Kitty Hannon

Kitty went to be Housekeeper to the priest at Coundon. She was dedicated to him but towards the end of his working life he "went funny" and was retired to Benton near Newcastle. Kitty went with him. When he died Kitty returned to live with Sally and her brothers. After a life dedicated to looking after the priest it could not have been easy for her to settle back into family life but she did and continued her selfless approach to those close to her and would do anything for her nieces and nephews.

Nora Hannon

Nora married Leslie Finlay and lived in Bishop Auckland. Leslie was from a Methodist family but converted to the Roman Catholic faith. He was an accomplished engineer who started an apprenticeship with a local firm. Leslie would relate how the firm had a contract to build a bridge across a river in Africa. Leslie became concerned

Fig. 132 Nora Hannon on holiday in Ireland where she stayed with her Uncle Michael who is standing next to her in this photograph.

about the design and at home did some calculations that convinced him that the bridge would not be structurally sound for the load it had to carry. He told his employers of his concerns but they were apparently not interested and he left the Company. He became a bus driver but retained his love of engineering and had a workshop in his garden and became a member of the Model Club in Bishop Auckland. He was a very accomplished model maker and made beautiful working models, some powered by steam, and was often offered money to sell them which he declined. Eventually he accepted commissions from museums for specific models.

He made a model of the Flying Scotsman and having constructed the boiler wanted to undertake a pressure test so, waiting until Nora was out visiting, he set the boiler up in the kitchen, plugged the safety valve and proceeded to build up the steam pressure. His daughter, Maureen and the family's pet dog were in the adjacent room when there was suddenly a loud bang followed by long shrill screech. The dog jumped to its feet staring white eyed at the door, all its hair standing on end. Leslie shouted to his daughter in urgent tone "Don't open the back door!" When safe to do so, Maureen opened the back door to find that the safety plug had been driven out of the boiler letting a fierce jet of pressurised steam hit the kitchen door removing the paint in a long clearly demarcated strip. When Nora returned home and surveyed the damage she looked at Leslie and addressed him with her usual comment reserved for such occasions "Well I'll be damned, you are devoid of sense".

Fig. 133 Nora Hannon and Leslie Finlay on their wedding day.

The model was completed without further incident and used on the railway track installed by the Model Club in Bishop Auckland giving rides to local children until vandalism forced its closure. The model of the Flying Scotsman was later donated to a museum.

Fig. 134 Leslie Finlay with model steam railway engine he built.

Leslie's engineering skills extended to optical instruments and he made a microscope and an astronomical telescope. When he used the telescope in the garden Nora was always concerned that the neighbours would think he was a 'Peeping Tom'.

Leslie made some models for the Local Education Authority based in Barnard Castle which would be taken round to the schools for demonstration purposes. His daughter Maureen became a teacher and remembers one of them being brought to her school. When she told them her father had made the model they wanted him to come to the school but by then, sadly, he had died.

Open House

The Hannon house in Gordon Lane, Ramshaw was popular with the great grandchildren of Thomas and Anne Mattimoe. Those who lived in Bishop Auckland, Coundon and Chester-le-Street spoke with fond recollection of school holidays spent with the Hannons. All regarded these times as country holidays confirming that Ramshaw retained its rural atmosphere despite the close proximity of the coal mine. Children would sleep head to toe in the upstairs bedroom. Days would be spent playing in the fields. Delicious, wholesome meals were provided courtesy of Aunt Sally's excellent culinary skills.

Fig. 135 Nora (far right), Sally and Leslie on holiday in Ireland on a 'nice soft day'.

Country living could confront the children with the unexpected. Anne Mattimoe, policeman Frank's youngest daughter from Chester-le-Street recalled two aspects which, as a young girl brought up in a town, she found difficult. When presented with a boiled duck egg for breakfast she turned to her Aunt who had presented her with this delicacy and said "Aunt Sally, I don't eat blue eggs". In researching for this book Anne accompanied me to the Beamish Museum, who had kindly allowed us to search their photo library. We came across photos of an outside toilet or 'netty'. This prompted Anne to tell me the story of the time she was in the back yard at Gordon Lane when Aunt Sally called out from the 'netty' "Anne, get me some paper". Anne looked round then, and in words that showed how well her family lived on a policeman's salary, called back "Aunt Sally, I can't find any toilet paper". Aunt Sally replied "Well pass me a magazine". Anne looked round but could only find the Sacred Heart Catholic magazine so she called "Aunt Sally, I an only find the Sacred Heart" to which Aunt Sally replied "That'll do" and Anne duly passed the magazine under the door. Anne, as a young girl, was mortified by the incident and thought it was a sin and wondered to herself "How am I going to tell the Priest at Confession".

Sally Hannon insisted the visiting children went to church on Sunday at St Chad's, Witton Park which involved an hour's walk across the fields. Mary Haye, eldest daughter of policeman Frank Mattimoe in Chester-le-Street remembered the walk which she always enjoyed with the adults carrying the children when they became tired. Observance of fasting before Mass was insisted upon by Sally but the lack of food and the long walk was sometimes too much for the children. Mary remembers on one occasion accompanying the Hannons to church with her sister Ronnie when on entering the building Ronnie fainted and fell flat on her face. Sometimes there was the opportunity for a lift back to Ramshaw from one of the congregation who had a car otherwise it was an hour's walk back before breakfast.

All who stayed with the Hannon family were sure of a warm welcome, good hospitality and a happy time. Everyone who I spoke to regarded these visits as a special treat and many stayed every year during the school holidays.

19   Life Continues

Coal mining is no longer an employer of any significance in the Bishop Auckland area. Railey Fell, or West Tees as it became, closed in 1939; Randolph Colliery closed in 1965; Eldon lane Colliery closed in 1932; Leasingthorne closed in 1965. Opencast mining brought a brief resumption of the industry in the 1980's bringing more noise and dust than had been seen during the industry's heyday in the area. This activity quickly came to an end and the land has been restored so that today little evidence remains of the areas mining past. The countryside around Ramshaw and Evenwood is beautiful and peaceful. The fells are now the domain of the rambler.

The railways, tramways and collieries of Ramshaw have long since disappeared but if we stand on the site and look over the Gaunless valley, as the writer for the Newcastle Chronicle did in 1873, the view is remarkably unchanged. The view of fields and woods with distant Cockfield and nearby Evenwood and its cemetery would have been recognisable to that writer. The chimneys of the engine rooms and the smoke from the pit heaps have disappeared but the three 'pit rows', Methodist chapel and Bridge Inn of Gordon Lane so admired by the writer still stand. The beck still runs through Gordon Gill down behind the houses of Gordon Lane though the cottages of *'Little Ireland'* were demolished in the 1950's after a long period of being unoccupied.

The descendants of the original *'Little Ireland'* families have continued to thrive. Three more generations have been born. They have spread across the country following opportunities and careers, however Ramshaw, Evenwood and other villages surrounding Bishop Auckland still maintain a strong presence from these families. I think Thomas Mattimoe and Ann Gaffney would be proud of their descendants who live to the values they were brought up to believe in and instilled in their own children. Despite the difficulies and tragedies that they and their subsequent generations endured, the joy and happiness far outweighed these sadnesses and vindicated that difficult decision Thomas and Ann made in 1867 to bring their young family from the country of their birth, leaving family and friends, to begin a new life in England.

I have been fortunate to meet many of Thomas and Ann's descendants and am pleased to confirm that the tradition of offering a warm welcome to visitors and, of course, a bite to eat is still very much alive. I regret that a narrow view of family history led me to focus on my direct ancestors and as a result I missed the opportunity to speak to others who would have given further fascinating insight into the times in which my ancestors lived. I am grateful to those I have met for the time and information they gave to me. My experiences as I toured around Co. Durham have given me much enjoyment and armed me with many stories to reflect upon in the future.

A book such as this can never be complete. I am sure that as I write this conclusion Angela, without whom this book would not have been possible, has thought of other people it would be useful for me to speak to but a line must be drawn in order that the story of the families of *'Little Ireland'* can be shared with others.

There is always more to be done. That is the joy of family history. Perhaps the archives in Dublin beckon to see whether any more can be added to the research begun by Col. Mattimoe. Perhaps other branches of the family deserve some time. Whichever option I choose I hope it brings me into contact with people as good and as welcoming as those I have met in the research for this book.

Fig. 136 Aerial view of Gordon Gill taken in May 1964. Traces of the cottages occupied by the Mattimoes when they first moved to Ramshaw can be seen in the bottom right of the photograph. The roofless lean-to buildings are all that remained at this time but the outline of the cottages can be made out running in front of these lean to ruins through to the building above them in the picture. The farmhouse in the centre of the picture still exists though now much improved with a beautiful garden laid out around the rill which leads down to Gordon Beck. The beck itself can be seen running across the top righthand corner. The bank beyond the beck was covered in sweet smelling yellow gorse every Spring and, despite the intervening opencast mining in the 1980's still retains some of these bushes.

Appendix A – Irish Records

Dioscese of Elphin Census 1749

Parish	Townland	Names	Occupation	Children	Servants
Ardcarne	Cloonhibir	Thady Mullimoe & wife	Cottier		
		Bartholomew Mullimoe	Cottier		
		Connor Mullimoe	Cottier		
		Glibert Mullimoe	Cottier		
Boyle	Boyle	Luke Mattimoe & wife	Shopkeeper	1 under 14	1 woman
		John Mattimoe & wife	Pumpowner	3 under 14	
	Doon	Michael Mattimoe	Farmer	3 under 14	
		James Mattimoe & wife	Farmer	2 under 14	1 woman
Drumcollum	Coolboy	Mark Mattimoe	Farmer		1 male
		James Mattimoe	Farmer	2 under 14	2 female 1 male
		Laurence Mattimoe	Farmer	3 under 14	
		Laughlin Mattimo	Farmer	1 over 14	
		Patrick Mattimoe	Farmer	2 over 14	
		Maurice Mattimoe	Farmer	1 over 14	
	Brickliffe	Patrick Mattimoe	Farmer	5 under 14	
Kilmacalane	Knockroe	Tha. Mattimo	Farmer	3 under 14	
Sligo	Sligo	Owen Mulloremoe	Cottier		

Tithe Applotment Records, 1823-1834

Ardcarne

Townland	Name	Type of Land	Area
Augha	Barth. Mattimo	Second quality	1 acre
		Third quality	1 acre
	Pat Mattimo	Fourth quality	1 acre
		Second quality	1 acre
		Third quality	1 acre
	Peter Mattimo	Fourth quality	1 acre
		Second quality	1 acre
		Third quality	1 acre
	John Mattimo	Fourth quality	1 acre
		Second quality	2 acres
	John Mattimo (2)	Third quality	1 ¾ acres
		Second quality	1 acre
		Third quality Fourth quality	1 acre
			1 acre
	Barth. Mattimo (2)	Second quality	1 acre
		Third quality	1 acre
Bridgecartron	James Mattimo	Fourth quality	1 acre
		Second quality	2 acres
Bridgecartron	Peter Mattimo	Third quality	2 ¾ acres
		Fourth quality	2 ½ acres
Danahonna	Pat Mattimo	Third quality	2 acres
Derrada	John Mattimo	Fourth quality	2 acres
		Third quality	3 acres
	Philip Mattimo	Fourth quality	2 acres
		Third quality	3 acres
		Fourth quality	2 acres

Ballysadare

Townland	Name	Type of Land	Area
Gisaneena	Darby Mattimoe		11 acres
	Darby & Pat Matimoe		10 acres
	Terence Matimo		3 acres
	Farrell Matimoe		9 acres

Ballysumsighan

Townland	Name	Type of Land	Area
Coolboy	Martin Milmoe	Gross	8 acres
		Neat	7 acres
	Bryan Milmoe	Gross	11 acres
		Neat	10 acres
	Bridget Milmoe	Gross	11 acres
		Neat	10 acres

Boyle

Townland	Name	Type of Land	Area
Aghacarra	Thomas Mattimoe		5 acres (est.)
	Michael Mattimoe		5 acres (est.)
	Pat Mattimoe		5 acres (est.)
Doon	James Mattimoe		4 acres (est.)
	Peter Mattimoe		6 acres (est.)
	Pat Mattimoe		3 acres (est.)
	Peter Mattimoe		5 acres (est.)
	Matthew & James Mattimoe		2 acres (est.)
Deerpark	Michael & Pat Mattimoe		3 acres (est.)

Calney

Townland	Name	Type of Land	Area
Shannpark	James Milmoe		5 acres

Cloonoghill

Townland	Name	Type of Land	Area
Ballinvally	Pat Millmow with Laurence McGarry	Arable	20 acres
		Bottom Pasture	5 acres

Kilbryan

Townland	Name	Type of Land	Area
Smatternagh	Domenic Matimo	Second quality	1 acre
		Third quality	½ acre
		Fourth quality	½ acre
		Untitheable	1 acre
Aughnanerim	John Mattimo	Untitheable	4 acres

Kilmactranny

Townland	Name	Type of Land	Area
Clooneen or Cabragh	Luke Matimoe	Arable	3 acres
		Bottom pasture	1 acre
		Curragh	1 acre
		Bog	4 acres
	Peter Matimoe	Arable	5 acres
		Bottom pasture	1 acre
		Curragh	1 acre
	Widow Matimoe	Bog	7 acres
		Arable	1 acre
		Curragh	¼ acre
Carrowcashel	Michael Matimoe	Moory	9 acres
		Mountain	2 acres
		Bog	¼ acre
Coolmorley	Pat Matimoe	Arable	5 ½ acres
		Upland & moor	1 acre
		Bog	1 acre
Cloonenhue	Thomas Matimoe	Arable	5 ½ acres
		Moory	½ acre
Derrienaslim	Bartly Matimoe	Arable	3 acres
		Inferior arable	2 ½ acres
		Upland arable	5 acres
		Road	½ acre
		Bog	1 ½ acres
Nockmore	James Mattimoe	Arable	24 acres
	Hugh Matimoe	Upland	83 acres
	Bernard Matimoe	Moory	13 acres
	Bernard Matimoe jnr	Road	1 ¼ acres
	Thomas Matimoe	Bog	13 acres
	James Matimoe jnr		(totals for all occupiers)
	Bartly Matimoe		
	+ 10 others		
Treanmore	Thomas Matimoe	Arable	50 acres
	Pat Matimoe	Upland	1 acre
	+ 3 others	Road	¼ acre
			(totals for all occupiers)

Kilmorgan

Townland	Name	Type of land	Area
Cloonlurg	James Milmo	Arable	6 acres
		Bottom Pasture	2 acres
Doormore	Farell Milmoe	Arable	4 acres
		Runny pasture	2 acres
		Red moor	1 acre
		Moor	3 acres
		Bog	1 acre
Kilmorgan	Michale Coleman & Milmoe	Arable	5 acres
		Bottom pasture	4 acres
Sackagh East	John Milmoe	Arable	1 acre
Drumcormack	Thady Mimoe	Arable	7 acres
		Bottom pasture	2 acres
	Bernard Milmoe	Arable	7 acres
		Bottom pasture	2 acres
	Charles Milmoe	Arable & pasture	10 acres
		Moory pasture	1 acre
Carrowkeel	Bartly & Martin Milmo		¼ acre

Note - Milmoe/Mattimoe families also appeared in the Tithe Applotment for Lissaneena.

Griffith's Valuation 1857-58

Ardcarne

Townland	Name	Type of Land	Area (a/r/p)	Immediate Lessor
Breanletter	James Mattimo	House(f) & garden	0/ 2/ 0	Michael Molloy
Aghoo	Bartholomew Moraghan	House(f) & small garden	0/ 0/ 0	John Mattimo
	Bryan Mattimo	House(d), offices & land	7/ 1/30	Edward King Tenison
	Mary Mattimo	House(d) & land	2/ 3/20	- ditto -
	James Mattimo	House(c), offices & land	25/13/49	- ditto -
	Margaret Mattimo	House(g), offices & land	0/ 3/32	- ditto -
	John Mattimo	House(d), & land	6/ 4/15	- ditto -
Bridgecartron or Derrycashel	Michael Mattimo	House(d) & land	3/10/ 0	Henry Boyd
	Winifred Mattimo	House(d), offices & land	12/ 1/ 0	- ditto -
	James Mattimo	House(c), offices & land	13/ 2/ 9	- ditto -
Derreenaseer	John Mattimo	House(d), offices & land (part bog)	20/ 0/ 6	Rev. Coote Molloy
	Gilbert Mattimo	House(d) & land (part bog)	10/ 3/10	- ditto -
Kilfaughna	Peter Mattimo	House(c) & land	9/ 1/22	William, Phibbs
Ballytrasna	James Mattimo	House(d) & garden	0/ 0/ 0	William Duckmont
Doon	Luke Mattimo	House(f) & land	3/ 1/10	Lord Lorton
	Patrick Mattimo	House(d), offices & land	17/23/58	- ditto -
Derryherk	Peter Mattimo	House(d), offices & land	19/ 2/30	Anne Neville
	Margaret Scanlon	House(f) & offices	0/ 0/ 0	Peter Mattimo
Derreenasalt	Patrick Matimo	House(d) & land	18 ½ acres	Rev. Coote Mulloy
	Michael Matimoe	House(f) & land	6 acres	- ditto -

Parish of Ballysadare

Townland	Name	Type of Land	Area (a/r/p)	Immediate Lessor
Lissaneena	Jeremiah Mattymoe	House(a), offices & land	32/16/17	Thomas Meredith

Boyle

Townland	Name	Type of Land	Area (a/r/p)	Immediate Lessor
Kilmacroy	Michael Mattimo	House(f) & land	8/ 2/ 6	Thomas Meredith
	James Mattimo	Land	0/ 1/30	Earl of Zetland
Lowparks	Terence Mattimo	House(d) & land	Half an acre	Lord Lorton
	Michael Mattimo	House(d) & land	Half an acre	- ditto -
	Luke Mattimo	House(d) & garden	0/ 1/ 5	- ditto -
Termon	Michael Mattimo	House(d) & garden		- ditto -
Aghacarra	Thomas Mattimo	House(d), offices & land	18/ 0/30	John Wolfe Flanagan
	Michael Mattimo	House(c), offices & land	3/ 5/ 0	- ditto -

Parish of Boyle

Townland	Name	Type of Land	Area (a/r/p)	Immediate Lessor
Cornameelta	James Matimo	House(c), offices & land	24/ 0 / 0	Lord Lorton

Drumcolumb

Townland	Name	Type of Land	Area (a/r/p)	Immediate Lessor
Coolboy	Michael Milmo	House(d), offices, herdsman's house & land	52/ 1/34	Eliza Tucker
	James Milmo	House(d), offices & land	30/ 4/57	- ditto -
	Luke Milmo	House(f), offices & land	4/ 0/30	- ditto -
Carrowcashel	Michael Milmo	House(d), offices & land	0/ 2/30	
Rusheen	Patrick Milmo	House(e), garden & land	4/ 0/50	

Kilbryan

Townland	Name	Type of Land	Area (a/r/p)	Immediate Lessor
Annagh or Drumarilra	Anne Mattimo	House(d), offices & land	10/ 2/24	Lord Lorton

Kilfree

Townland	Name	Type of Land	Area (a/r/p)	Immediate Lessor
Kilfree	Thomas Mattimo	House(d), offices & land	11/ 0/ 0	Charles Costelloe

Kilmacallan

Townland	Name	Type of Land	Area (a/r/p)	Immediate Lessor
Drummacool	Bart. Milmo	House(b), offices & land	35/ 4/34	
Rathmulpatrick	Bart. Milmo	House(f), offices & land	31/ 3/35	

Parish of Kilmactranny

Townland	Name	Type of Land	Area (a/r/p)	Immediate Lessor
Carrowcashel	Thomas Matimo	House(f), office & land	19/ 1/17	Thomas Meredith
Drumbeg South	Peter Matimo	House(f) & land	16/ 2/ 5	James McFadden
Adrline	James Matimo	Land	10/ 0/ 0	Earl of Zetland
Treanmore	Thomas Matimo	House(c), offices & land	30/ 1/25	Chas. J. McDermott
	Peter Matimo	House(b), offices & land	47/ 6/20	Mrs John and Dr Hart and Chas. J. Macdermott
	Patrick Matimo	House(d) & land	13/ 0/ 32	-ditto -
Knockmore	Bartly Matimo	House(d), offices & land	19/ 3/ 0	Robert Gough
	Michael Matimo	House(d) & land	10/ 3/ 0	- ditto -

Townland	Name	Type of Land	Area (a/r/p)	Immediate Lessor
Knockmore	Martin Matimo	House(d) & land	11/ 5/75	-ditto -
	Catherine Foley	Garden	0/ 2/ 0	Martin Matimo
	Bridget Corcoran	House(f) & garden	0/ 1/30	Martin Mattimo
	Mary Matimo	House(f) & small garden	0/ 0/ 0	John Ballentine
	John Matimo	House(d) & land	17/ 9/103	Robert Gough
	Timothy Sweeny	House(f) & garden		John Matimo

Kilmorgan

Townland	Name	Type of Land	Area (a/r/p)	Immediate Lessor
Cloonlurg	Hugh Milmo	House(c)		
Doomore	Patrick Milmo	House(d), offices & land	19/ 0/30	
Drumfin	Michael Milmo	House(b), offices and land	13/ 0/30	
Knockmoynagh	Charles Milmo	House(b), offices & land	19/ 1/49	

Kilronan

Townland	Name	Type of Land	Area (a/r/p)	Immediate Lessor
Alderford (village of Ballyfarnon)	Jane Mattimo	House & small garden	19/ 1/17 13/15/ 0	Rep. of Wm F McDermottroe

Kiltoghert, Co. Leitrim

Townland	Name	Type of Land	Area (a/r/p)	Immediate Lessor
Carickslaven	James Mattimore	House(f), offices & land	11/ 0/ 2	Sir Gilbert King

Toomour

Townland	Name	Type of Land	Area (a/r/p)	Immediate Lessor
Ballinhover	Michael Mattimoe	House(g)	0/ 0/ 0	Meredith Thompson

St. John's

Townland	Name	Type of Land	Area (a/r/p)	Immediate Lessor
Sligo town	Patrick Milmoe	House and yard		

(a) House assessed at £1-5-0
(b) House assessed at £1-0-0
(c) House assessed at £0-15-0
(d) House assessed at £0-10-0
(e) House assessed at £0-7-0
(f) House assessed at £0-5-0
(g) House of no value

Appendix B – Census of Gordon Gill, Ramshaw

Gordon Gill 1851 Census

Name	Relation	Condition	Age	Occupation	Where Born
Robert Marley	Head	Married	45	Rail Labourer	Durham, Evenwood
Elizabeth Marley	Wife	Married	44		Durham, Evenwood
Elizabeth Marley	Daughter		9		Durham, Evenwood
Robert Marley	Son		11		Durham, Evenwood
Margaret Marley	Daughter		4		Durham, Evenwood
Louisa Marley	Daughter		42		Durham, Evenwood

Gordon Gill 1861 Census

Name	Relation	Condition	Age	Occupation	Where Born
Richard Gair	Head	Married	47	Colliery Blacksmith	Durham, Lanchester
Margaret Gair	Wife	Married	45		Yorkshire, Mickleton
Thomas Gair	Son		21	Colliery Blacksmith	Durham, Evenwood
Elizabeth Parkin	Mother-in-law	Widow	75	Land Holder	Durham, Weardale
Patrick Cox	Head	Married	34	Coal Miner	Ireland
Elizabeth Cox	Wife	Married	34		Durham, Esington
Margaret Cox	Daughter		9	Scholar	Durham, Headlean
Mary Cox	Daughter		6	Scholar	Durham, Kellerby
Thomas Cox	Son		4	Scholar	Durham, Kellerby
Elizabeth Cox	Daughter		2		Durham, Cockfield
John Turbet	Head	Married	47	Coal Miner	Ireland
Ann Turbet	Wife	Married	37		Ireland
Mary Turbet	Daughter		12	Scholar	Scotland
Bridget Turbet	Daughter		10	Scholar	Scotland
Michael Turbet	Son		8	Scholar	Scotland
Margaret Turbet	Daughter		4	Scholar	Durham, Cockfield
Andrew Lee	Lodger	Single	27	Excavator	Ireland
Edward Holmes	Lodger	Single	40	Mason's Labourer	Ireland
John Galloway	Lodger	Widower	60	Farm Labourer	Yorkshire, North Riding
Martin McDonough	Lodger	Single	19	Coal Cleaner	Ireland
Joseph Foster	Head	Married	45	Coal Miner	Durham, Chester-le-Street
Mary Foster	Wife	Married	36		Durham, Evenwood
Cuthbert Cummins	Stepson		17	Putter in coal mine	Durham, Evenwood
Anthony Dodds	Stepson		15	Putter in coal mine	Durham, Evenwood
Mary Jane Dodds	Stepdaughter		14		Durham, Evenwood
Isabelle Foster	Daughter		4		Durham, Evenwood
Thomas Foster	Son		2		Durham, Evenwood
Peter Foster	Son		1 mth		Durham, Evenwood
Ralph Place	Head	Married	52	Colliery engine driver	Durham, Painshaw
Ann Place	Wife	Married	48		Durham, Painshaw
Mary Wardle	Daughter	Married	22		Durham, Thristleton
Maria Place	Daughter		17		Durham, Old Kelhoe

Name	Relation	Condition	Age	Occupation	Where Born
Alice Place	Daughter		14		Durham, Stranton
Elias Place	Son		12	Colliery engine fireman	Durham, Hartlepool
Ralph Wardle	Son-in-law	Married	20	Deputy Overman	Northumberland, Willington
Daniel Jackson	Head	Married	40	Coal Miner	Cumberland, Depington
Agnes Jackson	Wife	Married	31		Lancashire, Brugton
Martha Jackson	Daughter		6	Scholar	Durham, Barnard Castle
Mary Ann Jackson	Daughter		3		Durham. St Andrews
Elinor Jackson	Daughter		3 mth		Durham, St Andrews
John Philips	Head	Married	29	Coal Miner	Ireland
Mary Ann Philips	Wife	Married	22		America
John Heal	Head	Married	35	Coal Miner	Ireland
Bridget Heal	Wife	Married	27		Ireland
Ann A Heal	Daughter		9		Scotland
Mary Heal	Daughter		6		Scotland
Catherine Heal	Daughter		3		Scotland
Thomas Heal	Son		1		Scotland
James Oushrey	Brother-in-law	Single	32	Coal Miner	Ireland
Michael Gaffney	Head	Married	41	Coal Miner	Ireland
Ann Gaffney	Wife	Married	40		Ireland
John Gaffney	Son		13	Driver in Coal Mine	Scotland
Michael Gaffney	Son		12	Driver in Coal Mine	Scotland
Thomas Gaffney	Son		10	Trapper in Coal Mine	Scotland
Timothy Gaffney	Son		7		Scotland
Mary Ann Gaffney	Daughter		4		Scotland
Catherine Gaffney	Daughter		10 m		Durham, Evenwood
Michael Tarbut	Brother-in-law	Married	36	Coal Miner	Ireland
Michael Tarbut	Brother's son		9		Scotland
Patrick Tarbut	Brother's son		7		Scotland
John Gaffney	Head	Married	30	Coal Miner	Ireland
Mary Gaffney	Wife	Married	31		Ireland
Timothy Gaffney	Son		10		Scotland
Patrick Gaffney	Son		7		Scotland
John Gaffney	Son		4		Durham, Evenwood
Edward Gaffney	Son		2		Durham, Evenwood
Charles Gaffney	Son		2 wks		Durham, Evenwood
Thomas Dargue	Head	Married	38	Coal Miner	N'land, Allendale
Hannah Dargue	Wife	Married	33		N'land, Allendale
Joseph Dargue	Son		12	Driver in Coal Mine	N'land, Allendale
Robert H Dargue	Son		10	Driver in Coal Mine	N'land, Allendale
Elizabeth Ann Dargue	Daughter		7		N'land, Allendale
Mary Jane Dargue	Daughter		3		Durham, Newbeggin
Thomas H Dargue	Son		1		Yorkshire, Mickleton

228   Little Ireland

Gordon Gill 1871 Census

Name	Relation	Cond.	Age	Occupation	Where Born
Michael Gaffney	Head	Married	50	Coal Miner	Ireland
Annie Gaffney	Wife	Married	48		Ireland
Thomas Gaffney	Son		18	Coal Miner	Scotland
Edward Gaffney	Son		16	Coal Miner	Scotland
Mary Gaffney	Daughter		12		Scotland
Catherine Gaffney	Daughter		10		Durham, Gordon Gill
Annie Gaffney	Daughter		16	General Servant	Scotland
Thomas Mattimoe	Head	Married	32	Colliery labourer	Ireland
Ann Mattimoe	Wife	Married	28		Ireland
Patrick Mattimoe	Son		15	Coal Miner	Ireland
John Mattimoe	Son		12	Coal Miner	Ireland
Thomas Mattimoe	Son		11	Scholar	Ireland
Peter Mattimoe	Son		5	Scholar	Durham Bishop Auckland
Stephen Mattimoe	Son		1		Durham Bishop Auckalnd
George Hodgson	Head	Widower	41	Colliery Deputy	Durham, Woodside
William Hodgson	Son		18	Coal Miner	Durham, Hett
John Hodgson	Son		16	Coal Miner	Durham, Witton Castle
Elizabeth Hodgson	Daughter		15		Durham, Toft Hill
Sarah Ann Hodgson	Daughter		11	Scholar	Durham, Toft Hill
Martha Hodgson	Daughter		9	Scholar	Durham, Toft Hill
Margaret Hodgson	Daughter		7	Scholar	Durham, Toft Hill
George Hodgson	Son		5		Durham, Toft Hill
Mary Ann Pearson	Servant	Widow	38	Servant	N'land, Preston
Thomas Place	Head	Married	25	Brakesman	Durham, Easington
Ann Place	Wife	Married	24		Durham, Heighington
George Thompson Place	Son		3 mth		Durham, Gordon Gill
Elia Thonpson Place	Head	Married	51	Engineman	Durham, Fatfield
Jane Place	Wife	Married	52		Durham, Houghton-le-Spring
Meggey Place	Daughter	Single	18		Durham, Merton Colliery
Stephen Place	Son		15	Scholar	Durham, Merton Colliery
Sarah Place	Daughter		12	Scholar	Durham, Merton Colliery
Isabell Place	Daughter		8	Scholar	Durham, Evenwood
Charles Hannan	Head	Married	22	Coal Miner	Ireland, Enniskin
Bridget Hannan	Wife	Married	20		Scotland, Monklen
Patrick Cox	Head	Married	40	Coal Miner	Ireland
Elizabeth Cox	Wife	Married	45		Durham, Hetton
Thomas Cox	Son		14	Coal Miner	Durham, Killerby
Elizabeth Cox	Daughter		12	Scholar	Durham, Cockfield
Sarah Jane Cox	Daughter		9	Scholar	Durham, Gordon Gill
John Edward Cox	Son		6	Scholar	Durham, Gordon Gill
Robert Cox	Son		3	Scholar	Durham, Gordon Gill
Peter Malone	Lodger	Single	31	Mason	Ireland
John Tarbert	Head	Married	60	Coal Miner	Ireland, Roscommon

Name	Relation	Cond.	Age	Occupation	Where Born
Anne Tarbert	Wife	Married	55		Ireland, Roscommon
Michael Tarbert	Son	Single	18	Coal Miner	Scotland
Margaret Tarbert	Daughter		14	Scholar	Durham, Cockfield
Joseph Forster	Head	Married	53	Coal Miner	Durham, Chester le Street
Mary Forster	Wife	Married	45		Durham, Toft Hill
Isabell Forster	Daughter		14		Durham, Windmill
John Thomas Forster	Son		13	Scholar	Durham, Aycliffe
Margaret Ann Forster	Daughter		9	Scholar	Durham, Gordon Gill
William Forster	Son		8	Scholar	Durham, Gordon Gill
Betsy Forster	Daughter		7	Scholar	Durham, Gordon Gill
Richard Gair	Head	Married	58	Blacksmith	Durham, Lanchester
Margaret Gair	Wife	Married	54		Durham, Mickleton
Thomas Gair	Son	Single	31	Blacksmith	Durham, Evenwood
Sarah Jane Hodgson	Servant		14	Servant	Durham, Ramshaw

Gordon Gill 1881 Census

Name	Relation	Cond.	Age	Occupation	Where Born
Thomas Mattimoe	Head	Married	47	Coal Miner	Ireland
Ann Mattimoe	Wife	Married	46		Ireland
Patrick Mattimoe	Son	Single	23	Coal Miner	Ireland
John Mattimoe	Son	Single	21	Coal Miner	Ireland
Peter Mattimoe	Son		15	Rapper boy	Durham Bishop Auckland
Stephen Mattimoe	Son		13	Scholar	Durham Bishop Auckland
Anne Mattimoe	Daughter		9	Scholar	Durham, Evenwood
James F Mattimoe	Son		5	Scholar	Durham, Evenwood
Michael Gaffney	Head	Married	67	Coal Miner	Ireland
Ann Gaffney	Wife	Married	65		Ireland
Thomas Gaffney	Son	Single	29	Coal Miner	Scotland
Catherine Gaffney	Daughter	Single	20		Durham, Evenwood
John Smith	Head	Married	45	Blacksmith	Durham, Winlaton
Catherine Smith	Wife	Married	44		Durham, Gatehead
Elizabeth Smith	Daughter		14	Scholar	Newcastle
Walter Smith	Son		12	Scholar	Newcastle
Catherine Smith	Daughter		9	Scholar	Newcastle
Thomas Smith	Son		6	Scholar	Durham, Winlaton
Edith Smith	Daughter		4	Scholar	Durham, Toft Hill
Lillian Smith	Daughter		2		Durham, Evenwood
Joseph Foster	Head	Married	63	Coal Miner	Durham, Chester le Street
Margaret Foster	Wife	Married	57		Durham, Etherley
Isabella Foster	Daughter	Single	24		Durham, Aycliffe
William Foster	Son		17	Coal Miner	Durham, Evenwood
Mary Jane Foster			2		Durham, Evenwood
Michael Gaffney	Head	Married	30	Coal Miner	Scotland

Name	Relation	Cond.	Age	Occupation	Where Born
Mary Gaffney	Wife	Married	27		Northumberland, Blyth
Thomas Gaffney	Son		5	Scholar	Northumberland, Coupen
Michael Gaffney	Son		3		Durham, Evenwood
John William Gaffney	Son		7 mth		Durham, Evenwood
Patrick Cox	Head	Married	53	Coal Miner	Ireland
Elizabeth Cox	Wife	Married	54		Durham, Esenton
Sarah J Cox	Daughter	Single	19		Durham, Evenwood
John E Cox	Son		16	Coal Miner	Durham, Evenwood
Robert Cox	Son		13	Coal Miner	Durham, Evenwood
John Thomas Foster	Head	Married	22	Coal Miner	Durham, Pitlireen
Ann Foster	Wife	Married	21		Durham, Toft Hill
Mary Jane Foster	Daughter		5 mth		Durham, Evenwood
Jane Place	Head	Widow	60		Durham, Houghton-le-Spring
Isabella Place	Daughter	Single	19	Dressmaker	Durham, Evenwood
Alice Place			7	Scholar	Durham, Evenwood
William Hodgson	Lodger	Single	28	Coal Miner	Durham, Hetton

Gordon Gill 1891 Census

Name	Relation	Cond.	Age	Occupation	Where Born
Stephen Mattimoe	Head	Married	23	Coal Miner	Durham Bishop Auckland
Mary E Mattimoe	Wife	Married	23		Durham Bishop Auckland
Thomas E Mattimoe	Son		2 mth		Durham, Evenwood
Thomas Mattimoe	Head	Widower	58	Coal Miner	Ireland
Peter Mattimoe	Son	Single	25	Coal Miner	Durham Bishop Auckland
Annie Mattimoe	Daughter	Single	19		Durham, Evenwood
James F Mattimoe	Son		16	Coal Miner	Durham, Evenwood
Thomas H Mattimoe	Grandson		7	Scholar	Durham, Evenwood
Michael Gaffney	Head	Widower	75		Ireland
Thomas Gaffney	Son	Single	39	Coal Miner	Scotland
Catherine Gaffney	Daughter	Single	30		Durham, Evenwood
James Welsh	Lodger	Single	22	Coal Miner	Durham, Evenwood
Edward Gaffney	Head	Married	37	Coal Miner	Scotland
Elizabeth Gaffney	Wife	Married	32		Durham, Cockfield
Elizabeth A Gaffney	Daughter		12	Scholar	Durham, Evenwood
Cornelius Gaffney	Son		10	Scholar	Durham, Evenwood
John E Gaffney	Son		8	Scholar	Durham, Evenwood
Sarah J Gaffney	Daughter		6	Scholar	Durham, Evenwood
Thomas Place	Head	Married	42	Colliery Brakesman	Durham, Merton
Emma Place	Wife	Married	22		Durham Bishop Auckland
George T Place	Son	Single	20	Coal Miner	Durham, Evenwood
Stephen Place	Son		17	Coal Miner	Durham, Beechburn
Thomas Place	Son		15	Coal Miner	Durham, Evenwood

Name	Relation	Cond.	Age	Occupation	Where Born
William Place	Son		12	Scholar	Durham, Butterknowle
James Place	Son		8	Scholar	Durham, Morley
John Cox	Head	Married	26	Coal Miner	Durham, Evenwood
Annie Cox	Wife	Married	23		Durham, Evenwood
Elizabeth Cox	Daughter		4		Durham, Evenwood
George T Cox	Son		3		Durham, Evenwood
Florence Cox	Daughter		31		Durham, Evenwood
Elizabeth Cox	Head	Widow	65		Durham Easington Lane
Sarah J Cox	Daughter	Single	29		Durham, Evenwood
Robert Cox	Son	Single	23		Durham, Evenwood
Charles Marshall	Head	Married	65	Agricultural Labourer	Durham, Evenwood
Mary Marshall	Wife	Married	60		Scotland
James Oliver	Son	Single	22	Colliery Labourer	Durham, Etherley
Margaret A Marshall	Daughter	Single	21		Durham, Evenwood
John Mattimoe	Head	Married	32	Coal Miner	Ireland
Hannah Mattimoe	Wife	Married	32		Ireland
Stephen Mattimoe	Son		5		Durham, Evenwood
John L Mattimoe	Son		2		Durham, Evenwood
Francis A Mattimoe	Son		7 mth		Durham, Evenwood

Gordon Gill 1901 Census

Name	Relation	Cond.	Age	Occupation	Where Born
Peter Mattimoe	Head	Single	35	Checkweigher	Durham Bishop Auckland
James F Mattimoe	Brother	Single	21	Coal Miner	Durham, Evenwood
Thomas Hy Mattimoe	Nephew	Single	17		Durham, Evenwood
Thomas Hannon	Brother-in-law	Married	23	Coal Miner	Ireland
Ann Hannon	Sister	Married	28	Housekeeper	Durham, Evenwood
Ann Hannon	Niece		4 mth		Durham, Evenwood
William Stewart	Head	Widower	50	Deputy Overman	Durham, West Auckland
William Stewart	Son	Single	19	Coal Miner	Durham, West Auckland
Elizabeth J Stewart	Daughter		16		Durham, West Auckland
Minnie Stewart	Daughter		15		Durham, West Auckland
F Mabel Stewart	Daughter		12		Durham, West Auckland
Minnie Orton	Servant	Single	35		Durham, Spennymoor
James Orton	Son		17	Pony Putter	Durham, Spennymoor
Richard Wm Orton	Son		15		Durham, Spennymoor
Jesse Orton	Daughter		3		Durham, Spennymoor
Annie Orton	Daughter		1		Durham, Spennymoor
Joseph Handley	Head	Widower	50	Colliery Joiner	Yorkshire
J Wm Handley	Son		12		Durham, Shildon
Maud Mary Tuck	Daughter	Married	19	Housekeeper	Durham, Shildon
Robert Ernest Tuck	Son in law	Married	22	General Labourer	Yorkshire, Nearham

Little Ireland

Name	Relation	Cond.	Age	Occupation	Where Born
John G Heslop	Head	Married	23	Coal Miner	Durham, Evenwood
Kate Heslop	Wife	Married	20		Durham, Evenwood
Alice Heslop	Daughter		1 mth		Durham, Evenwood
Edith Anderson	Sister in law		15	Hose Maid	Durham, Evenwood
Mary Place	Head	Widow	26		Durham, Mount Pleasant
Thomas Place	Son		4		Durham, Toft Hill
John Mattimoe	Head	Married	40	Deputy Overman	Ireland
Bridget Mattimoe	Wife	Married	40		Ireland
Stephen Mattimoe	Son		15	Colliery Screen Boy	Durham, Evenwood
John Leo Mattimoe	Son		12		Durham, Evenwood
Francis A Mattimoe	Son		10		Durham, Evenwood
Mary Ann Mattimoe	Daughter		6		Durham, Evenwood
George Robinson	Head	Married	34	Coal Miner	Durham, Evenwood
Annie Robinson	Wife	Married	34		Durham, Evenwood
Thomas Wm Robinson	Son		11		Durham, Evenwood
John Alfred Robinson	Son		5		Durham, Evenwood
Ralph Robinson	Son		4		Durham, Evenwood
Albert Robinson	Son		1 mth		Durham, Evenwood
Stephen Mattimoe	Head	Married	33	Coal Miner	Durham Bishop Auckland
Mary Ellen Mattimoe	Wife	Married	32		Durham Bishop Auckland
James Fr. Mattimoe	Son		9		Durham, Evenwood
Ann Mattimoe	Daughter		7		Durham, Evenwood
Mary Eveline Mattimoe	Daughter		4		Durham, Evenwood
Joseph Mattimoe	Son		3		Durham, Evenwood
Elias Place	Head	Married	52	Colliery Engineman	Durham, Hartlepool
Margaret Place	Wife	Married	45		Durham, Evenwood
Ralph Place	Son		16	Colliery Bank Boy	Durham, Evenwood
Margaret J Place	Daughter		13		Durham, Cockfield
Elizabeth M Place	Daughter		13		Durham, Cockfield
George Bertram Place	Son		8		Durham, Cockfield

Bibliography

Elsie Anderson, May Birch, Kathleen MacMillan, Kathryn and Kevin Richardson, John Smith	*Evenwood's Heyday – A Colliery Village, 1896-1918*
Barr, James	*The Lost Spanish Galleons and Treasure in Donegal*
Hebden, Derek J	*Bishop Auckland – 100 years ago*
Hickey, Frank	*St. Wilfred's, Bishop Auckland* Bishop Auckland College
Keegan, John	*The First World War, an illustrated history* Hutchinson
Kerr, Donald	*The Catholic Church and the Famine* The Columba Press
Kee, Robert	*Ireland, A History* Abacus, 1995
Laurie, Barbara	*Bishop Auckland in the 1850's* Ceddes Print & Design, Sedgefield
MacLysaght, Edward	*Irish Families - Their Names, Arms and Origins* Irish Academic Press
MacLysaght, Edward	*More Irish Families* Irish Academic Press
Mattimoe, Cyril M	*The Origin of the name Mattimoe* The National Library of Ireland, Dublin
Mattimoe, Cyril M	*The Surname Mattimoe and its variant Milmo* The National Library of Ireland, Dublin
Mattimoe, Cyril M	*North Roscommon –its people and past* Roscommon Herald, Boyle
McCarthy, Tony	*The Irish Roots Guide* The Lilliput Press
McPhail, Helen and Guest, Philip	*Battleground Europe Saint Quentin 1914-1918* Pen & Sword Books
Mcmanners, Robert Wales, Gillian	*Shafts of Light* &
O' Tuathaigh, Gearoid	*Ireland Before the Famine 1798-1848* Gill and Macmillan
Percival, John	*The Great Famine* BBC Books, 1995
Pols, Robert	*Family Photographs 1860-1945* Public record Office Publications
Temple, David	*The Collieries of Durham Volume 1 and 2* Trade Union Printing Services Ltd.
Stapleton, Jim & De Cuellar, Francisco	*The Spanish Armada 1588, The Journey of Francisco De Cuellar*

Index

Aghacarra, Co. Roscommon, 20, 39, 40, 52
Albanagh, 14
Ardcarne, Co. Roscommon, 12, 29, 33, 36, 37, 39, 40, 48, 62-63, 65
Arigna, Co. Roscommon, 35, 58, 68
Armstrong,
    Anne 'Annie' nee Mattimoe (1906-1968), 122, *122, 126,* 201
    Brian, 201
Aughanagh, Co. Sligo, 12, 13, 46, 52, 63, 135
Ballinafad, Co. Sligo, 10, *15,* 20, 62
Ballinamuck, Co. Longford, 35, 68
Ballindoon Friary, Co. Sligo, *13*
Baxter, Anne nee Mattimoe, 184, 217
Bell, John, 182
Bell, Julia nee Mattimoe, 182, *183*
Bingham, Sir Charles, 18, 19, 20
Bingham, Sir John, 14
Bishop Auckland, Co. Durham, 74-79, *78*
Bishop Auckland Cemetery, 1, *6, 191*
Bishop Auckland Employment Committee, 166
Bishop's Palace, Bishop Auckland, 74, 77, 78
Black and Tans, 160-161
Bowes Close, Ramshaw, 82, *103,* 111
Boyle, Co. Roscommon, 8, 12, 21, 23, 28, 32, 35, 46, 52, 54, 56, 59, 60-63
Boyle Abbey, 17, *17,* 18, 19
Boyle Workhouse, 59
Brehon Code, 14, 17
Brian Boru, High King of Ireland, 10
Brian, King of Connaught, 12
Bridge Inn, Ramshaw, Co. Durham, 7, *122, 198*
Bridge Street, Bishop Auckland, 76, 77
Bricklieve, Co. Sligo, 8, 9, 33
Brunswick Clubs, 48
Busby, Sir Matt, 195
Bushey, Hertfordshire, 2, 3
Cambrai, Battle of (1917), 150-151
Carrick-on-Shannon Workhouse, 61
Carrigeenroe, Co. Roscommon, 19, 40, 60, 67
Carrowkeel, Co. Sligo, 8, *9*
Carterthorne Pit, 165
Catholic Association, 45
Catholic Emancipation Act, 47, 48
Catholic Relief Act, 33
Chiltern Avenue, Bushey, 2, 3, *5*
Coatbridge, Scotland, 92
Collooney, Co. Sligo, 20, 27, 60
Coolboy, Co. Sligo, 27, 28, 29, 32, 39, 65
Composition Act, 1823, 39
Compossicion of Connaught, 17
Connaught Rangers, 42, 161, 164
Conor, King of Connaught, 14
Conyers, Sir Clifford, 20, 21
Corn Close, Bishop Auckland, 75

Cornwallis, Lord, 35
Coronation, 1, 188
Costello, Tomas Laidir, 18
Cox, Patrick, 92
Crannog, 8, *9*
Cromwell, Oliver, 23, 29, 31, 32, 48
Curlew, Battles of the, 20, 21
Curlew Mountains, 16, 20, 36
Daykin, Lucy, 148
Defenders, 33, 34, 36, 48
Dermot, King of Moylurg, 14
Deputy Overman, 88
Dermot McMurrough, 15
Dillon, Earl of Roscommon, 24
Doon, Co. Roscommon, 29, 33, 39, 56
Donnelly, Martin, 5, *126, 133,* 134, 181, *181,* 182, *182*
Doyle, Maureen nee Finlay, 211, 216
Eales, Mary nee Mattimoe, 192, 196, 197
Eldon Colliery, 1, 132, *132,* 166, 218
Elizabeth I, 17, 20, 30, 31, 42
Elphin, Census of the Diocese of, 27, 32, 39, 64
Evenwood Cemetery, 102
Evenwood Prize Silver Band, 125, *125,* 165
Faction fighting, 54
Famine, The, 36, 57-65
Fearnley, Evelyn nee Mattimoe (1915-1974), 201
Fenianism, 70, 128
Field Punishment Number 1 (FPN1), 151
Finlay,
    Leslie, 215, 216, *216, 217*
    Nora nee Hannon, *214,* 215, *215,* 216, *216,* 217
Fireman, 89
Fitzgerald,
    Caroline, 42
    Col. Henry Gerald, 42, 43
Flight of the Earls, 21
Foley, Mrs nee Donlan, *134*
Gaffney,
    Ann, nee Tarbert (1821), 91, 92
    Edward 'Teddy', 99, 109, 114, 116
    Elizabeth nee Cox (1859-1914), 132
    John (1831), 91, 98
    Mary nee Stanton, 92
    Michael (1816), 76, 90, 92, 99
    Thomas, 112, 124, 125
    Sarah Jane nee Cox, 92, 103, 112, 124
Gallowglass, 14, *14,* 16
General Strike, The, 167-169
Gordon Gill, Ramshaw, 90, 91, 95, 96, 98, 102, 111, 112, 114, 120, 127, 176, 206
Gordon Lane, Ramshaw, 95, *139,* 203, 204
Gray,
    Anne nee Ferrall, 135
    Betty, 1, *2, 185*

Index

Gray,
    Elizabeth nee Haigh (1862-1936), 135, *136*
    James (1855-1888), 135
    James (c.1798), 135
    John William 'Willy' (1884-1927), 1, *6*, 135, *135*, 136, 137, *137*, 188, 189, *189,* 190
    John 'Jack', 1, *2*, 3, 137, *189*
    Margaret nee Conway (1832-1910), 135
    Margaret 'Peggy', 1,*2*, 4
    Mary (1887-1911), 136
    Mary, 1, *2*, 3, *185, 189, 190*
    Monica, 1, *2, 3*, 4, *185*
    Nora, 1, *2*, 4, 5, *190*
    Molly (nee Mattimoe), 1, 2, *3*, *4*, 6, 104, 112, *113, 128, 133*, 135, *135*, 137, 178, 180, 188, *189* ,190
    Peter (1823-1898), 135, 191
    William 'Laurie', 1, *2*, 4, *189*
Griffith's Valuation, *40, 41,* 65
Haggerleases Branch line, 90, 91, 95, 163, 203
Haigh, Alice Inman (1875), 137
Haigh,
    George (1872), 137
    John (1835-1918), 136, 137
    John William (c.1864), 136
    Louisa (1866), 137
    Maria (1878), 137
    Mary nee Purtill (1839-1913), 136, 137
    Mary (1868), 137
Hannon,
    Annie nee Mattimoe (1872-1928), 99, 102, 103, ***106-107***, *118*, 121, *121*, 127, 128-130, 139, 204, 206
    Bartholomew (c.1800), 119
    Bernard, 206, 208, 208, 213
    Elizabeth Ellen (1905-1921), 128, 164, *164*
    Frank (1882-1942), 117, *121*
    Frank, 112, 213, *213*
    John (1901-1980), *83, 85, 121*, 206, *206*, 208, 210
    Joseph 'Joe' (1906-1983), 128, 212,2 13
    Kathleen nee McCrory, 112, 187
    Katherine 'Kitty, 165, *165*, 175, *214*, 215
    Lucy (nee Hannon, 6, 206-207
    Mary (1902-1922), *123*, 128, *165*
    Matthew (c.1857), 65
    Mattie (1915-1915), 128, 139
    Michael (1871-1954), 117 ,119
    Pat, 206
    Sarah 'Sally' (1903-1974), 128, 211, 212, *212*, 217, *217*
    Thomas (1878-1928), 117, 119, 121, *121*, 127, 128, 130, *137*, 142, 204, 206
    Thomas 'Tom' (1908-1965), 128, 213
Haye, Mary nee Mattimoe, 184, 185, 187, 188, 217
Hedge-schools, 50
Hodgson, Margaret Jennifer 'Jenny' nee Gray(1882), 136, *136*
Humbert, Gen., 29, 34, 35, 55, 68
Hunter, Alice nee Gray(1885), 136
Insurrection Act, 1822, 38
Jackson, Jonas, *101*, 115
Killala, Co. Sligo, *11*, 29, 31, 35
Kilmactranny, Co. Sligo, 12, 27, 29, 39, 44, 62

Kilronan, Co. Sligo, 8, 9, 12, 36, 68
King,
    Edward, 42
    Lord, 27,
    Sir Henry, 42
    Sir John, 17, 23, 42
    Mary, 42, 43
    Robert, Viscount Kingsborough, 42, 43
    Robert Edward - see Lord Lorton
Kinsale, Co. Cork, 21
Knocknaskeagh, Co. Sligo, 65, 117
Knockroe, Co. Sligo, 33
Knockvicar, Co. Sligo, 12, 16, 18
Leasingthorne Colliery, 169, 182, 192
Leeholme, Co. Durham, 132, 192
Lissaneena, Co. Sligo, 27
Lloyd, Col., 24
Local Board of Health, Bishop Auckland, 74
Lorton, Lord, 18, 33, 39, 40, 42, 43, 46, 47, 48, 57, 60, 61, 65
Lusitania, 134
McDermot,
    Brian Og, 18
    Conot Oge of Aghacarra, 19, 20, 21
    John, 33, 36
    Turlough, 18
    Una Bhan, 18
McDonagh, Mary (c.1760), 52
McLoughlin,
    Anne (c.1800), 52
    Anne (c.1830), 40, 69
McLysaight, Edward, 26, 104, 119
Mass Rocks, 22, *22*, 50
Mattimoe,
    Ann nee Gaffney (1834-1888), 66, 67, 70, 73, *74*, 77, 96, 102, ***106-107***, 108, 132
    Annie (1894-1918), *194*, 195
    Caroline 'Carrie' nee Samms (1890-1947), 129
    Cornelius 'Con' (1901-1978), 128, 192, *194*, 196
    Col. Cyril, 8, 26, 27, 29, 32
    Elizabeth 'Lizzie' nee Kelly (1876-1957), 122, 124, 200
    Esther (1909-1984), 122, 201, *201*, *214*
    Frank (1874-1939), 99, 102, 103, ***106-107***, *126* , *137*, 211, *211*
    Frank (1890-1952), 1, 2 ,4, 112, *113, 133*, 137, 142, *146*, 186, 187, *187*, ,204, 206
    Francis, Frank (1914), 137
    Ginny nee Haws, 186, *186*
    Hannah nee Donlan (1858-1914), 104, *104, 106-107*, 112, *113, 133*, 137
    Hannah nee Smith (1892-1974), 148, 149, 159, 160
    Harold (1908), 128
    James (1749), 33
    James Francis 'Frank' (1892-1918), 112, 142, 148-159, *149,* 160, *194*
    John (1858-1922), 67, 77, 96, 102, 105, ***106-107***, 112, *113, 126,* 130-132 ,*133*, 139, 178, 180, 181, 191
    John Leo (1888), 2, *113, 133*, 185, 186
    Joseph 'Joe' (1898-1958), 112, *194*, 195
    Luke (1749), 33

Mattimoe,
  Mark (1749), 32
  Mary Eveline (1896-1915), 112, *194*, 195
  Michael (1749), 33
  Mary (c.1835), 52
  Mary (1859), 67
  Mary (1911), 201
  Mary Ann nee Rutter, 102, 105, *106-107*, 108, *109*, 130, *130*,173, 174
  Mary Ellen nee Hagan, 108, 112, 128, 142, 160, 192, *194*, 195, 196
  Mary Redfearn nee Parmley, 102
  Matthew (1762), 52
  Michael (1876-1877), 99
  Minnie nee Smith, 195
  Nellie (nee Welsh), 137, 187, *187*, 188, 206
  Patrick (c.1800), 52
  Patrick (1831), 52
  Patrick (1855-1911), 67, *77*, 96, *99*, 102, 105, *106-107*, 108, *109*, 124, 129, 130, *130*
  Patrick 'Pat' (1912-1977), 122, 201
  Peter (1867-1931), 75, 103, *106-107*, *122*, 123-125, *125*, *126*, 130, 143, 198, 200, *200*
  Peter 'Pete' (1910-1946), 122, 201
  Sarah Jane nee Ferguson, 128, 130
  Sarah nee Wilson (1870-1920), 139, 178
  Stephen (1870-1950), 76 ,102, *106-107*, *126*, 130, 131, 160, 171, 192, *194*, 195, 196
  Stephen (1885-1952), 105, *106-107*, *113*, *126*, *133*, *146*, 147, 184, *184*, 185, *185*
  Stephen (1885-1939), *106-107*, *109*, 130, 131, 212
  Thadius (1749), 33
  Teresa (1913), 142
  Theresa (1906-1911), 130,131
  Thomas (1833-1900), 12, 39, 40, 51, 52, 55, 63, 65-67, 69-72, 75, *76*, 77, 96, *106-107*, 109, 120, 132
  Thomas (1861-1871), 67, 98
  Thomas (1883-1956), 102, 103, *106-107*, *126*, *129*, 132, *140*, 142, 182-184
  Thomas Edward (1890-1896), 112
  Thomas 'Tom' (1914-1974), 122, *169*, 201
  Thomas 'Tommy' (1904-1973), 128, *194*, 195
  Timothy 'Timmy' (1903-1927), 128, *194*, 195
  Veronica 'Ronnie', 184, 185, 187, 188, 217
  Winnie (1915), 142
Milmo, Darby, 27
Milmo(e), Patrick, 27, 28
Miner's strike 1892, 112
Miner's Strike 1922, 165-166
Molly Maguires, 56, 60
Moore, James, 101, *101,* 170
Moran, Jackie, 161, 192
Moylurg, Ireland, 8, 10, *10*, 12, 13, 14, 16-19, 23, 32, 42
National Schools, Ireland, 51
Norwood Colliery, 90, 95, 98, 111, 114
O'Connell, Daniel, 45, 48, 54
O'Donnell,
  Hugh 'Red Hugh', 19, 20, 21, 22
  Rory, Earl of Tyrconnell, 22
O'Moran, Jacque, 24

O'Moyle, Green, 18
O'Neill, Hugh, Earl of Tyrone, 20, 21, 22
O'Rourke, Brian, 20 ,21, 22
Peacock,
  Jane (nee Mattimoe), 5, 108, *109*, 130, 207, *207*, 208
  Joe, 207, *207*, 208, 209
Pale, The, 16, 29
Parsons, Frances, 43
Penal Laws, 24, 33, 45, 46
Pony putter or driver, 82, *83*, 84, *84*
Proddy Mats, 197
Quadrini, Mr, *209*, 210
Railey Fell Colliery, Ramshaw, 80, *81*, 90, 93, *103*, 111, 114, 127, 129, 131, 168, 169, *172*, *176*, 204, 218
Ramshaw, Co. Durham, 90, 91, *94-95*, 97, *110-111*, *162-163*, 168, 170, *202-203*, 207
Ramshaw School, 93, 99-101, *101* 108, 114, *115*, 116 -117, *131*, 144, *214*, *215*
Randolph Colliery, 114, 166, *167,* 168, 171, 203, 218
Ribbon-men, 36, 48
Rock, The, 13, 16
Rockingham, 18, 40, 42, *43*, 46 47, 62
Rory O'Conor, High King of Ireland, 14, 15
Rory, King of Moylurg, 16
St. Chad's, Witton Park, Co. Durham, 108, 174, 175, 176, 177
St. Joseph's, Coundon, Co. Durham, *140-141*
St. Osmund's, Gainford, Bishop Auckland, 102
St. Quentin, battle for, 157-159
St. Teresa's, Carrigeenroe, Co. Sligo, 69
St. Wilfred's, Bishop Auckland, 6, 26, 75, 102
San Esteban, 31
Scotswood Pit disaster, 176
Seagrave, Angela, 210
Seagrave, Tom , 85, 204
Smith, Esther (1916-2002), 159
Spanish Armada, 18, 30, 31
Strathmore, Earl of, 90
Strawboys, 66, *66*, 67
Stockton and Darlington Railway, 74, 90, 95
Strongbow, Earl of Pembroke, 15, 16
Sweat House, 11, *11*
Teig, brother of Turlough last King of Moylurg, 20
Teig of the Towers, 13
Tithe Applotment Survey, 27, 28, 32, 39, 40, 52
Tone, Wolfe, 34
Trefcon British Military Cemetery, 159
Trinity Island, Lough Key, Co. Sligo, 12, 18, *19*
Turlough Mor, High King of Ireland, 14, 15
Turlough, King of Moylurg, 16, 18
Wanless, Elizabeth nee Cox, 92, 109
Ward,
  James, 201
  Jane nee Mattimoe (1905-1967), 122, 201
  Peter, 201
Weatherley, James, 170, 171
White-Boys, 36, 47
Wild Geese, 24
Zeppelin raid on Ramshaw, 143-145, *144*